AF228457

"John Carona's commitment to public service and community association management is evident throughout this book. His thoughtful guidance encourages those of us in similar roles to stay proactive and solution-focused. It's a meaningful reminder that strong communities are built through collaboration, awareness, and a willingness to adapt."

—**ANTHONY RODRIGUEZ**, chairman, Miami-Dade Board of County Commissioners; owner, Florida Advanced Properties

"Communities, large or small, are complex machines both physically and psychologically. In this volume, John brings together all the elements—from the physical infrastructure to the rules to leadership to the underlying legal architecture—to demonstrate what it takes to build and maintain a truly successful community that meets owners' physical, financial, and emotional expectations."

—**TOM SKIBA**, CEO, Community Associations Institute (CAI)

"John Carona is single-handedly redefining the future of community association management. As an industry pioneer and innovator, he's set the standard for success—and this book reveals exactly how leaders can govern effectively and unearth the true power of community."

—**MIKE PACKARD**, PCAM, CPM, thirty-year instructor and former national president, Community Associations Institute

# IN THE COMMON INTEREST

## Unlocking the Potential of Community

3

# JOHN CARONA

GREENLEAF
BOOK GROUP PRESS

Published by Greenleaf Book Group Press
Austin, Texas
www.gbgpress.com



Distributed by Greenleaf Book Group

For ordering information or special discounts for bulk purchases, please contact Greenleaf Book Group at PO Box 91869, Austin, TX  78709, 512.891.6100.

Design and composition by Greenleaf Book Group and Mimi Bark
Cover design by Greenleaf Book Group and Mimi Bark

Publisher's Cataloging-in-Publication data is available.

Print ISBN: 979-8-88645-382-9

eBook ISBN: 979-8-88645-383-6

To offset the number of trees consumed in the printing of our books, Greenleaf donates a portion of the proceeds from each printing to the Arbor Day Foundation. Greenleaf Book Group has replaced over 50,000 trees since 2007.

Printed in the United States of America on acid-free paper
25 26 27 28 29 30 31 32    10 9 8 7 6 5 4 3 2 1
First Edition

To the inspiring and engaging servant leaders at Associa
who strengthen communities daily while unlocking
their potential for an even brighter future.

# CONTENTS

# INTRODUCTION

Every successful individual knows that his or her achievement
depends on a community of persons working together.

—PAUL RYAN,
Former Speaker, U.S. House of Representatives

More than ten years ago, I put pen to paper to explain how community associations worked and how their residents promoted community through their common interests. It was my hope that providing an overview of the core functions and operations of a community association could empower their residents and boards of directors with information about the mechanics of these modern communities. While writing *Embracing the New American Community*, little did I know it marked the birth of this three-volume saga of *In the Common Interest*.

Four years later, I applied the same principles to explain my company's vision of providing service to the thousands of neighborhoods we are privileged to serve daily. *In the Common Interest 2: Embracing Five Star Customer Service* focused on our approach to customer service and provided insights on how to embrace a five-star customer service model.

My goals are similar in this third book. In the years since my first effort, the important role that community associations play in connecting neighbors and providing a framework for a vibrant and engaging community experience has become increasingly clear. That insight motivated me to engage in this opportunity to remind community leaders and the millions of residents they serve that community matters—and why.

As former speaker of the House, Paul Ryan notes that successful individuals rely on communities of people working together. For community associations, there could not be a truer statement. Each day across the globe, millions of volunteers and the professionals who support them work to demonstrate the power of community for residents in homeowners associations, cooperatives, and condominiums. In the United States alone, close to one in four residents make their homes in community associations. They do so for a variety of reasons, including the role community associations play in protecting and enhancing the value of their homes. To support their efforts, I decided to take the time to remind those living in and leading community associations of the importance of their work. In today's age of division and social media, it is important to remember that community matters.

Community associations remain the first choice for millions of homebuyers each year. In addition to underscoring the important work they do and how residents appreciate their effort, I am happy to share my team's experience in helping our clients use the community model to unlock their true potential. Together, we learned that community matters when those engaged in creating it focus on matters of community, not on personal, competing, or unrelated agendas. That is why I focus herein not only on the often-overlooked good news about community associations, but also on areas important to ensuring their present and future success.

As we undertake this journey, we will explore the core concepts of community, which is the basis upon which we organize our society. It is also the means by which many of us connect with each other. It is where we live, raise our children, and enjoy our leisure time. It is home. We then will examine four areas that are key to unlocking a community's potential, namely, successful communities, community challenges, alternative outcomes, and future plans.

We begin with an overview of the concept of community. From history, we learn that community is a defining characteristic of human civilization. Over time, concepts of community have emerged, grown, and evolved to their present-day status. For millions of homeowners, this includes living in community associations.

Perhaps, it is the tension between our desire as North Americans to cling to the notion that we are all rugged individuals and the equally powerful desire to be part of a community that is the source of many memes about community associations. In our examination of community associations, however, one fact stands out: They are appreciated by their residents.

Beyond concepts, there are four keys that residents and boards can use to unlock the potential of their communities: what makes successful communities, addressing community challenges, finding alternative outcomes, and future plans.

The first key relates to what makes community associations successful. This includes ensuring that board actions are effective. Board members serve the residents of the community. Ensuring their role is understood by them and by residents is important to building success. Because they are volunteers with limited time, hiring professional community managers to handle day-to-day operational functions can help them focus on governance. Clearly, in their quests to improve their communities, they are not alone. Successful boards leverage the assistance of an arsenal of professionals to support their success.

For those who have served on boards, the second key should sound familiar, namely, dealing with challenges. This starts with the familiar "challenging resident." Most boards know the type. No matter what action or outreach they undertake, the resident opposes it. They should be heartened, however, by our sharing strategies they can implement to mitigate or resolve the issues created by such residents.

Another part of this challenge occurs when the problem is reversed: It focuses on what happens in a community when the board is the problem. While a harder nut to crack, leveraging professional support and focusing on the needs of the community can help overcome a board that is off-track.

Finally, unlocking a community's potential also means planning for the unexpected. Disasters can strike anywhere, and making sure the community is prepared from a financial, communications, and operational standpoint is key to preserving and protecting it.

The third key is working to find ways to effect alternative outcomes. Community association leaders often wish they could impact outcomes of problems they face or issues they address. Often, they can. To do so, they must realize that part of the problem is how community associations are covered by news media. Despite the overwhelming data indicating residents are satisfied living in community associations, when the reporters call, they can create impressions of the contrary and pose challenges for boards.

Knowing how to respond and the best ways to tell a community's story can put the board in charge of the narrative. Similarly, working to build a sense of community often gets put on the back burner while handling the day-to-day tasks of governing an association. Unlocking the true power of the community, however, can happen only when community engagement is part of the equation. Engaged residents are happy residents and have a better sense of the full array of benefits derived from a well-run community.

Finally, finding alternative outcomes requires the community to create a vision for its future and a means to measure progress. Setting community goals and planning how to achieve them also highlight the role of the association in building community and enhancing property values.

When it comes to making community matter and addressing matters of community, we need to keep an eye on the future. This is the fourth key to unlocking a community's potential. Community associations are positioned to continue to help meet the housing needs of millions each year. Understanding that the preferences of residents change over time can help boards continue to meet their needs.

What is more, each year, the government plays an increasingly larger role in how community associations operate, thereby directly impacting their future viability. Fortunately, board members and residents of community associations are best positioned to inform federal, state, and local officials about what regulations would best enhance their success. Having served as a Texas state senator and representative, it is my pleasure to share my experience-based insights into this important topic.

The many thoughts and the advice I share in this book are intended to prepare board members and residents to reflect on which keys to success would best suit their needs. They can then put the pieces together to pursue improving and creating a community that serves the needs of all residents.

I agree with former Speaker Ryan's belief that achievement depends on a community of persons working together. Community matters: It not only binds us to our neighbors in a common sense of purpose and support, but also requires attention to the very issues that keep us moving forward. May this book serve as a reminder of the important work that community volunteers engage in every day and provide insights into ensuring communities will continue to matter for years to come. I hope you enjoy it and deem it beneficial.

# CONCEPTS OF COMMUNITY

A journey of a thousand miles begins with one step.

—LAO TZU,
Chinese Philosopher

## PART I INTRODUCTION

Every journey has a starting point, and as the Chinese philosopher Lao Tzu noted, "A journey of a thousand miles begins with one step." As we begin our discussion about the important work of building community, we need a baseline from which to pursue our ambitious goal.

Community associations play an important part in today's housing market. They provide a framework for engaging residents when technology, political divisions, and other factors seem to be pulling us apart. Today's challenges can be informed by remembering why community is important. This is why we begin by focusing on the concepts that comprise it.

In laying the foundation for our discussion, Part I will examine three fundamental areas of community. In chapter 1, we will establish a working definition of community as a place to live. After establishing that baseline, in chapter 2, we will review the economic and social changes that led to the emergence of the community association model. Finally, using our understanding of community and the framework of community associations, in chapter 3, we will look at factors that, in my experience, have supported the development of successful communities.

While the definition of community has changed over time, the need to engage with our neighbors and connect with each other has not. Together, the chapters of Part I will illustrate the central importance of community in our lives and remind us of our ability to build successful communities.

## CHAPTER 1

# Emerging Concepts of Community

We were born to unite with our fellow men,
and to join in community with the human race.

—MARCUS TULLIUS CICERO,
Roman Philosopher

## CHAPTER INTRODUCTION

Community is a fundamental element in our lives, but as a concept, it is amorphous. It can be a collection of people or a group with shared interests, religion, lifestyle, political leanings, or numerous other factors. While the concept of community evolves continually, the common element at its core is a sense of belonging.

Humans are social creatures. We thrive on interactions and find a sense of comfort in a group setting. As Cicero notes, "We were born to unite with our fellow men, and to join in community with the human race." Increasingly, however, traditional approaches to community are ebbing. Demands on family time, the impact of social media, the cost of living, political divisions, and other challenges are shuffling our notions of community while creating new pathways through which humans can connect. These changes create a window for us to envision new ways to use existing community structures to connect with our neighbors. The apparent accelerating pace of change adds a sense of urgency to this task: In other words, we need to build community now.

Adopting an operational definition of "community" is an important first step toward defining our connections in the twenty-first century. Given the more than forty-five years I have devoted to building the leading provider of community association management services, my focus on community, for purposes of this discussion, centers on the residential buildings or neighborhoods many of us call "home."

Using this focus, we can then look back at communities over time to paint a picture of how communities evolve to meet their residents' needs. Finally, we can glean from our definition and historical framework the key elements that are critical to developing successful communities.

## DEFINING COMMUNITY

Sociologists and other scholars who devote themselves to defining community will continue to debate related issues within the broader context of human settlement. Generally, they define community as a social structure of like-minded members united by commonalities. These commonalities may include a similar status or shared interests, values, and social norms. The community members collaborate to organize activities in a localized geographic area, or they may be united by a common bond without regard to time or location.

For the purposes of this treatise, however, the context of community is the place where one lives, the people who live nearby, how their neighborhood is governed, and the ways in which residents can find a sense of belonging. Working within this framework, we define the elements of community in a way that enables us to look at the broadest concepts that unite residential communities.

At its core, community can be defined as a group united by proximity, common purpose, and social norms (see figure 1.1).

## Community: United by Proximity, Common Purpose, and Social Norms

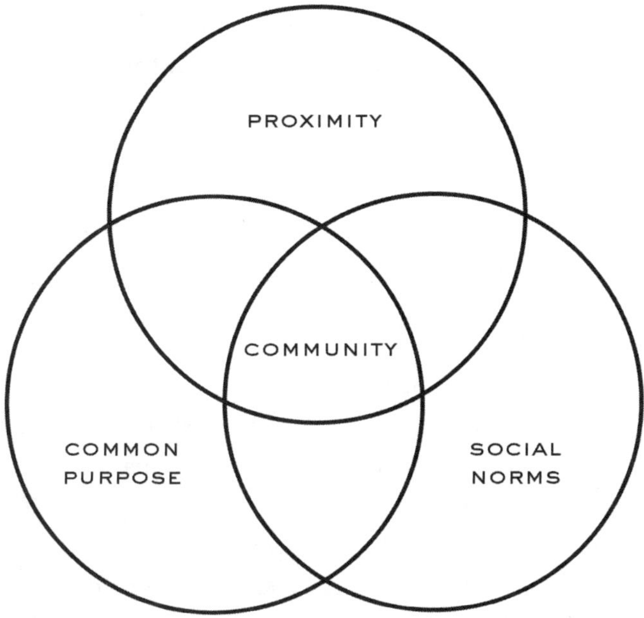


Figure 1.1: Community: United by Proximity, Common Purpose, and Social Norms

### Proximity

Finding literal common ground is an obvious foundation for a community. Beyond practicality, other needs draw people together to create a living space. Proximity facilitates face-to-face interactions, making it easier for neighbors to communicate. It also enables spontaneous gatherings, activities, or other events to strengthen relationships. In more challenging times, it also provides greater "safety in numbers."

While proximity is a fundamental defining quality for looking at groups residing together, it also provides benefits to the community. It facilitates, for example, efficiencies that can propel a community forward.

In a culture of economic sense, the concept of proximity has been a driving force in revitalizing American cities over the last thirty years. Professionals and the "creative class" have been drawn together for the benefits that accrue from being proximate to each other. Such concepts were explored in depth by authors, including Richard Florida in *The Rise of the Creative Class.*

Most importantly, when an individual chooses to live near others, that decision can create a sense of group membership and belonging. It helps fulfill the natural tendency of humans to seek connection with each other, which is as true today as it was for Cicero.

## Common Purpose

From early settlers to contemporary retirees, common purpose has been the glue that has bound a community. A shared vision of how a group wants to live and organize itself creates a space where people can bond in pursuit of that vision.

The founding of Plymouth Colony, in what is now Massachusetts, illustrates the role of common purpose as a foundation of community. Seeking greater religious freedom, passengers on board the *Mayflower* set out from England in 1620 to establish a new community and start a new life. After two months at sea and low on supplies, those colonists found themselves on the cusp of a Northeastern winter. Rather than continuing to their desired destination of Virginia, they docked at the coastal lands near what is now Cape Cod.

The uniting element of the passengers was to establish a community in which they could practice their religion more freely. Their common purpose united them in their goal as they reached their new land.

Correspondingly, common purpose is a hallmark of the many active adult communities throughout North America. Their residents aged fifty-five and older are united in the common purpose of ensuring an active retirement. They further this purpose by offering numerous clubs and amenities as residents find comfort and support in working with their neighbors to help preserve active lifestyles.

A common purpose also underscores Cicero's insights: We are born to unite with our fellow humans. In early communities, this element may have been as fundamental as safety, evolving into a wide range of common purposes over time. Unity in our pursuits provides us with a sense of belonging—a sense that we are part of something bigger than ourselves. From that sense of belonging, we derive a connection that grows into loyalties, bringing us even closer in our pursuits.

## Social Norms

How we behave when we are alone can differ from when we are in a group setting. In today's vernacular, this might be considered courtesy, but in primitive days, aligning one's behavior with the group could be a matter of survival. At that time, for example, group members might have been prohibited from needlessly poking bears—literally!

To preserve social cohesion, a community needs social norms to provide boundaries for the behavior of its members. Over time, such norms emerge organically and reflect the mean of acceptable behavior within the group.

Let us revisit the example of Plymouth Colony to see this element in action. Before setting foot on land, the colonists created the *Mayflower Compact*, which documented the founders' common purpose. That purpose was defined as "working to establish equal laws, ordinances, acts, constitutions, and offices . . . as shall be thought most meet and convenient for the general good of the colony."[1]

Impressively, the first achievement of these brave souls, after a months-long, dangerous sea voyage, was to establish the means to set social norms for their new community.

Today, we see this element in multiple hierarchies that harken to the *Mayflower Compact*. Constitutions, laws, ordinances, acts, and rules are all manifestations of social norms. When laws are silent, ethics, manners, and tradition help establish community boundaries. To thrive, a community needs to create a safe space for its residents—a space in which social norms bind them.

## IDENTIFYING ELEMENTS OF COMMUNITY

Defining *community* as "a collection of people living in proximity with a common purpose and united by shared social norms" is the foundation for discussing its elements. Because these organic bonds emerge when people choose to live together, they are essential to our analysis of building community by identifying its more formal, structural elements. By this, I mean elements that go beyond defining community to provide a more formal, operative structure. Building on our definition, we can identify structural components that include boundaries, infrastructure, rules, communication, social frameworks, and governance. This elemental framework is the basis from which we support the residents, provide shared space, and offer a formal means of achieving connection.

## Boundaries

Boundaries are a critical element of a residential community. They literally are the lines limiting the space within which the community exists. Community boundaries define the area within which the three definitional factors of proximity, common purpose, and shared social norms are aligned.

The boundaries of a community should enable its residents to feel secure in their homes and shared spaces. Some communities also have a common aesthetic that further unifies residents and contributes to the area's overall character. Clearly defined community boundaries often promote resident interaction, facilitating their cohesion and enhancing "good neighborliness." Relatedly, when neighbors understand the role of common spaces within their community and their responsibilities to them, they are more likely to feel comfortable interacting and supporting their community's quality of life.

## Infrastructure

Shared physical infrastructure is another critical element of a community. More specifically, infrastructure is a physical element or space that serves the needs of the community and provides a nexus to connect residents. It comprises all community-wide physical elements provided for the mutual benefit of its residents.

Today's concept of community infrastructure evokes images of roads, sidewalks, and perhaps clubhouses, but hundreds of years ago, in the Middle Ages, it could have included items seemingly mundane today. A great example of this element from long ago is the communal oven. Historians find examples of community ovens going back centuries. These ovens enabled members of the community to cook staple foods more easily and likely created significant efficiencies due to the time and effort otherwise needed to maintain fires and the investment in time and materials needed to build primitive cooking structures.

While we have traded our communal kitchens for modern appliances, many common infrastructural elements of communities' pasts remain relevant. Elements such as roads, walking paths, parks, and recreation areas are considered essential by most residents today, especially because those common spaces enable them to connect and socialize.

## Rules

If shared social norms are an element in defining community, then rules are their expressed version and serve to provide an element of regulation for communities. Rules authorize the community to establish and maintain order and to ensure a balance between residents' rights and their responsibilities to the community at large. They also contribute to the health of the community by providing standards for acceptable behavior, defining a process for the continued development of the community, and outlining methods for maintaining the well-being of residents.

From the past to the present, rules have been the instrument for moderating behavior in communities. Written rules with their "thou shalts" and "thou shalt nots" delineate acceptable actions for community residents and enhance harmonious co-existence. Relationships can be strained, for example, if residents worry their property and well-being are not being protected or respected. That is why, throughout time, we have seen rules regarding subjects such as curfews, trespassing, stealing, speed limits, and even noise regulation. By explicitly describing behavior expectations, rules promote peace and harmony.

Rules can define community membership and dictate who can enjoy its benefits. All residents, for example, must help support their common areas. This requirement has changed over time, from initially requiring residents to volunteer to maintain the common areas to today's universal practice of paying assessments for this purpose.

## Communication

As Cicero noted, man is a social creature, striving to make connections. Building community requires connections with neighbors and that requires communication. To go beyond a mere collection of homes in an area, residents need to relate to each other. Such connections foster trust, mutual understanding, and unity. In the broadest sense, communication means the ability to converse with neighbors. This has evolved over time, from the town crier of days gone by to today's ability to electronically exchange ideas, information, and opinions in real time.

Communication facilitates relationships. Historically, communication might have been focused on basic needs such as security and access to resources. Today's neighbors, however, likely discuss a wide range of topics. As they interact and get to know each other better, they gain insight into each other's values and thought processes. This helps them find the common ground that unites community residents and enables them to benefit from their diverse experiences.

Using available channels of communication also facilitates the engagement, coordination, and collaboration essential to maintain the community through collective problem-solving. Again, the more residents can communicate and connect with each other, the greater their sense of belonging.

## Social Frameworks

Communication among members of a community is critical, but it does not happen in a vacuum. It is impacted and supported by another important element of community, namely, social frameworks.

A social framework is an infrastructure that promotes engagement and unity within the community. Such frameworks are usually the result of a proactive effort by community residents or community leaders.

As we will examine in later chapters, community associations provide a social framework in many areas, ranging from board meetings to clubs and social functions. In a larger sense, these mechanisms emerged to address practical issues within communities. For me, they stir images of groups of community elders gathering to make decisions for their community, to collaborate in addressing community challenges, or even to plan an annual festival or important community ritual. Such a framework might have comprised structures that emerged organically from connections in the community to facilitate resource gathering or production of goods for its members.

Social frameworks allow residents to organize in furtherance of their wants or needs for their community. They allow like-minded persons to form groups or subgroups to support their greater good or perhaps merely an activity that provides amusement or comfort.

## Governance

How a community is governed can impact its overall health, cohesion, and development. Ships do not steer themselves—at least, not yet.

Similarly, a community cannot operate and evolve without a governance element.

Governance is the mechanism that facilitates maintaining and nurturing a community by creating and enforcing rules. It can be embodied in a single individual or held by a collective board, but it represents the delegation of community-wide decision-making to a select group. What is more, governance provides structure by ensuring decisions for the community are made efficiently to benefit the entire community.

Several years ago, a popular costume drama on public television followed the machinations of an aristocratic family in early twentieth-century England. One of its subplots traced the changes from England's manorial system to its more modern entrepreneurial economy. It was interesting to note how the lord of the manor and his family provided employment for the community around the manor, assisted in resolving disputes, and even helped provide health services for residents of the vast estate. This, of course, was the backdrop to dramatic love stories, betrayal, and general intrigue; but underlying that was an illustration of how communities were governed in one region more than one hundred years ago.

Today's governance structures are highly variable. From federal and state government officials to city council members and, more recently, community association board members, many leaders have ideas or proposals for creating, amending, and enforcing the rules we need to ensure harmonious communities.

Building successful communities requires a framework of elements that ensure the community has a defined physical space; infrastructure to support residents; rules to ensure acceptable behavior; and a governance structure to oversee, maintain, and meet the community's evolving needs. This is not a definitive list but, rather, an identification of the fundamental elements that support building successful communities.

## OUTLINING CHALLENGES TO BUILDING COMMUNITY

The desire to live in a community seems universal and timeless. This does not mean all individual communities weather the challenges of time. The world is littered with the ruins of failed communities and civilizations. Ironically, many of us spend time and money to tour them, pondering their wonders and demises.

As we define community and identify its essential elements, it is appropriate to take time to examine the challenges of building it. Such challenges arise from factors such as the loss of common purpose, cultural and economic changes, environmental issues, and evolving personal preferences. Examining these factors should help us find ways to resolve them in our own communities.

## Loss of Common Purpose

Common purpose is a defining factor for community. It answers the question of why people want to live together and what they expect to achieve in this endeavor. When a community is aligned in its vision, residents are united in a common pursuit. If that common purpose atrophies, however, the resulting loss of a sense of belonging can undermine social cohesion because the underlying objective that drew residents together no longer exists.

The loss of common purpose can also impact a community by fostering apathy. A new community with attractive amenities and young families is likely to be united in purposes such as maintaining a community pool, playground, or recreational facilities that meet the needs of families. Young professionals among them may be eager to engage civically to help lead their community. Look ahead twenty or thirty years, however, and that common purpose may be gone. Residents are now aging in place, retired, or perhaps on a fixed income, and their children have probably moved on with their lives. Amenities are no longer new, but rather aged and needing repairs. With the common purpose of a family-focused community much less relevant to residents, the same may be true of their common ties.

## Cultural and Economic Changes

Cultural and economic changes both facilitate and undermine building community. Our history is rich in examples of cultural and economic challenges to building community. From the Great Migration to the emergence of the Rust Belt and the rise of the Sunbelt, all were driven by cultural and economic changes.

Starting in the early twentieth century, for example, the United States saw a significant movement of people of African descent from Southern states to the North and the Midwest. Driven by the desire for better opportunities and to escape the oppression of racist segregation policies of the Jim Crow era, more than six million African Americans moved to places such as Chicago, Detroit, Philadelphia, and New York. This Great Migration led not only to the loss of culturally significant rural African American communities in the South, but also to the emergence of new community structures that had significant cultural impacts at the newly more populated destinations.

Similarly, the rise of global trade starting in the 1970s had a significant community impact in the United States. The increased importation of less expensive manufactured goods such as cars and steel, for example, dramatically impacted the Midwest. The decline even led to the creation of the "Rust Belt" label to refer to the once vibrant but now empty and decaying communities around cities such as Detroit, Cleveland, Gary, and other industrial centers. Relatedly, displaced workers and those coming of age during this time sought to secure their futures in more desirable work climates in the South and West.

Maintaining community during cultural or economic change creates numerous challenges. Changing cultural expectations can impact social norms, which, in turn, impact social ties in a community. Similarly, changing economic circumstances can impact the viability of the community when fewer financial resources are available to support community needs. Building community in these contexts requires focusing on overcoming inequality and finding a renewed sense of inclusivity among community members.

## Evolving Personal Preferences

In the late 1970s, there emerged a growing trend of people looking to America's great cities to build their futures, shunning the comfortable, but perhaps homogenized, experience of suburban communities. Cities such as New York, Philadelphia, the District of Columbia, and others saw reversals of population declines. More and more young professionals explored the benefits of urban communities. Once boarded-up neighborhoods gentrified and attracted a new wave of business investment in the form of shops and trendy cafés. Residents of urban communities enjoyed the diverse experiences and backgrounds of their neighbors and of recreated or reinvented neighborhoods.

Then, in 2020, something happened that altered residents' personal preferences. This change came in the form of the historic COVID-19 pandemic, especially from 2020 to the end of 2021. Suddenly, residents of densely packed urban communities reevaluated their options. The health risks imposed by living in close quarters with neighbors triggered a reevaluation of urban living. Even more impactful, the emergence of fully remote or hybrid work sites allowed urbanites to explore options to live in more bucolic settings at lower cost and without the lengthy commutes.

Building community during a time of changing personal preferences creates challenges. Individuals may begin to prioritize their own interests over the values and collective goals of their communities. As priorities change, community residents may seek new types of communities that align with their newly emergent requirements. This can lead to a sense of instability within communities as members come and go based on their changing needs and desires.

## Environmental Issues

Environmental issues often vary by region, season, or circumstance. Whether a natural disaster, such as a lack of rainfall, or a consequence of human behavior, such as air pollution, each impacts the community.

### Drought

Drought has been a significant challenge to community building. Water is an essential element of life, and communities cannot exist or thrive without an adequate supply of clean water. Historians often cite evidence that historic droughts were a contributing factor to the decline of civilizations such as the Maya. Their city-states were scattered about modern-day Mexico's Yucatan peninsula. In this limestone landscape, water resources are primarily found in sinkholes or cenotes. Lack of adequate rainfall triggered a demographic crisis and led to the abandonment of Maya communities.[2]

Today, communities across the desert Southwest of the United States are facing similar challenges. Ongoing drought is stressing existing water supplies and resulting in mandates for industries and residents to reduce water usage. This is impacting fast-growing communities across the Southwest as they attempt to reconcile growth with existing resource limits.

### Wildfires

Wildfires impact communities as well. Within just a matter of years, two vibrant communities were devastated by wildfires. Paradise, California, was destroyed during the fast-moving Camp Fire in 2018, resulting in the loss of most housing and commercial areas of the community. Likewise, the historic and culturally important town of Lahaina, Hawaii, was destroyed by a wildfire in 2023. In both cases, recovery efforts are expected to take many years.

## Hurricanes

Hurricanes can flatten communities, and their recovery can take many years. Several years ago, many of our clients in the Florida Panhandle were impacted by Hurricane Michael, a massive Category 5 hurricane. Almost all communities in the impact zone were hit, and many were completely destroyed. I recall seeing photographs of a townhome community near the shore and feeling dismayed that the only evidence that families had lived there were the concrete slabs that were used to support homes. While many of the communities in the area have recovered, some could not navigate the cost and complexity of rebuilding.

## Collateral Impact

The collateral impact of environmental challenges impacts communities as well. More frequent and stronger hurricanes are roiling windstorm insurance markets and increasing costs for homeowner and community insurance policies. With environmental-driven impacts projected to accelerate in coming years, communities need to reckon with their impact.

## CONCLUSION

Given our established understanding of community, it is important we take steps to nurture communities that meet the needs of individuals in the twenty-first century. As we navigate the challenges of modern life, including the demands on our time, the impact of cultural change, and the complexities of economics, we must seek opportunities to connect with our neighbors and foster a sense of belonging. By leveraging our existing community ties, we can create spaces that facilitate meaningful interactions.

Drawing on my experience in community association management, I have seen the power of community to bring people together and create a sense of home. By focusing on the unique needs and dynamics of residential communities, we can learn valuable lessons about building successful and sustainable communities for the future. Understanding the key elements that contribute to community success, including strong communication, inclusive decision-making processes, and a shared sense of purpose, we can lay the foundation for vibrant and resilient communities that enrich the lives of all who inhabit them.

The concept of community is ever-changing, but its core principle, of fostering a sense of belonging remains constant. As we continue to redefine and reimagine community for the twenty-first century, let us draw on the lessons of the past and the insights of the present to create communities that are inclusive, supportive, and empowering. By embracing change and the diversity of our communities, we can build a future in which everyone feels a sense of belonging and connection. We can begin by looking at how these factors contributed to the development and growth of community associations.

---

## QUESTIONS TO CONSIDER

1. What memories do you have of the first community in which you resided?

2. How do you define "community," and how has that definition changed over time?

3. What do you consider critical elements of a community? How would you rank them?

4. How have cultural or economic changes impacted your community in the last ten years?

5. If you have lived in a community that experienced a disaster, how was it impacted, and what coping and recovery strategies were implemented?

6. Do you have suggestions regarding how communities can prepare for, respond to, and recover from a disaster?

# Evolving the Concept of Community

*Growth is never by chance; it is the result of forces working together.*

—JAMES CASH PENNEY,
Founder, JCPenney

---

## CHAPTER INTRODUCTION

James Cash Penney may have been discussing the retail industry, but his words apply to community associations, particularly because the concept of community continues to evolve over time in response to forces working together.

During the twentieth century, for example, the powerful forces of industrialization, investments in infrastructure, and growing prosperity in the United States came together to impact where and how people lived. The transition from an agrarian to an industrial society pushed them to live in cities. Likewise, postwar policy changes impacted the types of housing that would be built. Moreover, a desire for a better quality of life contributed to the evolving concept of community. Together, these factors contributed to the emergence of modern community associations, including condominiums, community associations, co-ops, and planned communities.

At its core, the concept of community is based on where one lives, his or her home, and the neighborhood where that home is located. Seemingly simple, the complexity of this concept reflects the many options available, the rapidity with which homeowners can move to another locale, and the remarkable speed with which new technology and service products are offered widely.

As community associations continue to gain ground as a primary housing option for millions of Americans, their role as a nexus of connecting neighbors and the need to ensure they operate effectively become critical elements for a community's success.

## UNDERSTANDING THE EMERGENCE OF COMMUNITY ASSOCIATIONS

During the United States' engagement in World War II, new housing was put on hold to preserve raw materials for the war effort. At the conclusion of hostilities, the United States faced not only the challenge of a housing shortage, but also the need to invest in the long-neglected national infrastructure. This dynamic set the stage for an evolution in the housing market that would give rise to modern-day housing with common ownership elements, such as a community association or condominium.

In the postwar years, a new concept of community emerged as millions of returning veterans needed housing. Largely spared from the devastation of the war, the economy of the United States was booming. The middle class was surging, and people generally desired a better life with more space and more choices than what was available in crowded cities.

The advent of the national interstate highway system also supercharged the development of suburbs as President Dwight Eisenhower's Federal-Aid Highway Act of 1956 impacted dense urban areas. It spurred an urban renewal program that sometimes eliminated well-established neighborhoods, especially as newly constructed highways displaced one million persons. Concurrently, the increased mobility and connectivity funded by congressional and state legislative appropriations facilitated choosing suburbia as a way of life.

## Early Community Associations

Most historians trace the development of the community association model to a humble potato field on Long Island. This was where builder William Levitt set out to build a residential community known as Levittown and filled it with modest, attractive homes. The homes were a perfect fit for service members, who could finance them with low-interest loans provided by the Servicemen's Readjustment Act of 1944, commonly known as the G.I. Bill.[1]

Unlike the developments that preceded it, Levittown had distinguishing characteristics. Its developers worked to implement rules that would preserve the character of the community. Although the community had neither governing documents nor a board of directors typical of a modern community association, those would come later. Nevertheless, historians point to Levittown as one of the earliest community associations in the United States.

Federal legislative changes continued to facilitate the growth of the community association model. In 1963, for example, the Federal Housing Administration adopted policies that authorized insurance for lenders who issued mortgages for condominiums or homes in a community association.

With these changes, the growth of community associations continued to build momentum. By the late 1960s, most states had adopted some form of state statutes governing condominiums in the form of Horizontal Property Acts. These laws provided a framework for future condominium development and addressed emerging issues of displacement when former apartments were converted to condominium housing.

## Modern Elements of a Community Association

As highways continued to expand into the rural areas beyond city centers in the years that followed, the community association model continued to be perfected.

Today, the term "community governing documents" broadly refers to the documents that establish and outline the governance of a community association. They include several critical elements reflected in the following steps taken by the developer:

- The developer submits a plat or plan to local authorities. This document maps out the land usage within the community that is to be built.

- Then the developer files articles of incorporation. The articles are intended to bring the association to life and establish it as a nonprofit entity with the authority to govern the community.

- Equally important, the developer files a document known as covenants, conditions, and restrictions (CC&Rs). It contains additional regulations of land use within the community that include outlining the use of common areas and establishing rules that bind the unit owners to the community.

- Finally, bylaws are developed that serve as the user manual for the community association board of directors' authority and governing processes.

## Appeal of Community Associations

The governing documents may seem like a rather ponderous collection of legalities, but they evolved to serve a larger purpose. As the middle class boomed in the postwar years, many people sought a better quality of life. A community association, with its ability to engage residents in a common ownership model, worked to meet that desire.

Rules in the community worked to guarantee the sizeable investment in homeownership would be protected. Their purpose was to ensure the residential nature of the community, help preserve the look and feel of the neighborhood, and provide a mechanism to enforce violations.

Beyond rule enforcement, the community association model also empowered communities to offer an array of amenities. In earlier community associations, such amenities typically consisted of only an attractive neighborhood sign or perhaps a community pool. Today, community associations offer an array of amenities that defy the imagination. They include security features such as entry gates, equestrian stables, fitness centers, golf courses, spas, and, in very specialized communities, even runways so residents can fly to the community and park their airplanes or helicopters by their residences.

Another appealing feature of community associations is that they move decision-making from city hall to the clubhouse. A community association is governed by its residents. The governing body of the community association is its board of directors. The board comprises elected representatives who own a home or unit within the community, providing a highly effective means of governance.

When decisions that impact the neighborhood are made by its residents within the boundaries of the community itself, they facilitate the engagement of the residents themselves. In fact, long-term studies of community association residents indicate this is a key element of community association living. Relatedly, a report issued by the Foundation for Community Association Research consistently has found that 87 percent of respondents felt their boards of directors served the best interests of their communities.[2]

## Growth of Community Associations

The appealing aspects of community associations are critical to understanding their emergence as a housing model. The market and homebuyers seem to agree. My first publication, *In the Common Interest: Embracing the New American Community*, provided industry data about the growth of community associations in the United States. Ten years later, a second look at these data confirms the continued growth in this sector (see table 2.1).[3]

| Year | Communities | Housing Units | Residents |
| --- | --- | --- | --- |
| 1970 | 10,000 | 701,000 | 2.1 million |
| 1980 | 36,000 | 3.6 million | 9.6 million |
| 1990 | 130,000 | 11.6 million | 29.6 million |
| 2000 | 222,500 | 18.8 million | 45.2 million |
| 2010 | 309,600 | 24.8 million | 62.0 million |
| 2020 | 358,000 | 27.5 million | 74.1 million |
| 2023 | 365,000 | 28.2 million | 75.5 million |

Table 2.1: 2023 U.S. National and State Statistical Review, Foundation for Community Association Research. Reprinted with permission of the Foundation for Community Association Research. Learn more by visiting foundation.caionline.org or by calling 888-224-4321.

The growth of community associations reflects not only the preferences of home buyers, but also a shift in priorities for more efficient use of limited space for housing and a desire for belonging to a community that meets the needs and desires of today's families.

## CONCEPTUALIZING COMMUNITY ASSOCIATIONS

Understanding community associations requires understanding their structure, variety, and governance. Lifestyles will vary among communities, and so will the roles and responsibilities of their boards of directors.

### Community Association Structure

Many new homes constructed in the United States today are built in community associations. While this term may be familiar to many readers and was addressed in my previous *In the Common Interest* books, I would be remiss not to provide at least a quick look at what a community association is, what types of community associations exist, and how they are governed.

## What Is a Community Association?

"Community association" is a broad term that covers many types of communities. Despite their variety in the marketplace, they are defined by common elements.

### Mandatory Membership

First, a community association has a mandatory membership component. This means that upon purchasing a home or unit in a community association, the owner of record becomes a member of the association. This process is automatic, and the owner is subject to the community's governing framework.

### Mutually Binding Documents

Second, a community association is characterized by documents that mutually bind the owner to the association and the association to the owner. To state it more constructively, the documents create a set of rights and responsibilities for both the owner and the association.

More specifically, the documents that create this relationship include the community's articles of incorporation, the CC&Rs, and the bylaws. Cumulatively, these documents serve as a handbook for members of the association to use to govern their association, maintain the common areas, and ensure day-to-day operations.

### Lien-based Assessments

Lien-based assessments are the final element that helps define a community association. All owners in the association pay assessments and support the cost of maintaining common elements, amenities, insurance, and management of the community itself. This common ownership element of a community association benefits all home-owners, and all are responsible for contributing to cover the cost of maintaining the community.

Assessments are mandatory, not optional, and in many cases, they are lien-based. This means that if a homeowner's assessment obliga-tion becomes past due, the association may place a lien on his or her property to ensure recovery of the funds owed.

## Types of Community Associations

The variety of community associations helps create a market to meet the needs of a variety of buyers. Purchasers can select from a nearly limitless array of amenities, housing styles, or price points to help meet the needs of their families, budgets, or desired lifestyles. This is the market in action, working to provide a variety of products to meet as many needs as possible. While this is a very broad view of the types of community associations, it provides a firm basis to under-stand their structure and common ownership nature.

As a practical matter, there are three types of community associa-tions, namely, condominiums, planned unit developments, and stock cooperatives. Although similar in having mandatory membership, binding documents, and lien-based assessments, they can vary in the type of housing provided and how the common ownership elements are structured.

### Condominiums

Condominiums are an interesting ownership model. Purchasing a condominium unit is essentially buying space within a larger struc-ture that includes everything from the unfinished surfaces of the interior inward—in other words, a condominium unit.

Condominiums exist in many forms. They can be high-rises, mid-rises, or even garden-style buildings. Many townhome developments are also considered condominiums. Generally, members of the association commonly own the infrastructure that supports the individual units in a condominium, and residents own the interiors of their respective units. The lobby, hallways, and any amenities are also commonly owned and referred to as common elements.

## Planned Unit Developments

A planned unit development (PUD) is typically a collection of single-family homes, though owners may share parks, pools, or other amenities. A PUD can also include commercial space, condominiums, single-family homes, and stock cooperatives, and it may resemble a small city. The common areas of the community are owned collectively by the association. The land that the member owns includes the rights, such as mineral rights, that often accompany land ownership.

## Stock Cooperatives

A stock cooperative is a unique entity. Unlike a condominium or a PUD, a stock cooperative is a corporation. The corporation owns all the elements of the property, including the residential units. A buyer in a stock cooperative does not purchase the unit itself but rather purchases shares in the corporation that entitle him or her to occupy a unit in the cooperative. A person living in a cooperative leases the unit from the corporation by owning shares in it.

## Governance of a Community Association

Community associations are self-governing entities. A community association is governed by a board of directors that is elected by the residents.[4] The board ensures the ongoing operations of the association, enforces the rules of the community, engages with business to serve the community, and hires management to oversee day-to-day operations.

Although the board's powers are defined in the foundational documents of the association, they may be further restricted by local, state, or federal laws. From a governance standpoint, community associations place governance as close to the citizenry as possible, empowering neighborhoods to make decisions impacting them.

## ENSURING THE EFFICACY OF COMMUNITY ASSOCIATIONS

Successful boards of directors embrace challenges related to interacting regularly and effectively with homeowners. This includes not only dealing with varying perceptions about their roles and functions, but also implementing lessons learned about well-run communities.

## Perceptions of Community Associations

One key to ensuring a community association serves its residents well is understanding current perceptions about community associations. True or not, these perceptions influence homeowners' understanding of the role and function of their community and its governance. On the surface, it seems safe to say there is a general lean to the negative in the perception of community associations. The good news, however, is that the bigger picture is both more complex and far more positive. Understanding these perceptions facilitates recognizing opportunities for better community governance.

A popular internet meme sarcastically notes that the plural for a certain type of pushy, know-it-all person is "homeowners association." This meme sums up the challenge and the opportunity for community associations to shape perceptions about their missions. If exposure to community associations were limited to reports in local television news, a viewer could not be blamed for casting a skeptical eye on their role in neighborhood governance.

The challenge for many community associations is that the board's engagement with residents is typically limited to enforcing rules or collecting mandatory assessments needed to operate the community. Additionally, the long-held belief that a family's home is its castle contributes to the initial skepticism about all governance-related actions of community associations.

The good news is that such stories do not capture the entirety of the experience of living in a community association. In fact, while most negative reports about community associations are anecdotal, the Community Associations Institute (CAI), the membership group representing those living and working in community associations, has undertaken long-term surveys that paint a different picture. CAI's Foundation for Community Association Research (FCAR) publishes a biennial survey that captures data related to overall satisfaction with community association living. Consistently over time, the results indicate a vast majority of the more than 75 million residents of community associations are pleased with their communities.

**Key data points include the following:[5]**

- 89.85 percent of community association residents rate their satisfaction with living in a community association from neutral to very good.

- 87 percent of residents have positive relationships with their communities' boards of directors.

- 86 percent of residents have reported positive experiences with their community managers.

- Only 13 percent of respondents reported the existence of a homeowners association would negatively impact a purchase decision.

The Foundation for Community Association Research's Homeowner Satisfaction Survey is an excellent source of industry data. The publicly available survey data go back nearly a decade, and the satisfaction numbers have remained relatively steady.

This seeming dichotomy between negative perceptions of community associations and data indicating most residents have an overall positive experience can be helpful from two perspectives.

First, the negative narratives around community associations may cause residents to believe they will have difficulties interacting with their community associations. Second, the data indicate the reality is far different, as most residents report positive experiences with their community associations.

Seen through the lens of ensuring efficacy in a community association, the conflicting data can be useful in countering the initial bias or concerns residents may have about living in a community association. They can empower boards to leverage this dichotomy by focusing on the needs of residents and providing responsive, consistent governance. In turn, their doing so will result in better communities that are increasingly perceived more positively.

## Elements of a Well-Run Community Association

One of the most rewarding aspects of my career has been observing community association boards of directors work to create engaging communities for their residents. Their efforts align perfectly with the value of self-governance that connects residents across North America. Over time, three elements have become hallmarks of successful communities: dedicated board volunteers, engaged residents, and an overall focus on the community.

### Dedicated Board Volunteers

As self-governing entities, community associations rely on volunteer homeowners to run for and serve on boards. Having engaged in public service for a significant portion of my career, first as a member of the Texas House of Representatives and then as a Texas State Senator, I know the importance of giving back to the community. It requires a commitment of precious time and a lot of fortitude.

Each year, more than 600,000 homeowners serve on their community association boards of directors. The value of their volunteered time is easily in the billions of dollars. The managers at my company and I take great pride in supporting their success.

A dedicated board of directors is truly the key to a successful community, but what defines a successful board?

First, a successful board is committed to the overall development of the community. The focus is on enhancing the quality of life for the residents by diligently setting budgets, adopting policies, enforcing rules, and engaging residents. While on the surface, these tasks may seem rather mundane or even tedious, in practice, they are anything but.

For many community associations, uncertainty in the insurance markets and recent bouts of inflation have put pressure on budgets. Faced with fiscal responsibilities to maintain or enhance the community's standard of living, board members may have to increase assessments, causing residents to balk. For boards, producing a budget that adequately covers operational expenses and funds reserves is essential. When faced with the need to increase assessments, boards can mitigate pushback by ensuring residents understand why an increase is necessary. In short, effective boards do their homework not only by attending to the business of the association, but also by engaging residents in a dialogue about what they are doing—and why.

A sign of a truly dedicated board is openness to continual improvement. Many community associations are complex entities, and some could even be considered small cities with budgets to match. Although board members are volunteers, they may need specialized training to be effective. They can select from a variety of training programs offered, usually free, by industry groups such as the Community Associations Institute, the Institute for Real Estate Management, or local law firms specializing in community association law.

A dedicated board of directors also plans for the future. Such planning includes developing successor board members. This can be challenging, and time constraints and negative perceptions of community associations can create headwinds for success.

Too often, problems in community associations arise when board members serve too long. Long-term service with little thanks or support can breed entitlement that can create problems in any community association. Creating a process for developing future board members can keep a community's governance fresh. This can include appointing committees charged with tasks ranging from architectural review to social functions. Residents who get a taste of the governance process and enjoy it may be great future board members.

## Engaged Residents

Engaged residents are another hallmark of a well-run community association. Ensuring residents understand the role of the board and focusing on responsibilities beyond mere rule enforcement are good starting points.

In today's culture, time is a precious commodity. Even the most dedicated homeowner in a community association may struggle to find time to attend board meetings or even to review board minutes. Communicating key elements of the board's work is crucial for residents to understand the rationale behind board decisions.

## Community Focus

One of the main advantages of living in a community association is the framework it provides for neighbors to connect. There is the obvious connection that is made through mandatory assessments and enforcement of rules, but for a community to truly thrive, using that framework to create social engagement is critical.

As a management firm for thousands of community associations, all of which focus on strengthening their respective communities, Associa works to facilitate such engagement. We sponsor, for example, National Night Out (NNO), which is designed to connect communities with local first responders. This event promotes safety and understanding between the community and local police agencies.

Other enjoyable opportunities are community-wide events, community clean-up days, holiday parties, or activities that suit the culture of the community. Cumulatively, they reflect a distinguishing characteristic of a dedicated board, namely, a community focus that reflects a holistic approach to its well-being.

## Ensuring a Well-Run Community

Many years ago, an ad featured a popular celebrity advocating for a health club. Its message was that if a good body came in a bottle, everyone would have one, clearly making the point that worthwhile outcomes require significant effort. The same is true for boards that work hard to build a well-run community. While there is no one-size-fits-all approach, boards can take broad actions that set them on paths to success.

### Listening and Observing

A critical starting point is listening and observing. Many communities get stuck doing things because that is how they have always been done. It does not necessarily have to be that way, however.

A good example of the benefit of observing can be seen in rules. Rules are important in community associations. As mentioned earlier, close to 90 percent of residents feel good about their communities for reasons including rules, amenities, and connection with neighbors—but the values, priorities, and needs of a community change over time.

Clotheslines are a good example of changing times, values, and practices. There was a time when clotheslines were the only option for drying clothes. Then, the modern convenience of electric or gas dryers emerged, and consumers welcomed the time savings and greater convenience. As a result, the previously popular clotheslines became somewhat of an anachronism and were often considered an eyesore.

Many associations built in the 1960s and 1970s banned clotheslines, but today higher energy costs and greater environmental awareness are pushing some to rediscover this old practice. Good for them. The point is that values and preferred practices can change over time, and rules in the community can and should change with them.

The question is, how can a board know if a rule is no longer valued by the community? Observation. Listening.

A rule that is violated or criticized consistently or vehemently may no longer fit the community's needs. When such an observation occurs, the board can listen to residents and determine whether to adapt or evolve the rules to meet the community's changed needs.

**Engaging and Surveying**

A more proactive means of ensuring a well-run community is engaging residents in as many ways as possible that they consider convenient and appealing. Today's technology empowers boards to take the pulse of the community in near real-time. At Associa, we partner with companies such as TownSq that provide applications (apps) to facilitate community operations and foster greater communication. These apps include survey tools that engage residents to ensure the board focuses on things that matter to the community.

Engagement does not stop with surveys. One of the best measures of a well-run community is engaging its residents in social activities. Block parties and holiday celebrations are the most obvious, but there are endless ways the community association can facilitate residents' connection with each other. Too often, that simple practice is an untapped potential in a community association.

**Adapting and Evolving**

Finally, another sign of a well-run community is adaptability. One of the many false narratives about community associations is that they are too rigid. While that may be true for some, I have not seen that as the norm. The aforementioned examples illustrate the point. The values of a community change over time. A rule that was sacrosanct twenty years ago may no longer meet the needs of the community. We saw this with the clothesline example.

An adaptable community is a resilient community because it can see what no longer works and can change focus to meet the current needs of residents. This is not an argument of change for change's sake, but rather a reminder that, as self-governing entities, community associations have a built-in ability to be self-adaptive as they evolve to meet changing needs.

## CONCLUSION

Community associations emerged during a unique historical time when the powerful forces of industrialization, investments in infrastructure, and growing prosperity in the United States came together to impact how and where people lived. Cultural, legislative, and even historical changes cumulatively contributed to the development of a housing model with elements of common ownership. They evolved into a variety of types that include condominiums, planned unit developments, and stock cooperatives.

The common ownership model binds the residents, provides rights and responsibilities for the association and the homeowners, and places the governance of communities in the hands of the residents. Although reported negative perceptions of community associations can color the expectations of those buying into the community association model, data indicate the experience is largely positive.

To protect and foster neighborhood governance, boards must work hard to listen, observe, engage, and adapt the community association to meet residents' current needs. Most importantly, the common ownership model of community associations provides a nexus to connect neighbors. As their needs and interests change, so will community associations.

## QUESTIONS TO CONSIDER

1.  How have you enjoyed your experience living in a community association?

2.  How does your experience living in a community association compare to living in a neighborhood without a community association?

3.  What elements of living in a community association do you most appreciate?

4.  Do you consider your community association to be well-run? If so, why? If not, what are your suggestions for improvement?

5.  If you could change one thing about your community association, what would that be?

6.  Does your community have any rules you consider silly or unneeded? If so, would you eliminate or amend them?

7.  What rules in your community do you consider essential or particularly important?

## CHAPTER 3

# Building a Successful Community

We cannot live only for ourselves.
A thousand fibers connect us with our fellow men.

—HERMAN MELVILLE,
American Author

## CHAPTER INTRODUCTION

"Success has many fathers." This proverb is true in any collective effort, including building community. As Herman Melville notes, we are connected by thousands of fibers. The rich tapestry of our communities is likewise constructed of many threads. Among these threads are effective boards, informed residents, and a community committed to avoiding the repetition of negative stereotypes.

Community associations benefit from dedicated volunteers who serve on their boards and oversee their governance. Each year, hundreds of thousands of volunteers give their time to serve their communities. The value of their dedication is immeasurable by most standards. In our role as managing agents, several traits of effective boards stand out. Understanding the elements of what makes an effective board is a part of building a vibrant, successful community.

For residents of community associations, understanding their rights and responsibilities within the community is essential. Knowing the rules, the process of challenging them, or even providing the ability to adapt rules over time can facilitate engaging residents in a community association. Ensuring that residents understand both their rights and responsibilities supports a community's success.

Finally, a key element in building a successful community is recognizing warning signs that the community has lost sight of its goals. Such a sign can be the emergence of behaviors that reinforce negative stereotypes of community associations. Understanding these signs can help prevent communities from going off course. The success of a community is intricately woven from the dedication of its volunteers, the informed engagement of its residents, and the vigilance in recognizing deviations from its core goals. Together, these elements form the fabric of a vibrant, successful community committed to dispelling negative stereotypes in pursuit of common harmony.

## EMBRACING TEN ELEMENTS OF EFFECTIVE BOARDS OF DIRECTORS

Effective boards require focus and dedication. In chapter 2, I briefly highlighted some of the characteristics that help ensure a well-run community. Here, I explore this issue in more depth, based on my observations from more than forty-five years of managing community associations. While each board is unique, and the following list is by no means exhaustive, the ten elements are typical of many of the successful communities we manage.

### Diversifying Expertise

The diversity we find in our communities is a source of strength. By diversity, I mean not only the persons of different races, ethnicities, genders, ages, religions, disabilities, or orientations who reside in community associations, but also their diversity of experience.

An effective board has membership that spans professions, occupations, and life experiences. The demands of the boards vary and touch on finances, due process, rules enforcement, and community engagement. A community benefits when residents with diverse work or life experiences volunteer for board service. They provide institutional knowledge that allows board members to work to their strengths. A board member with accounting experience, for example, can help colleagues walk through the budgeting process, while one who is a teacher can help explain board actions to the larger community.

Such membership diversity can bring a variety of perspectives to decision-making and help reduce blind spots in which board members otherwise would be unaware of critical issues. A board comprising only older residents, for example, could fail to plan activities for families with young children, while one without religious diversity might err in scheduling an election on a spiritual holiday. These faux pas can be easily avoided by ensuring diversity on boards of directors.

## Understanding Documents

Community association boards are the governing entities of communities. The governing documents authorize them to make decisions on behalf of their communities. The proverbial buck stops with them. This authority extends to setting budgets, enforcing rules, engaging contractors to serve the community, and much more. To be effective, a board must have a common understanding of its role, the scope of its authority, and its responsibilities to the community at large. It needs to be accountable, and only by understanding its role can it achieve this goal.

Although it may sound simple, the best way to achieve an understanding of the board's function is to have the board review the governing documents annually with a focus on the bylaws and rules. This exercise in focus will ensure the board does not drift from its explicit mission. It can also bring to light rules that may no longer fit the community's values.

Interestingly, Nevada requires all elected or appointed board members to certify they have read and understood the governing documents within ninety days of assuming their positions.[1] Whether required by statute or not, this common-sense action is a best practice that keeps boards focused on the key issues of their communities.

## Leading by Example

One of the many challenges for boards in the post-pandemic environment is civility. We have all seen the erosion of civility in the last few years. In earlier times, we could look to state or federal leaders to provide examples for navigating disagreements regarding policy matters. Today, we are confronted with disagreements and divisions whenever we turn on the news or dive into our social media streams. That said, the board sets the tone for the community.

An effective board strives to lead by example in its language, tone, and temperament while acting as a collective entity, not as individuals. This means individual board members have no authority, and a board acts by a majority of its members. In any democratic process, a board member will sometimes be in the majority and at other times in the minority. Respecting the process and working to execute majority decisions is not only demanded by principles of leadership, but also required by board members' duties to their communities.

Likewise, focusing on the agenda items for the board meetings and using tools such as *Robert's Rules of Order* facilitates focusing debates on issues, not personalities. Comments made by board members or residents that are directed at others rather than at the issue at hand can be ruled out of order. If the board sets an example, residents will have a framework for disagreeing without being disagreeable.

## Improving Continually

Increasingly, it seems as if every tool we use needs a frequent update, including our computers, phones, and even our cars. Unfortunately, when it comes to changes in regulation or priorities in our communities, there is no update patch for boards. As noted, there are many technical demands on board members. An effective board is one that makes time to engage in continuing education about its roles and responsibilities. This is a critical measure of an effective board because it exists and functions within an evolving environment. Each year, for example, state legislatures consider hundreds of legislative measures that impact community associations. What is more, changing prices or technological advancements may impact the reserve funding needs for future projects. Successful boards understand that change is as continual as it is inevitable, and they educate themselves accordingly.

Although the task of continuing education may seem daunting, the reality is that board training and education opportunities are available widely, often free. Industry attorneys, community management firms, and membership organizations such as the Community Associations Institute regularly provide in-person and online board education courses. Impressively, they do remarkably well in updating course content to reflect changing requirements in community management.

## Being Consistent

The rules typically adopted by community associations help enhance and protect the value of the homes within them. That said, rules also are the greatest source of tension between boards and residents. No one likes to get called out for breaking a rule, and violators must be assured they are not being singled out. Their acceptance of rule enforcement is enhanced when they are confident the board is implementing rules fairly and consistently and responding just as fairly and consistently to any available appeals from fines or other consequences.

The most important element of rule enforcement that often gets lost is its underlying goal—compliance. It is easy for a resident to take a rule enforcement action personally instead of objectively, especially when a violation results in a monetary fine. To mitigate this problematic possibility, the board can first begin by adopting and announcing a regular schedule of community inspections. Second, it can ensure violation notices include a description of the related appeal process or a method to inform the board the violation was resolved. Finally, a board can provide exceptions to rule enforcement in unusual circumstances, thereby providing some grace to distressed homeowners dealing with circumstances beyond their control. An example is waiving the fine for homeowners who were dealing with a catastrophic illness and unintentionally failed to comply with a rule—but giving them a deadline for compliance. At the end of the day, boards should be consistent in their enforcement and always remember the underlying goal is compliance.

## Governing Transparently

For any governing structure, including community associations, transparency is a vital element. Residents should be given the resources to understand decisions made by their boards, the rationale for them, and the overall financial health of their communities. Transparency can be elusive, partly because it depends on the willingness of the audience to absorb the information provided. With that in mind, effective boards can meet their responsibilities by providing residents with sufficient information to understand the reasons behind the decision-making processes that impact their communities.

Many community association boards of directors rely on monthly meetings, minutes, and budget documents to keep residents in the loop about community developments. Providing copies of those documents is generally deemed sufficient to meet any legal requirements imposed by them or by state statutes. Supplementing this information with summaries published in community newsletters, websites, or social streams can be helpful and effective. This is especially true about budget matters. Many communities are struggling to deal with increasing expenses across the board, especially regarding insurance or other matters. It is one thing to mention these costs; it is another to provide a breakdown of the factors that may drive an assessment increase. Visuals such as a pie chart can illustrate the drivers for an assessment increase, thereby answering questions and reducing resistance to budget increases.

Likewise, boards can survey communities to gauge residents' priorities. Sometimes, survey functionality is incorporated into community applications to enhance interaction between boards and residents. These surveys can be excellent tools for getting the pulse of the community and for creating an environment in which residents perceive their board as listening to their concerns.

## Knowing Limits

For critics of community associations, it may come as a surprise that community association boards of directors are not all-powerful. The powers of a board are defined in the community's governing documents and may be modified by state or federal statutes. Effective boards understand their limited authority. It is not uncommon for a board to face issues that go beyond the scope of its role. An effective board knows its boundaries because it knows its governing documents.

Additionally, boards will sometimes encounter matters that may require the expertise of a licensed professional, such as an attorney, accountant, or engineer. Costs should not dissuade the board from seeking a consultation. In fact, such engagement is typically less costly than dealing with the consequences of substituting the board's judgment for expert advice.

## Considering the Future

Community association boards are under pressure to keep expenses in line. Assessment increases are unpopular but necessary for maintaining and insuring a community association. An effective board considers these expenses when planning by adequately funding reserves. Reserve funds are a portion of assessments set aside for the community's future repairs and upkeep. Unfortunately, they are often the first area neglected when boards look for ways to cut costs, which is short-sighted.

The value of property in a community association is linked to the maintenance of its common elements and amenities. Failure to fund for future repair or replacement often creates even greater and more expensive problems. Primarily, it can result in large special assessments when structural repairs are needed. In exceptional cases, as seen in the collapse of the Champlain Towers in Florida, the results can be devastating. Mortgage underwriters, such as Fannie Mae or the Federal Housing Authority, encourage communities to set aside 10 percent of their budget for reserves. Because that amount can vary depending on the financial health of the community association, a reserve specialist should advise boards about a proper path. Failure to plan wisely will ultimately undermine the community's health.

## Engaging Residents

Greater community engagement is needed in today's world. An erosion of civility, the isolation that comes from telework, and a general reshuffling of social norms are evident in the aftermath of the COVID-19 pandemic. As a result, many people crave connection. Effective boards recognize this and use the community association framework to engage their residents. Such engagement highlights the benefits of living in a community association and moves the focus beyond rules enforcement.

Associa prioritizes community engagement and facilitates it by offering a host of programs to our clients. First among these programs is Associa Supports Kids (ASK). Led by our mascot, Scout, we provide communities with giveaways, including coloring books, child-print ID kits, and toys they can use to liven a community event.

We are also the only community management company that is a national sponsor of National Night Out (NNO). This nationwide event promotes safety by connecting communities with local law enforcement. It also strives to meet an increasingly important goal, namely, improving the dialogue between law enforcement officers and the diverse communities they serve.

Helping neighbors is the most important path of community engagement. A community can be a source of support and solace when disaster strikes. To lead by example, Associa founded Associa Cares in 2007. It is a 501(c)(3) charity that provides direct financial grants to people who lose their homes during a natural or man-made disaster. Since its founding, Associa Cares has distributed more than $5 million to thousands of families in need. All efforts need not be so grand, however—having a committee to help ill or grieving neighbors by raking a yard or dropping off hot meals is a simple way to connect and show the power of community.

These highlighted programs are examples of how Associa supports engagement in our client communities. Boards of directors can tailor engagement to meet their community association's specific culture.

## Adapting to Change

"Adapt" is a word that appears frequently in this chapter. That is because it is a tool for effective governance that too often gets lost in the day-to-day challenges boards face. As we discussed earlier, however, preferences change over time, and what was an important focus of a community association twenty, ten, or even five years ago may not be as important today. Clotheslines were the example provided earlier, and today's emerging topics include electric vehicle charging stations, solar panels, and native landscaping.

One of the best features of a community association is that it places governance in the hands of the neighborhood. If a rule no longer suits the needs of the community, it can be changed. For community rules, this is an easier task that often requires only a simple majority vote of the board. If the restriction is in the governing documents, however, effecting change may be a more time-consuming process that requires a supermajority of residents.

That said, using the community governance structure to adapt to changing community needs is an effective means of demonstrating responsive, effective governance. Whether the change requires a majority of board members or a supermajority of residents, making it would be significantly easier than changing a local ordinance or passing state or federal legislation.

## DEFINING RIGHTS AND RESPONSIBILITIES OF RESIDENTS

The relationship between the community association board and residents is contractual in nature. Governing documents authorize the board to make decisions on behalf of the community, and residents have the right to enjoy community amenities and obligations to support the association through assessments and to comply with community rules. A contract works best when all parties clearly understand their rights and responsibilities. This ensures everyone is on the same page and sets appropriate expectations for behavior.

## Board of Directors' Roles and Responsibilities

Board roles and responsibilities are outlined in community governing documents and may be enhanced by appropriate state or federal statutes. This does not mean that all board members and residents have taken the time to read and understand them.

The relationship between the board and residents works best when the board's role and responsibilities are understood by all parties. It is a worthwhile exercise for a board to develop a summary of its responsibilities to share with residents, thereby facilitating their understanding of its role. This project can be done with the assistance of legal counsel to ensure the summary accurately captures the board's functions.

Interestingly, some state governments have produced documents that outline the authority of community association boards as a means of consumer protection. Illinois, for example, is among the states that produced a free document outlining the rights and responsibilities of association board members.[2] Such documents help establish clear expectations for both boards and community association residents.

## Residents' Rights and Responsibilities

A community's governing documents also define the rights and responsibilities of the residents of the association. Obligations such as complying with community rules and paying mandatory assessments are key among these. Too often, however, the rights of residents may be overlooked. It can be a helpful exercise for the board to develop a summary of the rights and responsibilities of community residents. Like the exercise in outlining the elements of the board's role and responsibilities, enumerating residents' rights and responsibilities establishes clarity of process and sets reasonable expectations in the community.

The importance of this enumeration is highlighted by the Community Associations Institute's (CAI) program focusing on the pillars of good governance. The preface of its program summarizes its goals as follows:

> *Community associations exist because they offer choices, lifestyles, amenities, and efficiencies that people value. Yet, with all of their inherent advantages, community associations face complicated issues, none more common than the challenge of balancing the rights of the*

*individual homeowner with those of the community as a whole. Issues often arise because of false expectations, misinformation, and misunderstanding. You can help ensure a more positive community experience by learning all you can about a community before you buy or rent a home in that neighborhood.*[3]

The publication provides an easily absorbed summary regarding the rights and responsibilities of the board and of community association residents. It reflects the expertise of industry professionals and is an excellent tool for boards interested in increasing their effectiveness.

## Civility

During the pandemic, a tragic crime in Atlanta drove home the need to restore civil discourse and will live forever in the hearts and minds of those who work in community associations. In August 2022, a disgruntled homeowner opened fire in a condominium complex, fatally shooting the property manager, Michael, and wounding the chief building engineer. The suspect also fatally shot her former supervisor.

As the leading management company, Associa considered this tragedy a wake-up call. In the weeks that followed, we worked feverishly to develop a framework for association boards and residents to use to help promote civility and enhance safety in community associations. The effort included a sample resolution about civility, a recommendation to engage with local law enforcement, and a suggestion that community associations participate in the National Night Out program discussed earlier. See the framework in Appendix A.

The civility pledge outlines the responsibilities of all the players in a community association. The document provides a framework that outlines prohibited conduct, establishes decorum at community meetings, imposes a duty of respect, and describes enforcement mechanisms. A board that models civil behavior and reinforces needed civility norms is a hallmark of an effective community association.

## RECOGNIZING THREE WAYS TO COUNTER STEREOTYPES OF BOARDS OF DIRECTORS

The negative stereotypes of community associations are strong. As discussed in chapter 2, there are many reasons for this. Effective community governance requires board members to understand such negativity and consciously strive not to reinforce it.

In such an environment, it is tempting and relatively easy for a disgruntled homeowner to take a dispute with the board to the local media. Sometimes, a reporter is more than willing to spin another tale of an alleged community association abuse. An effective board counters this risk by paying attention to a few fundamentals, including those discussed here.

### Flexibility

Enforcement, rules, and assessment obligations exist for a variety of reasons. The board has a duty to maintain and enhance the community and, relatedly, for enforcement related to rule violations or assessment delinquencies. That said, the board can work with its counsel and take appropriate action to ensure compliance that considers the entirety of the circumstances.

Consistent enforcement of the rules helps ensure community harmony, but it should not come at the expense of common sense. Times and situations sometimes justify enforcement with compassion. A good example involves a single resident being treated for a significant health matter who temporarily falls out of compliance by not keeping the lawn mowed. Rather than issue a violation, the board can provide flexibility to allow the resident to come into compliance or, better yet, find a neighbor who may be willing to help. Such fact patterns are rare, but if board members know about a unique situation at play and compassionate flexibility is in order, then lending a hand can work to highlight the spirit of community.

Another area that creates controversy for community associations is enforcing lien rights for assessment delinquencies or even proceeding with foreclosure to recoup past-due assessments. All residents are responsible for paying their fair share for operating communities. Cumulatively, the impact of individuals who fail to pay those obligations is that it increases the costs for all other homeowners. Accordingly, effective boards find an appropriate threshold to initiate foreclosure as a resolution to assessment delinquency.

We have all read stories or heard about a board that initiates a foreclosure for a nominal past-due payment. While such instances are rare, they exist. These actions sometimes drive further governmental regulation of board authority and reinforce negative stereotypes about community associations. Some states have gone as far as to impose thresholds for past-due accounts before action can be taken.

As each community's needs are different, boards should be prepared to set benchmarks before taking the drastic action of enforcing lien rights. Given the tools available to collect past-due assessments, boards should consider less obtrusive options such as payment plans before taking the ultimate action.

## Mutual Respect

Members of a community association board of directors are responsible for respecting their fellow board members. They should be united in their goal of preserving and enhancing the value of the community, even if they visualize different pathways to achieve that goal.

Although composed of individual members, a board acts collectively through majority votes. Once a board formally approves a matter, its members should support the actions taken or, at the very least, not undermine the ability of the board to implement the results. This duty of mutual respect among fellow board members, however, does not preclude dissenting members from working within the board framework to change or repeal approved actions with which they disagree.

It is helpful to remember that the behavior of individual board members impacts the perception of the entire board and the community association. Board members should strive to put the community first and refrain from allowing personalities to trump policy debates.

## Positive Reinforcement

Too often, the relationship between residents and their boards is strictly negative. When a resident's first contact with a board is a violation letter, the relationship begins on a negative note.

Effective boards seek to change this dynamic by simple actions of positive reinforcement, such as establishing a welcome committee and providing new residents with welcome baskets that feature donated items or coupons from local businesses. They can also organize programs to thank residents for their contributions to the community at large. These include announcing a resident Volunteer of the Year or Yard of the Month, rewarding good neighbors, and adopting other recognitions that are positive in nature. These activities not only connect residents of the community, but also highlight shared values among neighbors.

## CONCLUSION

Community associations exist in many forms. Likewise, there are many pathways to building a successful community. It begins with recognizing the connections between boards and residents. A successful community has taken the time to understand and facilitate these connections. For boards, building a successful community is, in part, an exercise in self-awareness. A successful board engages in introspection to ensure it focuses on effectively meeting the needs of the community.

For residents, living in a community association is not a spectator sport. It requires understanding the benefits and the responsibilities inherent in the common ownership structure of community associations, particularly as they relate to the importance of day-to-day operations and the reasons for board actions. Finally, building a successful community also requires board members with compassion who can look beyond the simple enforcement of rules and respond to challenges with an appropriate level of awareness. These multiple elements can best be addressed by focusing on what is best for the community, considering the lifestyles, values, and preferences of its residents.

## QUESTIONS TO CONSIDER

1. Does your community association board of directors represent you effectively? If so, what are some examples of its effectiveness? If not, how can it improve?

2. If you serve or have served on a community association board, what experiences or insights helped you serve residents more effectively? If you have not served, would you consider doing so?

3. Are there additional ways your board can keep your community informed about its work?

4. What are some of the ways members of your board of directors set good examples by their leadership and responsiveness? How can they improve in this regard?

5. What steps can be taken to engage more residents in social activities or in other community-oriented events?

6. As a resident of a community association, do you have a good understanding of your obligations to the community, as well as its obligations to you?

7. What actions can be taken to ensure mutual respect and civility are the norm during your community-wide meetings?

8. How can your community's board of directors provide regular and meaningful positive recognition to residents?

# SUCCESSFUL COMMUNITIES

There is no power for change greater than
a community discovering what it cares about.

—MARGARET J. WHEATLEY,
American Writer and Management Consultant

## PART II INTRODUCTION

There is an inflection point when a group of leaders realize their power to promote positive change. For community associations, a collaborative board of directors is often the key to building a successful community. For many boards, defining that success can be an elusive goal. To harness the power Margaret Wheatley speaks of, success and positive change can be achieved by board members who understand the issues and needs that residents care about and hope their elected leaders will address.

Boards do not operate in a vacuum. Building successful communities requires their members to look beyond their expertise to help ensure their effectiveness, find the right management support, and hire professionals needed to achieve their communities' goals.

The process begins with some introspection. A board can and should adopt a philosophy of continuous improvement based on its foundational understanding of its role within the community. Knowing the scope of their authority can help ground board members and focus their efforts on their missions. A commitment to improving their skill sets can prepare them to face potential challenges collectively and effectively. Their willingness and ability to set aside personal differences in the best interest of residents keep their focus on the community rather than on internal politics.

One means to enhance a board of directors' success is to engage professional management. Firms like Associa exist to handle the day-to-day operations of a community, which allows the board to focus on governance. A fundamental understanding of the board's role is helpful, as is having a grasp of the support professional community management can provide.

Finally, knowing the range of professionals and professional services available to support the board's vision can help demystify the process of finding their assistance when needed. When the right professional is found, having a basic understanding of the contracting process and key terms to protect the community is a logical next step.

As the board begins a project with a hired professional, looking at best practices for interacting with consultants can accelerate progress and promote collaboration.

While Part I of this book focused on the important role community plays, Part II highlights how board members can utilize their talents and hire professionals to collaboratively build a successful community. Its three chapters provide an overview of how boards of directors can enhance their effectiveness while collaborating with the right management and other professionals to achieve their visions and build successful communities.

## CHAPTER 4

# Ensuring an Effective Board

If your actions inspire others to dream more,
learn more, do more and become more, you are a leader.

—JOHN QUINCY ADAMS,
Sixth President of the United States

## CHAPTER INTRODUCTION

A board of directors is the cornerstone of a community association. It functions as the decision-making body for the community and provides the leadership needed to build and sustain a vibrant community. As former President Adams noted, as leaders, their actions should "inspire others to dream more, learn more, do more and become more." Because of their central leadership roles in community associations, boards are essential in any effort to build community.

Ensuring an effective board is critical. Working toward that goal requires understanding the role of the board, creating and highlighting pathways for board members to educate themselves, and, finally, focusing on ways board members can work together.

Many of the challenges we see in community associations stem from misunderstandings about how they operate. Knowing the roles boards of directors play in our communities is fundamental to our efforts to build community. Generally, they are the elected bodies empowered to make decisions for their community associations. Their roles can be conceptualized more easily by looking at the scope of a board's authority and the source from which this authority originates.

Understanding a board's role is a great point of departure, but we should not lose sight of the many challenges its members face. They are primarily volunteers who are responsible for the governance and operations of a corporate entity, their community association. This requires knowledge in many disciplines that range from accounting and budgeting to conducting and participating in meetings, adopting rules, and even settling disputes among neighbors. Providing board members with the needed resources to improve their knowledge will help strengthen their ability to continue to inspire others.

Finally, understanding the board's role and educational opportunities can facilitate our discussion about how board members can best work together to accomplish their common goals. Boards consist of a variety of members with many perspectives, backgrounds, experiences, and political leanings. Such diversity of thought can be a double-edged sword, either positively providing an array of perspectives to inform decision-making or negatively creating needless obstacles to finding common ground. Collectively, understanding a board of directors' role and enhancing its opportunities for education and collaboration will add to our arsenal of community-building tools.

## UNDERSTANDING BOARD ROLES

Community associations grant decision-making powers to boards of directors. Board members are elected by residents and oversee the day-to-day needs of residents. The board's authority is not absolute but, rather, limited by various sources, including its governing documents. To understand the role of the board in a community association, it is helpful to understand the board's authority, the sources for that authority, and the responsibilities board members have to their communities.

## Board Authority

As the decision-making body for community associations, the board runs the show. A community association is a corporate entity, which means that from a legal standpoint, it has legal rights such as those a person might have. This provides a practical mechanism for community governance by allowing decisions to be made by a group representing the interests of the community.

In most cases, a community association board can act on behalf of the association regarding a variety of matters. This typically includes the power to collect assessments, issue fines and late fees, execute contracts, adopt budgets, enforce rules, and exercise other powers that may be enumerated in the community's governing documents. It is especially important for board members to acknowledge their powers are not unlimited, but, instead defined by a variety of sources, including governing documents and state and federal laws.

A board is also a collective entity. Binding decisions made on behalf of communities must be determined by a majority vote of the board, not by individual action. Once a decision is made, however, all members are bound by it.

## Sources of Board Authority

To fully understand its role, an effective board must also be cognizant of the sources of its authority. A basic understanding of the community's governing documents, applicable state and federal statutes, and even case law can shape what the board can do. Effective boards understand this dynamic and work to stay abreast of developments. For a board's actions to be enforceable, it must act within the limitations of its authority and mandate.

Understanding the interplay among these sources of authority helps ensure the board's actions are appropriate and legal. When there is a conflict between sources of authority, the higher one takes precedence. This means, for example, that powers defined in bylaws can be changed by state law, which, in turn, can be changed by federal statute.

## Governing Documents

The community's governing documents typically include its articles of incorporation; covenants, conditions, and restrictions (CC&Rs); and bylaws. Cumulatively, they outline the powers of the board. Generally, the board is established by articles of incorporation, and its authority is defined in the bylaws. A good rule of thumb is that bylaws are an operational manual that spells out what the board can do and how it is supposed to carry out its functions.

Governing documents are specific to a community association and can vary depending on the size and nature of the development. They can give the board power to levy fines, enter contracts, hire professionals, set budgets, and exercise other powers needed to protect and enhance the value of property in the community association.

## State Law

Board authority can also be shaped by state laws. Because they are a higher authority, state statutes can supplement, modify, remove, or otherwise limit the authority defined for the board in its governing documents. This interplay can be illustrated in the following examples:

*Consider the situation of a board limited in its actions by powers granted to it in the community association's governing documents. Over time, the needs for board authority may evolve, but the board cannot act beyond those limitations without amending the documents or having its power extended by statute.*

*Many states have adopted state condominium or homeowners association acts that include an enumerated list of board powers or a mandate that certain provisions related to boards be included in any governing documents. Such laws supplement the governing documents of a community and provide additional authority to the board.*

Board powers can also be restricted by statute. A great example of this can be seen in state actions to curb board authority regarding a range of topics. An increasingly popular area of regulating board powers reflects the changing values about the environment. At the time many associations were built, aesthetic preferences disfavored installing clotheslines and solar installations or changing the property in other ways that might impact the look and feel of the community. As resident priorities changed over time, many legislatures adopted laws restricting a community association board from regulating items such as clotheslines[1] or solar installations.[2]

## Federal Law

A higher authority than state laws, federal laws can impact boards similarly. In fact, many federal laws protect an individual's or a family's ability to purchase a home. Arising from the Civil Rights struggles of the 1960s, for example, the Civil Rights Act of 1968 includes sections referred to as the Fair Housing Act.[3] It is intended to ensure no one is denied housing due to race, religion, national origin, or sex.[4] Because it applies to community associations, the Fair Housing Act is a perfect example of a federal law that impacts community associations.

Like state legislatures, the U.S. Congress has passed laws limiting the powers of community association boards. The Freedom to Display the American Flag Act (2005), for example, prohibits community association boards from banning the display of the American flag.[5]

## Case Law

Courts of law play a related role in defining the powers of community association boards of directors. One of the functions of courts is to adjudicate disputes by applying the provisions of applicable laws to the facts of a disagreement and issuing a decision. Court decisions are considered case law that can impact the scope of a board's authority.

Case law can be more complicated than state or federal statutes because whether they apply to one, some, or all community association boards depends on the nature of the case, the court in which it is heard, and the questions addressed. While boards do not need to abide by court decisions in which they are not litigants, they should be aware of them. They should turn to their attorneys for advice about such matters.

In the final analysis, the role of the board is straightforward: It is the body that governs the community association.

## Board Responsibilities

Boards also have an important responsibility to the community. Because board members act on behalf of the interests of the entire community and handle community funds, they have a fiduciary duty to the people and entities they serve. This means board members, in their roles as community leaders, are obligated to put the interests of their communities ahead of any other interests they may have.

A fiduciary duty is defined as a relationship of trust and confidence between a person in a position of authority and others who are subject to that authority. In other words, board members should not use their positions of power to achieve personal gain or advantage and must put the interests of the association above any personal or emotional needs.

### EDUCATING BOARD MEMBERS

For community association board members, understanding the sources and scope of their authority and the extent of their responsibilities to residents comprise half the challenge. Although they are volunteers in service to their communities, their task is as important as it is challenging—and is not necessarily easy.

Continuing education is the key to their success. Their insight and experience as community association residents certainly will be the foundation from which they begin their board service, but their perspective will soon be colored by their new responsibilities and newly gained knowledge.

Effective boards provide a rich variety of opportunities for their members to learn in greater depth about subjects including what forces may supplement or limit their roles and actions. If they do not know already, they soon must learn the board's role is defined not only by community documents, but also by a panoply of state and federal statutes and even case law. The good news is that many educational resources are available to help board members understand their duties to the community and build an effective board. It does not end there, however.

Because board members are empowered to lead community associations, they benefit from having access to resources that assist them in tackling the many disciplines involved in governing community associations. They need a fundamental understanding of a wide range of topics that impact communities. Financial statements, budgeting, rule enforcement, conflict mediation, communication, presiding and meeting skills, and maintaining an association reserve fund are merely some of the topics board members need to deal with in their roles as community leaders. That is why effective board members educate themselves to serve their communities better.

While it may seem like a herculean task to arrange training and development for board members, a surprisingly rich ecosystem of membership organizations, government agencies, and professional management companies offer educational opportunities to community association board members for little or no charge. Such resources are valuable tools to ensure board members are best prepared to serve residents and build their communities more effectively.

## Membership Organizations

Numerous national, state, and local organizations serve the community association industry. These membership groups offer resources to improve the overall experiences of board members, residents, and professionals working in community associations.

The primary membership organization serving the industry is the Community Associations Institute (CAI).[6] Founded in 1973 for the express purpose of advancing excellence for community associations, CAI has more than sixty-five chapters globally. It offers not only a wide variety of in-person and online courses, but also an online bookstore with numerous titles addressing key board issues.

Equally important is that CAI awards a Board Leadership Certificate to community association board members who complete a set of courses specifically addressing key board leadership topics. Holding this credential helps build trust and confidence among residents and can be helpful when running for election to the board.

## Management Company Resources

Community association boards often hire professional community managers to assist them in community operations. I am proud that the company I built serves community associations across North America. We focus on empowering our board clients to be the best leaders they can be.

Recognizing the importance of that goal, we continually update and strengthen our continuing education program, which focuses on key issues for boards.[7] This includes our six-part program that addresses board roles, communication, budgeting, planning, and other topics. We offer these learning opportunities to both clients and potential clients.

Our tailored publications focus on topics such as hosting a successful board meeting, budgeting, maintenance, and assessment collection matters. We also regularly schedule webinars that allow participants to engage with experts by asking questions directly or through the online chat feature. Also popular are our online self-study programs, which allow them not only to log on at their convenience, but also to advance at their own pace.

## Professional Business Partners

Community association boards are supported by a host of professionals they can hire as needed or as ongoing consultants. These include attorneys, reserve specialists, insurance brokers, engineers, architects, and professional community managers.

Most of these professionals are qualified by virtue of certifications, education, or licensing that require a high degree of proven ability. Those committed to building strong communities typically offer education programs within their specialties for their clients or potential clients. Interested board members should feel free to reach out to these professionals to inquire how they can help in this regard.

## State Resources

Increasingly, state agencies are providing educational resources to assist community association boards of directors. While many of their programs may focus on the big picture of board service and may not be as focused or detailed as programs available from other sources, they can be helpful, especially for newly elected board members.

Florida and Nevada are among the states that provide such resources. In Florida, for example, board members must certify within ninety days of joining a board of directors that they have read and understood their association's governing documents and completed a board certification course. The state provides a list of certified training organizations that can assist board members in complying with these requirements.[8]

Similarly, Nevada's Real Estate Division publishes a handbook that provides an overview of the various requirements and responsibilities that accompany community association board service.[9]

## WORKING TOGETHER

Community associations work because of the millions of volunteers who step forward to serve on their boards of directors. With few exceptions, there is no prequalification required for board service; yet, as we have discussed, board members deal with a wide range of topics and personalities. Because the board is responsible for ensuring the successful operation of the community association, its ability to function effectively can determine whether the community is a pleasant place to live.

Serving on a governing body also means finding common ground regarding community matters and establishing bonds to promote board teamwork. An effective board finds ways to facilitate working together that can include defining board member expectations, creating a culture of respect, setting consensus goals, fostering team building, deploying technology, communicating interpersonally, hiring professional managers, and networking with other boards. These practices are mutually inclusive, not exclusive, and are described briefly.

## Defining Board Member Expectations

We have established the importance of board members knowing the scope of their board's role in their respective communities. Building on that knowledge, boards can establish expectations for them. One helpful avenue for accomplishing this is to offer an orientation session for new members and to announce it so interested residents can attend. The agenda should include a question-and-answer period as a means of addressing all concerns and providing all the information needed. Equally important, it should address the expectations residents have of board members—and vice versa—as well as the expectations board members have of each other.

Setting expectations keeps the board on track by helping its members understand their expected contributions and individual responsibilities.

## Creating a Culture of Respect

Sometimes, it seems that as a society, we have lost the understanding that we do not have to agree with others all the time or even like each other to work together toward a common goal. That said, an effective board, especially through its presiding officer, strives to create and maintain a culture of respect.

Board members are expected to engage in vigorous debates about key or controversial issues facing their communities, but they should focus on the issues at hand and avoid personal criticism or attacks—before, during, or after meetings.

Because boards set the tone for their communities, personal attacks between their members, even if related to policy issues, can be perceived as permissive behavior for how residents can treat the board and each other. When that happens, meetings can become increasingly contentious, and that negativity can carry forward to future meetings.

Boards should debate topics by focusing on their merits, voicing their support/dissent regarding a topic, and voting. Once a decision is made, board members should fulfill their duties by collaboratively executing the majority decision. If collegiality among board members becomes a challenge, it is helpful to remind each other they share and should embrace the most important goal of building a successful community. Reaching that goal is easier in a positive, constructive, respectful atmosphere.

## Setting Consensus Goals

Every community association board has a host of annual tasks it must perform. These can include adopting a budget, enforcing rules consistently, and reviewing architectural requests. Although such operational responsibilities are critical to the community association, boards can also set a consensus goal for the community. This does not have to be a complicated goal, but, rather, one that the board can coalesce around and support as a team, such as increasing residents' engagement or scheduling more social activities.

Board members will not always agree, perhaps even on the most basic decisions, and some issues can evoke great passion. Setting a goal that unites a board, such as increasing social activities in a community, can be a great way to establish team spirit and express appreciation for the skills each board member brings to the table.

## Fostering Team Building

Team-building exercises are typically designed to promote cooperation, communication, and trust. Boards can benefit from investing time in collaboration that allows them to problem-solve in a safe and enjoyable context. Benefits from these exercises include creating opportunities for shared experiences and improved relationships, understanding board members' individual skill sets, and instilling a sense of pride as a team member.

There is no need for risky team-building activities, such as falling backward from a platform into the arms of team members expected to catch you. What is needed are problem-solving activities that require listening, communication, interaction, and consensus. Perhaps the simplest exercise that meets these criteria is asking team members to organize themselves into a line chronologically based on the months and dates (not years!) on which they were born. Small groups can form a single line, while larger ones can break into subgroups that compete to finish first.

More typical activities include engaging in a community service project, participating in an escape room, or interacting in a relaxed social setting simply to allow board members to get to know each other better.

## Deploying Technology

The community association industry used to be a laggard when it came to technology, but times have changed—thank God! Community association boards have increasingly diverse options for implementing technology to facilitate and improve their community governance responsibilities. Tools such as TownSq can be deployed to streamline communication, send messages to the entire community instantly, resolve violations, and in some cases, even allow online voting.

Community websites or applications can promote transparency within the community by providing access to governing documents, agendas, board minutes, financial statements, budgets, schedules, and other information. These tools can help boards be more productive, especially by eliminating some otherwise routine tasks, such as responding to information requests. This, in turn, allows them to focus on enhancing the board's vision and motivation.

## Communicating Interpersonally

While technology can be employed to lessen the board's workload, it should not be a substitute for interpersonal communication. I am confident each of us has experienced having a well-intentioned text message or email communication interpreted to our disadvantage. Because readers often project their emotions more easily into emails, the best way to ensure your intended receiver understands your point of view and intent is to reach out personally. A telephone call or quick conversation has the added benefit of making a personal connection.

Interpersonal communication enhances understanding because the listener can hear vocal elements such as rate, volume, stress, and pitch; and the observer can read body language, including facial expression, gestures, posture, and appearance. Cumulatively, these verbal, vocal, and nonverbal messages are more likely to be interpreted appropriately. Such interactions help project a better overall picture of sincerity, reduce misunderstandings, and promote trust.

Relatedly, we have all heard and read, "It is not what you say; it is how you say it." Two persons can say basically the same thing, but the different ways in which they express it verbally, vocally, and non-verbally can result in completely different reactions. This outcome is explained by the communication research of Albert Mehrabian, who demonstrated that the communication of feeling (not of content) is based on 7 percent verbal (words), 38 percent vocal (voice), and 55 percent nonverbal (body language) aspects of the communication.[10] Community association board members who internalize this information and modify their communication accordingly can enhance their effectiveness and improve outcomes. Management companies often offer continuing education programs that help them do so.

## Hiring Professional Managers

It can be exceedingly challenging for board members to handle all the daily operational tasks in a community association, particularly if it is large. That is why many boards use professional community management companies to handle the day-to-day operational tasks of the community, thereby freeing the board to focus on governance.

A qualified professional community management company can focus on ongoing tasks, such as rules enforcement, maintenance, meeting notices, and billing, and can also assist with dispute resolution or other less routine aspects of the job. At Associa, we take great pride in the work our managers do to support community association boards in the daily operations of their communities.

## Networking with Other Boards

Many community associations exist alongside similar communities. Reaching out to other community association boards can be an effective tool to promote board cohesion and learn from the comparable experiences of others. Board members can learn valuable lessons from their peers, especially regarding matters that may be new to them but have been experienced and dealt with by a neighboring board. Such dialogue can be mutually beneficial, especially for gaining insight into overcoming obstacles to difficult projects and learning how other boards handled matters collectively.

## CONCLUSION

Simply stated, the board of a community association is the nexus around which the community coalesces. Working to ensure its effectiveness is one of the board's most important objectives.

As leaders, board members are well advised to take to heart the advice of John Quincy Adams and consistently take actions that inspire others to dream more, learn more, do more, and become more. His words capture the essence of members' responsibility for ensuring their board is effective. Using the authority vested in them by the community's governing documents, state and federal statutes, and case law, boards can more successfully navigate the complex landscape of serving their communities effectively.

Given the breadth of the topics a board may be required to handle, education is a critical component of improving its performance. Each member brings a skill set that can benefit the community, and cumulatively, the diversity of their skills has immense value. This is the foundation from which board members can gain the added knowledge they need to fulfill their roles effectively. Fortunately, there are rich educational resources tailored for community association boards, including membership organizations, management companies, professional business partners, and even state agencies.

Because a board of directors functions as a collective entity and makes decisions by majority vote, fostering a culture of collaboration and teamwork is vital. Working to set clear expectations, promote mutual respect, and establish consensus projects are essential strategies for ensuring a cohesive and efficient board dynamic.

A collaborative culture is reinforced by engaging in team-building exercises, leveraging technology, and prioritizing interpersonal communication. These activities strengthen bonds among board members and with residents of community associations.

Relatedly, networking with neighboring boards provides opportunities for exchanging knowledge, sharing experiences, and finding mutual support. Applying the lessons learned from board member peers to address common challenges can facilitate success while saving time and effort.

The journey toward building vibrant communities requires the efforts of dedicated and knowledgeable board members. By establishing a common understanding of the board's role, adopting continuing education goals, promoting effective collaboration, and networking, community association boards of directors can achieve their visions to govern effectively with foresight, integrity, and mutual respect in the best interests and well-being of their communities.

---

## QUESTIONS TO CONSIDER

1. How does your community association board of directors inspire you and other residents to do more for your community?

2. Through their words and actions, do your board members reflect an understanding of their roles and of their authority in serving your community? If so, how do they accomplish this? If not, how can they improve?

3. To what extent does your board employ continuing education and educational resources to do a better job in leading your community?

4.  When board members need answers to important questions that impact your community, do they turn to professionals or other resources for advice and assistance? If so, how satisfied have you been with the outcomes?

5.  What are some examples of how your board uses technology to facilitate and improve its responsibilities to your community? Do you have suggestions for how technology could be used more effectively to benefit residents?

6.  In what ways does your community's board of directors serve the community well?

7.  How do you evaluate your board members' abilities to reflect collegiality and mutual respect during discussions or debates, especially when they strongly disagree about issues?

8.  Are you satisfied with your board's attempts to foster a culture of respect among its members and between them and residents? If not, what advice would you give them for doing so?

## CHAPTER 5

# Hiring the Right Management

*The thing that lies at the foundation of positive change,*
*the way I see it, is service to a fellow human being.*

—LEE IACOCCA,
Former President of Ford and Chrysler Motor Companies

## CHAPTER INTRODUCTION

While the board of directors is the nexus of a community association, in many larger communities, volunteer boards increasingly find it difficult to undertake the daily operations of the community. Accordingly, hiring the right management is essential to their success.

Interestingly, I discovered this need early in my career when I was asked to manage a couple of condominium associations in Dallas. It is hard to believe that in the following forty-five years, the role of the professional community association manager has come into its own.

Professional managers and community management companies assist community association boards of directors in running their communities. I am always amazed that my initial effort to serve a handful of condominiums has grown into the leading community management firm in North America. Consistent with the words of Lee Iacocca, across our organization, our community managers continually strive to create positive changes by serving residents.

Community managers and the firms that employ them are increasingly important players in building community. With specialized training and relevant experience, a manager can assist boards in planning and conducting annual meetings, building a budget, tracking financial status, enforcing rules, and completing other tasks to keep the community running smoothly.

The manager works for the board of directors in service to the community. Comparable to misunderstandings about the role of a board of directors, there is some confusion regarding the role of the community manager. Understanding the role and responsibilities of the community manager is essential to building a vibrant and strong community.

A board that establishes the role of the community manager and seeks to hire one also should define minimum and preferred qualifications for applicants for the position. This is particularly important because most board members are volunteers with varying experience in hiring a professional. Agreeing on the manager's role and qualifications can facilitate the process of hiring professional management for their communities.

Understanding the role and qualifications of professional managers is the foundation from which to discuss the best ways to work with a professional community manager or community management firm. Community association managers have diverse backgrounds, specialties, and levels of experience. Knowing how to identify the right manager or management firm can ensure a productive working relationship. Similarly, knowing how to work with a professional manager can supercharge a board of directors' efforts in building a strong community.

## UNDERSTANDING THE ROLE OF COMMUNITY MANAGERS

A community manager is a professional hired by the board of a community association to direct its day-to-day operations. The services provided by the manager can vary. For smaller associations, the services can be as simple as maintaining the association's financial records. For larger ones, that may encompass thousands of homes, the manager can provide turnkey solutions, including hiring staff, organizing board meetings, keeping minutes, conducting inspections, and other functions required by the board.

There are many types of community associations, and community managers provide service levels to meet their specific needs. Most community managers work for a management firm, but others may be hired directly by the community board. To better understand the varying roles community managers can play, we will begin by examining their functions and types and the sources that define their scopes of authority.

## Functions of a Community Manager

Generally, a community manager supports the board of directors of a community association. Functions performed vary based on the type of community association, its size, and the needs of the board of directors. While their range of functions varies, their duties may include the following:

### Administrative Support

A community manager's primary role is to provide administrative support to the board of directors. This can include scheduling board meetings, providing required notices for community-wide meetings, keeping board minutes, and other activities to support the board's mission.

### Assessment Collections

A community manager, typically supported by personnel at the management firm that employs them, can collect assessments on behalf of the community. Cumulatively, the collections provide a stream of revenue to maintain certain amenities, purchase insurance, perform landscaping, fund association reserve accounts, and arrange special projects.

## Financial Reports

To be effective leaders and fulfill their fiduciary duties, board members must have insight into the community association's financial status. A community manager can not only produce financial statements, but also handle accounts payable.

## Community Inspections

To protect the value and aesthetics of the community and ensure rules are observed, a manager can conduct periodic inspections of the property. This process can include "drive-throughs" to note matters not in compliance with rules adopted by the board of directors.

## Rule Enforcement

A community manager can be a buffer between residents who violate rules and the board of directors that adopts and enforces them. This can minimize a difficult or negative situation, thereby facilitating future positive interactions between the parties.

If a resident is in violation of one or more rules, for example, the manager can send a notice encouraging him or her to take action to come into compliance with noted violations. The process typically begins with a friendly reminder that is followed by the imposition of fines if the matter is not resolved. If the resident contests the violation, the manager can work with the board of directors to schedule a hearing to adjudicate the matter.

## Bids for Services

A community manager can save the board significant time by handling requests for proposals to solicit bids for services. This process can focus on projects ranging in complexity from one-time, major construction or repair projects to more routine or regular services, such as landscaping or pool maintenance.

## Community Staffing

At the direction of the board, or if empowered by the management contract, the community manager may ensure the community hires employees to meet its needs. Usually requested by larger associations, community staffing can include everything from hiring seasonal workers needed to complete turnkey solutions to ensuring all permanent staffing needs in the community are met.

## Community Events

The community manager can organize a rich variety of large or small events, whether for all residents or targeted at a particular age or special interest groups. These can include holiday celebrations, community-wide cookouts, or other social functions designed to connect residents. Regardless of their purpose or venue, these activities typically are more successful when arranged by experienced professionals and their teams.

## Other Functions

The diversity of community associations results in a similar diversity in needs that can be filled by a community manager. Depending on the size of the community and the scope of the amenities, a community manager can oversee or coordinate a variety of staff. This can include lifeguards, on-site security and housekeeping personnel, lifestyle coordinators, food service staff, and even staff to operate equestrian centers.

## Types of Community Managers

Community associations come in all shapes and sizes. They can range from a small condominium association with a few units to a high-rise, or even to a large community housing thousands of residents. This diversity of community types in our industry resulted in our defining four classifications for community managers, namely, portfolio, on-site, large-scale, and high-rise. These are described as follows:

### Portfolio Manager

A small community association may not need a full-time community manager. In such cases, the board of directors may prefer to hire a portfolio manager who supports multiple communities and contracts for a set number of hours or specific services to be provided monthly. While the agreed-upon services may vary, they typically include assisting the board with scheduling meetings, bookkeeping, and enforcing community rules.

### On-Site Manager

A larger community association may require a full-time manager responsible for the community's daily operations. In such cases, the board of directors often hires a full-time manager who works on-site.

### Large-Scale Manager

Some community associations can be as large as a small city with multiple amenities, such as community centers, golf courses, equestrian centers, fitness centers, and, in some cases, even bus systems. Their managers may be considered large-scale managers and sometimes are referred to as general managers. Similar to on-site managers in that they work within communities, their functions are akin to those of city managers. They often are empowered by the board to hire support staff, oversee community operations, handle financial matters, and perform other assigned tasks.

### High-Rise Managers

A high-rise community association has a unique set of needs. That is why a high-rise community manager generally provides services beyond the typical bookkeeping, board support, and rules enforcement. Tall residential towers have many more technical needs that include heating and cooling, elevator banks, and exterior maintenance complicated by the height of the building. A manager working in such community associations may supervise personnel, including a concierge, fitness center instructors, or even on-site caterers.

# Sources of Community Manager Authority

Similar to their boards of directors, community managers do not have unfettered authority. Effective boards understand the role, scope, and source of authority of their respective managers, as well as their own obligations.

Understanding the manager's authority allows the board to ensure the community is provided with the management services it purchased. This understanding is the foundation from which board members can facilitate effective operations.

Depending on the type and scale of management services needed, board members can rely on three sources of authority that define the manager's role, namely, the management contract, the manager's employment agreement, and the manager's job description.

## Management Contract

The management contract is the agreement between the community association represented by the board of directors and the manager or management company. The contract defines the powers delegated to the manager in service to the community and can enumerate the functions the manager is expected to perform.

In other words, through the contractual arrangement, the board delegates functions it otherwise would perform to the manager. A limiting factor in this arrangement is that the community manager or management company cannot undertake functions that are not granted by the governing documents to the board of directors or the community.

## Manager's Employment Agreement

A board of directors for a larger community association may hire a community manager directly rather than work through a management company. In such cases, the employment agreement between the community association and the manager will define the functions to be performed by the community manager.

### Manager's Job Description

A community manager's job description is an internal document adopted by the board. It typically outlines the role and authority; duties and functions; and minimum education, experience, and other qualifications deemed necessary for this important management position. As a source of information about the role and authority of a community manager, it supports the employment agreement or management contract.

## DEFINING MANAGER QUALIFICATIONS

Because managers deal with a variety of subject matter areas related to their defined functions, they must be qualified to serve their respective communities well. At Associa, we ensure our managers earn the appropriate credentials as part of their preparation to meet our clients' expectations and to give them the confidence that they are qualified to do so.

When looking for the right managers, board members are well-advised to identify ideal qualifications based on the roles and functions they will be expected to perform. This process begins with understanding the qualities that make a good manager and the significance of the various professional designations adopted for the industry. Mastering this knowledge empowers a board of directors to find the best possible qualified manager to meet its community's needs.

## Qualities of Good Community Managers

The success of a board is often determined by the type of management it chooses. A strong manager helps leaders stay on task, fulfill their duties, and prepare the community for a bright future.

Managers may reflect different qualities at different levels of excellence, but they all should be strong in the following eight areas.

Specifically, all good community association managers should have a community service focus; be good communicators, goal-oriented, organized, professional, knowledgeable, and objective; and have financial expertise.

## Customer Service Focus

Providing exceptional customer service should be the top priority of every community association manager. Maintaining a positive customer-first attitude when dealing with board members and/or residents, regardless of the task at hand, is the key to their success.

Concerns, issues, or problems inevitably will arise during the day-to-day management of an association. Regardless of the circumstances or their seriousness, the manager must ensure everything runs smoothly, including while answering questions, resolving concerns, or responding to comments.

The customer service-focused manager will respond quickly and resolve issues timely. By striving to keep board members and residents happy, they also earn their loyalty.

## Effective Communicator

Effective internal communication is one of the most important elements in the success of a community. A quality community association manager should be easily accessible and facilitate regular, clear, and prompt communication with board members, service providers, and residents. This includes using the channels of communication preferred by their clients—whether email, text messages, website, telephone calls, in-person or virtual meetings, or others.

Equally important are managers who communicate effectively, listen, observe, and read intently. The ability to articulate a message is always considered of paramount importance, but frankly, only if that message reflects an appropriate understanding based on listening to and observing customers carefully, as well as reading their written messages thoughtfully.

## Goal-Oriented

Goal-oriented community association managers help boards of directors define goals for improvement whenever appropriate and desired. In helping a board plan and conduct board meetings, for example, a manager can help its members define goals related to deadlines for making documents available, whether to them or to residents; time devoted to activities such as public comments, executive sessions, or adjournment; and continuing education related to topics as diverse as roles and responsibilities of volunteer members, financial planning, or risk management.

Because they are professionals, managers improve their customer service by setting personal goals that empower them to do a better job. They can advance their careers and further their education, for example, by completing continuing education courses and by obtaining various credentials from the Community Associations Institute (CAI). Earning these credentials proves they're dedicated to providing exceptional service and prepared to serve and help lead their communities.

## Organized

From collecting assessments and negotiating contracts to attending meetings and managing projects, community association managers have myriad duties, many of which are top priorities. They must have solid organizational skills that allow them to complete tasks efficiently, access documents easily, and keep the association running smoothly.

Multitasking is essential, as are time management skills and the ability to delegate assignments to other qualified personnel. Relatedly, timelines with projected start dates, milestones, deadlines, and completion dates are helpful organizational tools used by managers who track their progress and evaluate their success.

## Professional

Professionalism is the hallmark of an effective community association manager. It is projected in countless ways, including demeanor, appearance, language, attitude, preparedness, and punctuality. More specifically, professional traits are defined in Associa's communication and customer service continuing education program as including capability, credibility, likability, reliability, respect, communication skills, and image.

The test of professionalism is to display it when conflicts arise or residents get angry. Regardless of the situation, a good community association manager should remain calm, composed, and professional. If matters escalate and cannot be resolved immediately, the professional manager navigates the conflict by buying time and changing the situational context for the exchange, perhaps by arranging to continue the discussion at another time and place. Time can then be used to advantage as the manager seeks answers to questions and solutions to problems. If necessary, he or she can turn to colleagues who have more expertise, either about the subject or regarding conflict management or conflict resolution. At no time should a manager be anything less than perfectly professional.

## Knowledgeable

Community association managers should be knowledgeable about every aspect of managing a community, especially their agreed-upon responsibilities and functions. At the risk of sounding academic while citing Bloom's Taxonomy, I believe they should demonstrate not only their mastery and comprehension of the relevant knowledge (information, standards, statistics, facts, etc.), but also their ability to analyze, apply, synthesize, and evaluate it for the board.[1]

Information may be powerful, but it is more useful when managers synthesize and evaluate it by developing generalizations that empower the board to make decisions based not merely on facts, but rather on their cumulative impact and interpretation. Knowledgeable managers do this as a matter of course.

At an absolute minimum, through their words and actions, managers should project their knowledge about the structure and operations of a community association, specific governing documents, and any applicable local, state, or federal laws. If they cannot answer a question, they should be able to get the answer or ask a professional partner or service provider who can.

## Objective

A community association is a nonprofit corporation designed to run as a business. Community association managers have a duty to act objectively, not subjectively, in the best interest of the association's membership—not of their own. Every day, in every way, in every dealing, they must treat everyone fairly and consistently, making decisions and recommendations based on standard practices rather than on personal opinions and preferences.

Questions about fairness, inconsistency, subjectivity, and preferential treatment are most likely to be raised regarding fines and compliance. Although managers may recommend exceptions for violation-based fines because of duress, health, or other compelling reasons, for example, they must take every precaution to uphold standards of accountability and responsibility. This means applying rules uniformly, fairly, and consistently. It also means being transparent about exceptions and their underlying rationale.

## Financial Expertise

Community association managers are typically responsible for many financial aspects of the association. They must have a clear, line-by-line understanding of the operating budget and reserve study and always be transparent about where the community stands financially.

More specifically, however, they must have the financial expertise to advise the board about how to meet its fiscal responsibilities and fiduciary duty to residents. Those hired by association management companies such as Associa have the benefit of access to experts who can help them address all financial matters, big or small, singular or recurring.

Always remembering that board members are volunteers who have diverse experiences and not all may have business backgrounds, managers must be prepared to bolster their financial expertise. They can be helpful in many ways, including arranging continuing education classes focused on topics, such as budget planning and execution, taxes, risk management, audits, forecasting, assessments, and revenue sources.

## Understanding Community Manager Designations

Partnering with a community manager allows community association boards of directors to run operations smoothly. Although community managers work closely with association boards of directors to provide many vital functions, including overseeing day-to-day operations, governance, maintenance, and finances, they typically are certified employees of management companies.

As a leading provider of community management services, Associa has earned some of the highest credentials in the industry, including the Accredited Association Management Company credential, Great Place to Work® certification, U.S. Best Managed Company, and more. Our recognitions are due to our 15,000+ team members who lead the industry with unrivaled education, expertise, and trailblazing innovation. As a company, we enthusiastically support our managers in their pursuit of professional development.

To advance their careers, further their education, and prove their expertise, many community managers seek industry certification and designations provided by CAI. CAI is an international membership organization that offers educational programs and professional designations for community managers and other industry professionals. It established the Community Association Managers International

Certification Board (CAMICB) as an international certification body for community association managers. Similarly, some states also offer or require community managers to obtain state-specific certifications and licenses.

Understanding these designations not only gives board members insight into the preparation and dedication of their community managers, but also could help them define minimum educational standards for those they hire.

CAI's international certification board offers the following four credentials. All who earn them are expected to complete additional required continuing education courses and adhere to CAI's professional code of ethics.

**Certified Manager of Community Associations (CMCA®)**

The Certified Manager of Community Associations (CMCA) certification is the entry-level certification for community association managers. It certifies the holder has demonstrated an understanding of the fundamental skills needed to manage a community.

To earn a CMCA designation, a manager must complete required courses on management fundamentals, have more than five years of experience in community management or hold a state-level certification, pass an examination, and be approved by CAMICB.[2]

**Association Management Specialist (AMS®)**

Considered the next progression in professional development after the CMCA certification, the Association Management Specialist (AMS) designation is for managers who demonstrate an advanced comprehension of issues associated with managing community associations.

To achieve the AMS designation, a manager must hold a CMCA; have at least two years of advanced management experience that must include administrative, financial, and facilities management; and complete advanced industry training courses.

**Professional Community Association Manager (PCAM®)**

Currently, the highest credential available for a community association manager is the Professional Community Association Manager (PCAM) designation. Highly regarded within the community association industry, it requires a significant investment of time to achieve.

Candidates for a PCAM designation must undergo a rigorous accreditation process. After earning CMCA and AMS credentials, they must complete a comprehensive case study focusing on an existing community association and have at least five years of industry experience.

**Large-Scale Manager (LSM®)**

A large-scale manager or LSM designation is issued by CAI to managers working in large-scale community associations, defined as having at least 1,000 acres and 1,000 housing units.

To achieve the LSM designation, a manager must demonstrate foundational competencies in association management, financial reporting, administrative support, and facilities management. An LSM candidate also must have the required experience or a degree in public or business parks and recreation management.

**State Licenses**

Several states, including Nevada, Virginia, Florida, Illinois, and Connecticut, license or require community association managers to register with state regulators.[3] Managers in those states must pass licensing exams or hold industry designations. This means a regulatory body mandates the training and any professional certifications they must obtain.

# WORKING WITH THE MANAGER OR MANAGEMENT COMPANY

For an association to be successful, the board of directors, residents, and management staff must work together to maintain a healthy partnership. It all begins by ensuring the board hires the right management company and then does its part to maintain a relationship that is as productive as it is pleasant.

## Finding the Right Management Company

Dedicated residents of a community association who volunteer to serve on a board of directors know the job of a director can be demanding. Focusing on governance matters while simultaneously handling daily operations can be a full-time commitment. That is why many boards engage the services of a professional community management firm.

Community management companies focus on assisting board members in successfully implementing their vision for the community. They handle an association's business affairs, coordinate accounting matters, direct maintenance needs, and perform other tasks required by clients. As the founder and leader of the largest such firm, I am proud our teams support diverse communities not only by performing these basic functions, but also by providing a nearly limitless range of services.

Finding the right management company, however, can be a challenge. Wise board members engaged in such a selection process should ascertain whether it is guided by values, committed to community, supported by professional expertise, strengthened by technological solutions, and dedicated to clients.

### Guided by Values

Although hiring a community management firm is a business decision, a board can learn a lot about one by considering its values. Many companies market their services as founded in corporate values, but boards should look through the hype to examine if the company puts those values into action.

The company I founded more than forty-five years ago has been guided by our values, and we take great pride in seeing them in action. In fact, inspired by customer service-focused companies, such as the Ritz-Carlton Hotel, we developed "The Associa Book" that reminds our teams about our values of service, innovation, family, integrity, and loyalty, which guide us daily and in the long term.

## Committed to Community

The value of the volunteer time given by the millions of community association boards of directors is staggering. Likewise, many residents also dedicate their time to serve as volunteers for community events or to serve on committees. This dedication to community service is the foundation of a healthy community.

Boards are best served by a community management firm that is equally committed to supporting strong communities. Continually inspired by community volunteers, at Associa, we honor and express our appreciation for them by demonstrating our commitment to community and how we live by our values. Perhaps the best example of how we do that is our founding and operating Associa Cares, which has distributed more than $5 million since 2007 to assist persons impacted by natural or man-made disasters. As the largest community-focused charity in the industry, it is self-sustaining and relies on the fundraising efforts of our teams.

Our teams also give back to communities through our Great Giveback program. Each year, our team members across North America volunteer their time to help local organizations in the communities we serve. To support their efforts, we provide them with paid time off to use for community service.

## Backed by Professional Expertise

When hiring a community management firm, the manager is the primary, but not the only, resource engaged by the community. The needs of a community can vary, and a manager backed by expertise within the firm can support the board of directors through a variety of challenges. A worthy community management firm can provide the board with accounting support, tips on community governance, advice on dealing with public relations matters, and assist the community with a range of technology-based solutions to support online payments and community-wide communication to promptly report maintenance needs.

## Strengthened by Technological Solutions

Technology continues to advance at an ever-increasing rate. As it evolves, it changes consumer expectations. When I began my career, for example, coupon books were the primary means of paying monthly association assessments. Similarly, communication between boards and residents was primarily through mail communication. Today, management firms can deploy technology that puts the power of community in the hands of residents. Community-wide instant communications, online payment of assessments, accessing important community documents, or even real-time access to resident account information are all standard expectations of community residents.

## Dedicated to Clients

No one is perfect. Humans are prone to making mistakes. Any company or any board can drop the ball, but the true measure of a firm's commitment to its clients is how it reacts when something goes wrong.

A dedicated management firm stands with its clients in times of crisis. The test of its dedication is how it partners with them to overcome issues that may occasionally arise in any professional relationship.

Standing by our clients is important. A great example of this can be seen in a client-impacting event that happened more than a decade ago. We uncovered a problem during a routine internal audit of one of our branches, informed the impacted communities, and made them whole. As a result, the impacted community associations remain our clients to this day.

Equally important, we applied our lessons learned and established the first Client Shared Services Center (CSSC), which centralizes accounting functions for most of our branches. Through it, we added internal controls and deployed state-of-the-art technology to serve our clients better and mitigate the risk of future misappropriations. This is what we mean when we say we stand by our clients.

## Maximizing Board and Manager Relations

The relationship between an association board of directors and the manager truly should be as productive as it is pleasant. This requires accentuating the positive by reinforcement and minimizing the negative through corrective actions. It also depends on mutual trust and respect and on a constructive attitude reflected through timely feedback and a futuristic outlook.

Occasionally, inexperienced members may believe inappropriately that the relationship between the board and a manager depends strictly on the latter's ability to carry out directives. In reality, it is a two-way interaction founded on an understanding of the boundaries within which they operate and of each other's roles and duties.

Board members can maximize their relationships with their community managers by being open-minded, identifying common objectives, maximizing meeting effectiveness, focusing on the community, and communicating effectively. These characteristics of effective board members can impact a relationship significantly for the better.

## Be Open-Minded

Serving on a community's board is not a task that should be taken lightly. It is a big job, and volunteers are not expected to be experts on day one. Newly elected board members, at times, can take an authoritarian or critical approach before developing a sound comprehension of their roles and governing procedures. In doing so, they risk turning a potentially productive collaboration into a stressful failure.

Rookies in every arena, whether in business or public service, are well-advised to assume their positions by rolling up their sleeves, listening, observing, and learning. By being open-minded and educating themselves, they will signal a positive response and promote harmony among fellow board members, residents, partners, and the management company.

## Identify Common Objectives

Identifying common objectives ensures board members and managers are on the same page. Adopting an annual plan consisting of agreed-upon projects, issues to be addressed, and execution processes is crucial for effective operations and continuity. Failing to have mutual expectations and distinct priorities and objectives among the board, committees, and management staff can result in confusion, uncertainty, and frustration.

## Maximize Meeting Effectiveness

Board meetings should be run efficiently and respectfully to enhance positive outcomes and effectiveness. Members should be prepared to engage in thoughtful discussion or debate and to ask meaningful, thoughtful questions as necessary. The most considerate, thoughtful, and best prepared among them will have read all meeting documents in advance, ask questions that require answers that will help and be of interest to all concerned, and not waste everyone's time by bringing up subjects that do not interest anyone else, are irrelevant, or have been discussed thoroughly on previous occasions. For best results, answers to simple questions should be secured before the meeting.

The board and management staff are required to meet regularly to confirm operations are running smoothly and ensure the community's success. This time is valuable, so it is essential to take steps to enhance meeting productivity. It is also important for board members to give management clear direction and avoid perpetually tabling action items.

## Focus on Community

When everyone focuses on community, everyone wins. Board members should never use their positions to further their personal agendas instead of what is most important to their communities.

A community association is a nonprofit corporation designed to run as a business. That means leaders have a duty to act in the best interest of the association—not of themselves. It is part of board members' fiduciary duty to separate themselves from any personal views and conflicts, as they can get in the way of making the right choices for the community and can disrupt management's role. Decisions should always be fair, consistent, and based on standard practices rather than on emotional opinions and preferences.

## Communicate Effectively

Effective communication is the foundation of strong communities. To ensure successful interactions, the board and manager should reach a consensus on the best channels of communication, who should be responsible for initiating and responding to communiques, and any preferences or limitations about frequency or regularity of contact or about prescribed days or times during which interaction can be expected. Some board members, for example, might prefer to be emailed during business hours and not after hours or on weekends. If so, community managers need to know.

Establishing an explicit communication process and system with the management staff holds both groups accountable and limits misunderstandings and disappointment.

## CONCLUSION

In the final analysis, the development of community association managers and management firms is evidence of the increasing demands and complexity of modern community associations. During the early years of my career managing a handful of condominium associations in Dallas, I never could have imagined the prominence of professional community management firms in today's marketplace. The role of community managers has become an indispensable resource for boards of directors' efforts to build community. They are critical partners who help volunteer board members by providing expertise in handling daily operations and fostering positive change in communities.

To be successful, however, board members need to understand the pivotal roles of managers. Capitalizing on specialized training and experience, community managers take on tasks ranging from financial management to rules enforcement, all while working to balance the needs of the board and of the community. To avoid misconceptions about the role of community managers, it merely underscores the importance of understanding their roles and responsibilities.

Defining qualifications for community managers also provides boards with the knowledge needed to hire the best professional assistance. Boards can make better-informed decisions when hiring a management company for their community by understanding the primary functions of the manager and the qualifications that support success.

Finally, a strong, productive working relationship between boards of directors and their community managers or management firms is paramount to ensuring the success of their community associations.

Identifying the right management provider and fostering effective collaboration can greatly enhance the work of the board of directors in nurturing a thriving community.

## QUESTIONS TO CONSIDER

1. If you live in a community association with professional management, how does this experience differ from other communities in which you have lived?

2. What are a community manager's most important duties and functions in serving an association? Is your manager performing all of them, or should the board ask for a higher level of service from him or her?

3. If you serve or have served on a community association board of directors, have you had to hire professional management for your community? If so, what qualifications did the board deem necessary for this support service?

4. Based on your experience and observations, do your board and manager understand the source and scope of your manager's authority? If not, how can this be improved?

5. What are your community manager's qualities and qualifications that help support the community?

6. How has using technology changed communication within your community association? Do you have suggestions for improving this process?

7. How has your community manager or community management company provided technological solutions as part of their contract? How has this improved your community?

8.  How would you evaluate the working relationships among your board members and between the board, manager, and residents? How can these relationships be maximized?

9.  Has your community transitioned from self-management to working with a professional community manager? If so, what have been the benefits?

## CHAPTER 6

# Engaging the Right Professionals

*Coming together is a beginning. Keeping together
is progress. Working together is success.*

—HENRY FORD,
Founder, Ford Motor Company

## CHAPTER INTRODUCTION

Operating a community association requires knowledge of and support across multiple disciplines. A community association may be self-governing, but it is not necessarily self-sufficient. An array of professionals is available to work directly with boards of directors on critical projects.

A holistic approach to hiring professionals facilitates the board's success by, to paraphrase Henry Ford, coming together, keeping together, and working together. The challenge for board members is to develop processes for understanding when their best option is to reach out for assistance and how to engage the right professionals.

Indeed, a methodical approach to finding the right professional is essential for the board's and residents' trust and confidence in those they hire and the likelihood they will succeed. While many tasks may be accomplished in a relatively straightforward manner, others require the engagement of a professional with specific training or credentials.

Gone are the days when one could turn to the Yellow Pages to get a list of potential partners. So are the days of simply handing off tasks to friends or residents who offer themselves as DIY experts and risk creating unneeded liability for the association. By approaching the process like a prudent corporation—and community associations are (nonprofit) corporations—the board fulfills its duty to the community.

Over the years, I have observed many boards navigate the process of engaging a professional.[1] Many of them understand initially—and others soon learn—that hiring qualified professionals limits the liability of the board. This protection for community association boards of directors arises from a legal doctrine called the business judgment rule. In short, when a board of directors is acting in good faith, in the best interests of the community, and with a level of care and inquiry a prudent person would use, its actions are largely protected. When confronted with an issue that requires input from professionals, seeking their advice and acting on that advice is interpreted as meeting the requirements of the rule. The most successful boards begin with a road map reflecting the types of expertise needed based on the nature of the project.

The board's next consideration is whether the expert needed is an attorney, certified public accountant, insurance agent, or another professional who must be licensed or hold other required credentials. If the need is identified and a candidate is chosen, the board must execute either an original or a ready-made contract with the professional, always including all necessary key provisions.

To facilitate success, board members must work with their hired professionals to define a mutually convenient method and timeline for regular communication, feedback, and an evaluation of the work to determine if the contract is completed and the board can sign off on the project.

## EXPLORING THE TYPES OF EXPERTS NEEDED

Community associations come in all shapes and sizes, so the type of professional support they need can vary from community to community. They all have basic needs, however, that may benefit from engaging a professional. Each, for example, is a legal entity that may need to consult with a qualified attorney from time to time. Most also have budgets and should set aside funds for future maintenance needs that may require them to engage a certified public accountant or a reserve specialist.

Some boards of directors hesitate to hire professional assistance because of perceived high costs or lack of knowledge about services needed or provided. Others, however, may prefer to rely on the expertise of board or community association members, whether paid or not. Exploring the types of professionals typically used by community associations can help those boards decide whether to hire professionals, and if so, what kind, under what circumstances, and for how long.

Generally, there are two categories of professionals typically hired by a community association. First are financial and legal professionals, such as lawyers or accountants, who must be licensed after meeting specialized education and licensing requirements that vary from state to state. Second are project- and service-oriented professionals who may have industry-issued designations or certifications but might not need a license to work in their areas of expertise.

A quick review of some of the most frequently hired professionals can help board members determine the types of business partners they can call on for support.

### Legal and Financial Professionals

Boards of directors will engage professionals to assist them with the ongoing operations and governance of their community associations. The variety of professionals serving community associations is as varied as the types of communities themselves. As nonprofit corporations that collect money from residents to serve the common good, however, most community associations sooner or later (if not always!) will need the advice of legal and financial professionals.

Attorneys, for example, can advise board members about the legality or interpretation of governing documents, or they can help them resolve a difficult dispute. Financial professionals, by comparison, can assist the board with issues and requirements related to filing taxes, budgeting, and ensuring funds are set aside for future repair or replacement projects. Because of the ongoing need to make decisions in these areas of responsibility, boards typically have an ongoing relationship with legal and financial professionals.

## Attorneys

As nonprofit corporations, community associations operate like businesses and regularly may have questions or concerns related to legal matters. In such cases, the board should hire an attorney.

Attorneys hold undergraduate and law degrees, although some have additional degrees, whether advanced legal degrees or degrees in other areas, and possibly at other levels of higher education. To practice law, they also must pass a rigorous test to be licensed by their respective state bar associations.

Board members who need legal advice would be wise to hire law firms or lawyers who specialize in representing community associations. They are best qualified to advise them about whether they are acting within the scope of their governing documents and in compliance with state and federal laws and applicable case law precedents. These professionals are often called upon when questions arise about whether a board is complying with and/or correctly interpreting the sources of their authority and when difficulties develop over personnel matters or disputes with or among residents.

Cost is often a factor that inhibits boards of directors from seeking legal advice, especially when some members perceive lawyers' hourly or retainer rates as exceedingly high. Those experienced with litigation, however, may see it as an investment and preventive measure rather than as an expenditure, simply because they realize the cost of seeking legal advice is universally less than dealing with subsequent lawsuits.

Building relationships with qualified counsel can result in benefits beyond attorney-client relationships, often including board training at little or no cost.

## Certified Public Accountants

A certified public accountant (CPA) is a professional who has a college degree in the field, passed the certified public accounting examination, and completed other licensing requirements adopted by a state board of public accountancy. CPAs are "number people" who can perform a variety of tasks for community associations.

The most common service provided by CPAs is to assist the board or management staff with preparing and presenting community financial statements. They can also review association financial statements to verify the appropriate information is being tracked and reported.

A critical function of CPAs is to audit a community's financial statements. During this process, the CPA reviews and tests processes to certify there are no material misstatements in the financials or inherent risks in the policies and procedures of financial management. They also work with community associations to draft and file tax returns and other regulatory filings required in a jurisdiction.

## Reserve Specialists

Reserve specialists are professionals who play critical advisory roles for community associations. Confidence in their expertise and experience can be enhanced when they achieve the Reserve Specialist designation offered by the Community Associations Institute (CAI).

Their assistance is needed because community associations are required to maintain the common areas of the neighborhood, including parks, swimming pools, golf courses, tennis courts, elevators, or other infrastructure. These elements have a limited useful life and eventually will need to be repaired or replaced. Accordingly, a reserve specialist or a qualified engineer works with the board of directors to review and analyze the physical and financial components of the community. This analysis is used to produce a reserve study that outlines a replacement schedule for key components of the community and provides a financial road map to ensure those funds are available when needed.

Generally, reserve specialists help community association boards plan and save funds over time to preclude future costly special assessments for maintenance and repairs.

## Project- or Service-Oriented Professionals

The range of professionals available to community association boards includes specialists who can assist with a given project or ongoing service. Architects and engineers, for example, can provide critical expertise that is important for successful, cost-effective, and less stressful construction projects or renovations. Ongoing service providers such as community managers or landscapers also provide recurring services to community associations.

Complex and extensive projects sometimes require project-oriented professionals to collaborate. Architects, engineers, and landscapers, for example, might need to develop complementary plans for large projects that include hardscapes and landscaping within a community association park that has other structures and features. In such cases, the community manager often facilitates their collaboration.

A board of directors should not shy away from engaging these professionals when needed, particularly because in most cases the work to be performed requires a level of expertise or training that board members (and often managers) do not have. Those who do should not be expected to volunteer their professional time and skills.

## Architects

Architects can advise community associations about a variety of topics. They can create plans for maintenance work on structures to ensure their compliance with community design guidelines. They can also create a scope of work for replacement projects that provides an accurate record of when and where work was done on structures within the community. Sometimes, they are asked to collaborate with engineers to recommend or make structural changes or repairs to common elements.

Many community associations have architectural review committees. These committees review and approve proposed changes to homes or units within a community association. An architect can assist in establishing such committees and provide input about compliance matters.

## Engineers

Engineers play an important role in ensuring structures meet building code requirements and are structurally sound. Because changes and repairs to a structure can impact its integrity, having an engineer review them both in advance and as they are made can preclude creating a risk or failure of the component or structure itself.

Engineers are often engaged to assess the safety and integrity of buildings and elements such as balconies, parking garages, and main structural supports. Their work and expertise help guarantee that buildings within the community are safe. As indicated earlier, they are sometimes hired to collaborate with architects in recommending structural changes or repairs to common elements.

## Landscapers

Landscaping services are often among the larger line items in a community association budget. Whether initiating projects or redesigning them, many companies can provide expertise regarding landscapes and outdoor living spaces, including design, installations, maintenance, hardscape construction, and irrigation.

While landscapers help make communities more aesthetically pleasing, their work can impact the community significantly. In addition to making common areas look their best, for example, landscape professionals can provide advice about plantings and hardscapes that reduce water usage, an increasingly important issue in many Western regions.

## Maintenance

Like an average homeowner, a community association typically has a list of items that need to be fixed or repaired. A burned-out light in the clubhouse, a broken fence needing repairs, and worn-out parking areas that need resealing are only a few of the tasks required to maintain common elements of a community association.

Especially in larger communities, boards of directors often hire a maintenance firm to perform needed repairs or scheduled maintenance. Implementing a proactive, ongoing maintenance plan instead of always waiting to repair damaged items prolongs the useful life of an association's common elements and can preclude more expensive replacement costs.

## Volunteer Professionals

Sometimes, newly elected boards of directors and new or small community associations worry about exceeding their budgets by hiring expensive professionals. To avoid that problem, they prefer to rely on the volunteer services of fellow board members or residents. If "volunteer professional" sounds like an oxymoron, it is because it usually is. Although perhaps acceptable on a very short-term basis, the arrangement inevitably will grow tiresome or problematic.

Residents may be delighted to volunteer their services to serve as elected representatives on a board of directors or to organize social activities, but in the long run, they likely will resent donating their professional talent for which they otherwise would be paid.

Additionally, licensed professionals may experience conflicts between their ethical duties to their jobs and their roles in their communities, especially if they are board members. Given the potential for conflicts of interest and liability to homeowners at large, board members should not be paid for services they provide to an association.

Hiring professionals to help boards of directors operate community associations is an expected responsibility. The cost is an investment in good management and in precluding future higher costs that result from not hiring advisors when needed.

## RESOURCES FOR FINDING PROFESSIONALS

The epiphany that professional help is required might be complicated by knowing where to start the search. Long ago, some of us simply turned to the Yellow Pages of our bulky printed telephone directories and started a round of cold calls. The task is easier for boards today, not only because they have a wider array of options, but also because of directories compiled by industry trade organizations and management companies. Associa, for example, continually builds an arsenal of providers that we make available to our clients. Our managers welcome opportunities to help board members find the right professionals for the right jobs.

The internet is also a great source of information about service professionals. Simply searching online for keywords such as "architects" or "landscapers" can result in a rich array of local options. Their websites often provide extensive information about their range of services and photographs of their projects. Equally important, reviews written by customers, whether happy or unhappy, can provide insight that is helpful in the board's decision-making process.

Finally, reaching out to neighboring associations can result in identifying potential effective partners for a community.

## Industry Trade Organizations

As the leading industry trade group for the community association sector, the Community Associations Institute (CAI) is a rich resource for boards interested in hiring professionals. Its membership comprises not only board members and community managers, but also professionals who serve community associations.

Particularly helpful are CAI's designations for some professionals beyond the community manager focus, including reserve specialists, attorneys, and risk management specialists. Attorneys with extensive experience and contributions to community associations, for example, can be designated fellows of CAI's College of Community Association Lawyers (CCAL). By comparison, professionals with extensive experience in community insurance risk management can earn designations as Community Insurance Risk Management Specialists (CIRMS).

CAI maintains an updated list that can help association boards narrow their search for credentialed professionals.[2] Many of these professionals have extensive experience and a track record of supporting community associations.

## Community Association Management Firms

A community association's management firm can be a valuable resource when searching for a professional. The most committed firms are pleased to provide additional resources to support a community's success.

Associa, for example, continually works with thousands of community association boards to find compatible partners. Over the years, we have built a stable of firms we trust to work with our valued clients. Our trust is based on our many years of experience with them and their successful track records.

## Neighboring Community Referrals

Building congenial relationships with nearby community associations has numerous benefits. Among them is the ability to share experiences with hiring professionals for specific community needs. Having such relationships and sharing information about responsive, effective professionals helps both boards in their quest to find the right providers for their communities.

## CONTRACTING WITH PROFESSIONALS

The importance of hiring the best professionals cannot be overstated. The likelihood of making the right decision is enhanced when employers take the time to search widely for candidates; reach out to industry organizations for suggestions; check references; and select the best candidates based on qualifications, experience, work ethic, enthusiasm for the job at hand, and character references.

If the board has taken the time to identify its needs, using the needs assessment as a scoring tool can help differentiate applicants and facilitate comparing their strengths and weaknesses. Beyond measuring and evaluating experience, it is helpful to review any professional's designations, certifications, licenses, and job-related insurance.

Board members should also look at any potential professional's engagement with the industry. One who supports community associations through trade organizations or community service demonstrates a commitment to building community.

After searching successfully for the right professionals, board members need to formally hire them. The engagement process commences with the execution of a contract between the professional and the community association represented by the board.

A contract is a mutual set of promises between two parties who pledge to undertake a specified action and consent to be mutually bound by the agreement. More simply, the board contracts with a professional who promises to undertake a project, and the board promises to pay for the services. Most professionals provide form agreements to their potential clients. While this is a common practice, a diligent board will take the time to review the proposed agreement, have it reviewed by legal counsel, and suggest appropriate changes, if necessary.

A contract review is a fundamental element of due diligence and common sense. It is always best to invest time before executing an agreement to identify any areas of ambiguity or address critical details. Once a board identifies the right professional for the task at hand, a sense of mutual expectation and excitement about the shared project typically follows. Because the board is getting the professional assistance it needs and the professional has a new client, everybody is happy. That makes this the best time to address details and ensure the contract properly addresses areas of mutual concern. That process can be more successful when paying attention to basics, such as defining the type of contractual relationship sought, clarifying the scope or scale of the project, and ensuring appropriate contract provisions are addressed.

## Defining Contractual Relationships

For community associations, the most common contractual relationships fall into two categories, namely, service and performance contracts, both of which can be auto-renewing. The names of these categories may vary among communities, but the concepts underlying them are straightforward: A service contract is typically for ongoing services to be provided over a defined period, while a performance contract is for one specific deliverable project to be completed within a specified time frame. Contracts can be as broad or specific as the parties desire, but they are far superior to verbal agreements. Examples of each are provided here.

## Service Contracts

The two most common service contracts community associations execute are for management services and landscape maintenance. The common nature of these contracts easily suggests the commonalities that define them, that is, they are for specific ongoing services to be performed periodically over time.

A community management contract, for example, is an agreement that a management company will provide specified management services for a set period at a certain price as agreed. Similarly, a landscape maintenance contract outlines the service the company will provide, where and how often it will provide it, and for how long the process will be repeated. While not complex arrangements, these types of contracts require specific provisions to provide clarity.

## Performance Contracts

While a service contract is characterized by its ongoing nature and recurring obligations, the performance contract is for a specific project, such as re-roofing a building or painting the façade of a clubhouse. It is characterized by a specific objective, start date, and end date. Once the objective of the contract is completed, the contract has been fulfilled. Like a service contract, the nature of a performance contract requires boards to review it for certain fundamental elements.

## Auto-Renewing Contracts

An auto-renewing contract is an agreement that renews automatically for an additional period if no action is taken to cancel or otherwise change it by an expressed deadline. Both service and performance contracts may be auto-renewing.

Boards should review contracts for language that provides for an automatic renewal. Typically, such contracts provide a notice period that requires notice of termination from ninety to thirty days before the agreement expires. If the notice is not provided, the contract is renewed for another term. If the board agrees to enter an auto-renewing contract, it should schedule the notice period and allow enough time to search for another provider if the incumbent does not meet the community's needs. Finally, if the board does not wish for the contract to be auto-renewing, it should request a contract with a simply defined term of service.

## Identifying Elements of Contracts

Once board members select a professional and determine whether they need a service or performance contract, they have parameters within which to determine the key elements of their agreements. The process begins as both parties identify the provisions they consider fundamental to the relationship. Together, they will flesh out the who, what, where, when, how, and how much aspects of a working framework for their agreement.

The most common key elements of contracts include scope of work, project and payment schedules, indemnity, dispute handling, and completion and sign-off. Wise board members rely on their attorneys to review contracts and ensure all necessary elements are included.

Please note: The overview of key contractual elements that follows is informational in nature and not intended as legal advice.

### Scope of Work

The scope of work defines the objective of the agreement. Generally, it spells out the objective to be accomplished, where the work will take place, and how the project will progress. For a service contract, such as one for landscape maintenance, the scope of work should include which areas are to be maintained and how often the work will be done. For a specific project, such as building repairs, the scope of work should include specific descriptions of areas where the work will be done and what the work will include. The scope of work is a road map that allows the parties to know what deliverables have been promised and where and when the work will be done.

## Project Schedule

The next logical step after defining the scope of the project is to outline the lifecycle of the contract. For a service contract, these terms typically would address how long the professional would provide a recurring service to the community, perhaps for one, two, or three years. It also should include how often recurring work will be done (for example, the grass will be mowed weekly during the summer).

For a performance contract, the time frame may dictate the day the work will begin and the expected date of completion. Such terms are critical, especially when the project will inconvenience the residents or require action on their part. Having clear start and end dates for a project will help the board inform residents about its duration and manage expectations and concerns about its impact.

## Payment Schedule

Contracts should include a payment schedule that reflects the specific set of actions the contractor will complete and the related terms of payment by the association. More specifically, they should specify when payments will be made for the work performed.

For specific projects such as roofing, for example, a deposit typically will be paid in advance to allow the contractor to purchase materials for the project. Beyond that, it is up to the parties to allocate a schedule of payments. Generally, however, paying the entire cost upfront can be problematic, especially because payment is often the only leverage a community association has in the process. That said, the contract should include a mutually agreed-to schedule, perhaps linking payments to completing important project benchmarks.

## Indemnity

Indemnity is another key element of a contract. It specifies who would be responsible if something were to go wrong during the work performed by the professional. Typically, contracted professionals are responsible for actions under their control. If a landscaping contractor is removing a tree that falls onto a neighbor's home, for example, an indemnity clause can hold the contractor responsible for rectifying the error.

## Disputes

The best time to determine how to handle disputes is before they occur. Investing time and money in hiring a professional should ensure a process for notifying parties and resolving disagreements, should they arise.

Many contracts include provisions that allow the contractor to cure or fix anything that does not meet the client's expectations. These provisions also include a process for notifying the contractor about any problems and a specific time frame within which the problem should be rectified. In effect, they create a process for responding to issues that may arise by establishing a clear framework for notification and resolution.

## Completion and Sign-Off

Boards of directors act collectively in making decisions for their respective community associations. When it comes to inspecting and signing off on a completed contract, however, boards need to consider whether to act in unison or to delegate the responsibility to a board member or the community manager. Because the final determination of contract completion is held by the board as the contracting entity, it is common for the community manager to decline execution to avoid any liability for contractor performance.

When the contractor's work is done, especially on a specific project, such as painting a clubhouse, the client typically undertakes a walkthrough to inspect it and determine whether the work was indeed completed. Because not all board members may want to take the time to do this, they need to reach a consensus in advance about what constitutes completion of the project, how that determination will be made, and who will make it. In many cases, they will delegate the authority to inspect and sign off on completion to one or more board members or to the manager. The decision to sign off on the project can be memorialized at a board meeting so the board will have a record of approving and closing out the agreement.

## Preparing the Contract

Contract development involves not only the parties involved, but also legal advisors. The board's attorneys should be involved in the process, whether they develop the document or review one written by others. In the end, board members should consider their attorney's recommendation before executing a contract.

Moving through the process of identifying a potential partner for a community project can be exciting. After meeting with potential providers, defining the relationship, and identifying important contract terms, board members are ready to begin the process of developing and negotiating a contract. This is a great point in the process to honor the carpenter's adage to measure twice, cut once. In other words, before the board executes a contract with the selected professional, it should make a final review of the objectives, budget, and critical contract terms.

### Project Objectives

After selecting the right person or firm, defining the professional relationship, and ensuring the inclusion of all key elements, the board's next logical step is to review anew and finalize the project's objectives. This is an appropriate time to consider any objectives suggested by potential professionals and to include any that may have been missed in the initial project outline. Ideally, the review should result in confirming the board members' consensus about the scope and objectives of the contract.

## Key Terms

After finalizing objectives, the board should ensure the contract also includes key terms needed to protect the board and set clear expectations of the parties.

For ongoing service projects, such as landscape maintenance, clear schedules indicating how often and where the work will be performed are necessary. Pricing terms should be clear and understood. The question of who is responsible for anything that might go wrong, indemnification, is another important consideration. The underlying point is that board members should read the contract to make sure its interests and important matters are addressed.

## Financial Considerations

The search for the right professional and the process leading up to the start of the project can be time-consuming, but every step is important and requires thorough consideration and review. This includes ensuring parties agree about the final cost estimates, payment schedules, and other financial matters. A final evaluation of the projected cost, available resources, and payments will help prevent delays or interruptions to the project.

## Board Review

The last step in preparing a contract is the board's broad review of all agreed-upon elements and any other considerations that may impact the project or its commencement or completion. This is a good opportunity to add, omit, or change aspects of the contract in the best interest of the community. It is also a good time to consider related action. For larger projects, for example, a communication plan for residents is a critical component, although it does not necessarily have to be included in the contract. Understanding and planning how to address the impact of the project on the community's day-to-day operations can help mitigate any issues that may arise.

## Attorney's Review

Having qualified counsel as a resource for a community association is important, especially when developing contracts. Attorneys often are called upon to develop contracts for important and complex projects, but boards also rely on standard documents used regularly by the parties involved.

Before executing a contract developed by management or provided by a potential professional, especially one that has a significant cost, the board should have its attorney review it and recommend it is ready to be signed. More specifically, board members should ask counsel to confirm the interests of the community are protected; to answer any questions about the meaning and impact of the contract terms; and to offer advice about potential difficulties, including handling disputes and dealing with a project that gets off track.

While some board members may complain about the expense of hiring lawyers, they should note that the cost of a contract review is significantly less than the cost of litigation, should the project fail or problems arise.

## INTERACTING WITH PROFESSIONALS

Just as important as developing a good contract is ensuring interaction with the person or company hired goes well. Establishing a working relationship early facilitates opening lines of communication and alignment of expectations.

Once the professional has been selected, taking the time to flesh out the project, timelines, and other aspects of the work will contribute to a timely and efficient process. Discussing the key terms of the contract and how the parties will interact is a good point of departure. In many cases, the professional engaged may be needed for additional future work, so establishing a solid working relationship from the beginning is helpful.

Whether the contract is for remodeling the community clubhouse, installing new landscaping, or even soliciting a legal opinion, building a collaborative relationship will facilitate the process moving forward with open lines of communication and agreed-upon expectations.

## Establishing the Relationship

A successful road map for interacting with consultants depends on establishing a productive working relationship. This begins at the very early stage of interviewing potential professionals to evaluate their qualifications and visions for the project. Discussing the contract and its key provisions can strengthen that bond by enhancing clarity of purpose and mutual expectations.

Equally important is establishing lines of communication that are mutually convenient and beneficial. Regularly communicating progress to board members facilitates their keeping residents informed, especially when projects result in limited access to areas of the community or questions arise that must be answered by an attorney.

Interacting with professionals may begin with a given project, but establishing constructive relationships with them often results in future collaboration. Ending the project on a positive note is enhanced by establishing realistic completion dates, celebrating milestones achieved along the way, and arranging a post-project examination to evaluate success and review lessons learned that can be applied to future endeavors.

Establishing a relationship with a professional starts during the search process that carries an element of excitement that can be the foundation for a constructive engagement. Success can be facilitated during collaboration to identify a project's objectives and the important elements of the contract under development.

The execution of the contract serves as the next opportunity to establish a strong relationship that will be enjoyed by the parties and be beneficial to the residents. It helps when everyone understands the needs and expectations of the project at hand and agrees on a point of contact for communication.

## Project Needs

Although the underlying need for the project should have been defined early during the contract development process, it should be reviewed with the newly hired professional. It should be clear that the board took the time to look at the matter from multiple points of view and included as many of its needs as possible and appropriate. If that needs assessment was employed to solicit professionals, prepare a request for proposal, and/or rate potential partners, it can also serve as the subject of an early discussion and bonding experience. Including enumerated needs in the contract should indicate that the board and professional were on the same page regarding the scope and nature of the project.

## Mutual Expectations

As early as possible after the contract has been executed, board members or their designees should meet to discuss mutual expectations regarding the scope of the project. This is also a good time for both sides to raise questions and discuss the culture and needs of the community.

## Point of Contact

If it is true that too many cooks spoil the broth, then it is easy to understand the importance of designating a single point of contact to manage the work of the professional. Often, that role falls on the community manager, but in smaller communities, a board member may do so. A single point of contact should result in more consistent and reliable communication between the board and the professional. This can be accomplished as the designee provides progress updates to board members and communicates questions or concerns to the professional.

The point of contact can also be empowered to review the work when completed to determine if the project is finished.

## Enhancing Communication

Effective communication is imperative for the success of a project. While too many think of it simply as a two-way channel to be used regularly or as needed, communication is far more complex. It entails appropriately employing every available traditional and electronic channel and every possible interpersonal and group site for exchanging and building upon information among professional partners, board members, and community managers. What matters most is selecting the most convenient, preferred, and cost-effective methods of communicating about day-to-day operations versus a myriad time-related factors such as timeliness, immediacy, urgency, and emergency.

Stakeholders in a community association project can expect to communicate via notes, memos, and progress reports; telephone and electronic media; small or large in-person meetings; and even on-site signage. Inevitably, there will be differences about how, when, and how often to communicate about project progress or problems. For daily exchanges, for example, some may prefer text messages, while others may prefer emails or telephone calls. The busiest among them may be interested only in the "big picture," preferring to receive progress reports as needed or at board meetings. Given these differences, it is important that professionals and the community association boards for whom they work agree on how and when to communicate, who should be involved in the process, and who will be the point of contact.

Simply exchanging information is not enough, however. Professionals and association representatives must have the ability to react to it, preferably in real time, by providing feedback, asking questions, requesting options for solving problems, or addressing concerns, etc. Such exchanges prove that communication is not merely two-way, but rather helical, as participants interact and figuratively build on their interactions.

## Recurring Meetings

There are two schools of thought about recurring meetings. One is that the professional and the board's designated point of contact should schedule recurring meetings at set times regarding the progress of the project. Their agenda would include update reports, issues that need attention, and question-and-answer sessions. This is especially important for projects that impact residents' access to common areas of the community or otherwise may disrupt the community.

The other perspective is that meetings should be held on an as-necessary basis at the most convenient time and place and should involve everyone needed to address agenda items. Those who favor this approach abhor "meeting for meeting's sake" based on a schedule rather than on need. (They probably would agree with proponents of short meetings who say tongue-in-cheek that chairs, food, and beverages should be prohibited and that the "one-foot rule" should be invoked. This rule allows presenters to speak as long as they want—provided they stand on one foot while talking!)

What matters most is that productive meetings function as venues at which progress reports can be made, timely issues can be addressed or resolved, and appropriate personnel can participate.

## Progress Reports

Progress reports help keep the board and the community's expectations in line and enable them to track progress and understand reasons for any variations from the schedule. As with meetings, they can be submitted based on an agreed-upon schedule, as needed, or in response to requests from the board. Their content should reflect the key objectives and terms defined in the contract and address issues such as unexpected delays due to back-ordered materials, pending permits, or problems discovered after work commenced.

Generally, the nature of the project can help gauge the frequency of the reports.

## Feedback Mechanisms

Feedback is an essential element of effective communication and critical to a project's success. Submitting or collecting it is not enough, however. There should be a mechanism for receiving it, responding to it, evaluating it, and when appropriate, for acting upon it. Without this mechanism, feedback is merely one-way communication, and instead of being productive can result in feelings of frustration, resentment, and alienation on the part of those who submitted it.

A project's success can be enhanced by feedback that helps the board and professionals identify issues they had not considered, gain insight into how the community is impacted, resolve residents' complaints or concerns, and consider constructive criticism. When the feedback is negative or even shrill, board members and professionals should step back, cut through the emotion to identify the logic behind the argument, and ask, "What if that critic is right?" If so, they should act accordingly.

To preclude residents from engaging directly with the professional, the board should establish a dedicated email address or telephone number for their use. This feedback should then be submitted to the vendor, and the appropriate person should respond to the resident who submitted the feedback.

## Community Updates

Although effective communication provides a framework for providing community updates, not every project requires the board or manager to keep residents in the loop. If the project creates an inconvenience for the community or otherwise impacts it significantly, however, updates issued regularly or as needed are strongly advised. These include projects such as resealing parking areas, repairing the pool or clubhouse, installing hardscape or landscape, or building a recreational center.

Using the communication channels and sites discussed earlier, a board representative or the community manager can provide timely updates about the project's progress to the community. Establishing a timeline and providing updates regularly will keep residents current about the project's status, manage expectations, and mitigate complaints caused by lack of information or by misinformation.

## Completing the Project and Learning Lessons

Completing a project provides a sense of closure and serves as evidence of the board's work in enhancing the community. Before closing out the project, however, a few key steps should be taken to avoid any issues that could emerge after completion.

Any project can have some items that need adjustment before declaring the work completed. If the board hadn't designated and authorized a point person to monitor day-to-day progress, complete the final review, and declare completion, this step could be complicated. Because the board is a collective body that acts through a majority, under those circumstances, the board would have to meet and act. If so, the importance of naming a designee could be a lesson learned for next time!

When the project is near the finish line, reviewing the promised deliverables, making any final adjustments, and preparing the final project file help guarantee a happy ending to the journey.

### Reviewing Deliverables

Anyone who has taken possession of a new home or had extensive work done on one knows the importance of doing a final review of the promised deliverables. Going through the scope of work and checking off the objectives is basic due diligence that helps identify any final adjustments or fixes that need to be made.

The board should have a clear consensus about whether a board member or the community manager can make the final judgment to sign off on completion. Once the final list of fixes is completed, doing a final inspection will complete the process and allow the contract to be closed out.

### Establishing Project File

Many states regulate the information a community association must retain as part of its community records, typically including copies of contracts for work in the community. Prior to closing out the project, the designated board member or manager should review the record-keeping requirements and confirm the documentation required to be retained is included in the project file.

Record retention requirements also mandate that certain files be kept for a set period. This should be noted on or in the file. Having a complete record brings the community into compliance with record retention requirements and guarantees a complete record will be on hand if any action needs to be taken in the future.

### Discussing Lessons Learned

An effective board committed to continuous learning will take time after project completion to engage in a final assessment and identify lessons learned. This discussion can identify areas in which the process worked well and others that could have been handled better. Such lessons can be applied to future engagements with other professionals and shared with current professionals for their edification.

If the project was complex and extensive, a resident survey for feedback could be helpful too. It could not only help identify areas the board may have overlooked, but it could also engage residents and give them the opportunity to have their feedback considered. What matters most is that lessons learned from a project be instruments for improving future experiences.

## CONCLUSION

A community association board of directors is required to deal with numerous tasks as part of its service. These tasks range from construction, maintenance, and landscaping to legal research and accounting, to name a few. Board members do not face these challenges alone, however. When they need advice, assistance, and support, they can explore an ecosystem of professionals and companies who specialize in community associations. Finding the right professionals to hire requires a bit of common sense and a general understanding of the process from commencement to conclusion.

Boards are empowered to execute service contracts to help them meet the needs of the community. This is essential because board members are not expected to be well-versed in every aspect of community association management. For inexperienced board members, demystifying the hiring process begins with a review of the most common professionals engaged by community associations and the related credentials that reflect their levels of industry-specific expertise. This category includes attorneys, accountants, community managers, and reserve specialists.

Once the board has found a professional or company that meets its needs, developing a contract with key provisions, including objectives and terms, is the next logical step. Involving those professionals in that process as early as possible is a hallmark of establishing a productive relationship with them, especially regarding specifics such as milestones, payment schedules, final review, determination of project completion, and feedback.

Depending on the complexity and cost of the project at hand, contracts should be developed or reviewed by legal counsel, especially to note any red flags or flagrant omissions. Skipping this step to avoid the cost would be penny-wise and pound-foolish.

A thorough, methodical, and communication-based approach to the solicitation, execution, and conclusion of the process supports a successful endeavor. Every project is a learning experience, and wise board members appreciate the lessons learned from it and look forward to applying them in the future.

As Henry Ford noted, working together is success. When board leadership and management reflect resident-focused planning, collaboration, communication, and feedback in hiring and contracting processes, that success is achievable.

## QUESTIONS TO CONSIDER

1. To what extent has your board of directors engaged professionals to assist the community? How did the board structure that hiring process?

2. What is the professional service your community association uses most often? How did the board maintain a productive relationship with those professionals?

3. Beyond a solid professional pedigree, what other qualities are important to you when professional support is hired for your association?

4. Has your board of directors ever had to terminate a contract with a professional? If so, what led to the termination, and what lessons were learned?

5. Does your board of directors regularly engage association counsel? If so, how does this benefit the board and the community?

6. Has your community ever undertaken a major project that inconvenienced or significantly impacted residents? If so, how did the board or manager handle communication with residents? Was there a mechanism for receiving and responding to feedback? If so, how would you rate it in terms of it being considered and productive?

7. What were the lessons learned from projects that did not go as planned? How did that learning experience help improve future projects?

PART III

# COMMUNITY CHALLENGES

Success is not final, failure is not fatal:
It is the courage to continue that counts.

—WINSTON CHURCHILL,
British Prime Minister

## PART III INTRODUCTION

Anyone who serves on a community association board of directors knows it can be a thankless task at times, but also that it can be a fruitful and rewarding experience. Building community requires an understanding of human dynamics and a near-infinite amount of patience. The pursuit of building strong communities is not a one-off task. It is a process that ebbs and flows as it encounters and overcomes challenges to progress.

As Churchill's wise words conceptualize, the pursuit of our goals is a process that requires courage to press on. This attitude can inspire boards to work through the inevitable obstacles that may emerge as they protect and enhance their communities. Such challenges are a normal part of any process, especially those relating to facilitating community because they relate to the sacredness of one's home.

Challenges come from a variety of sources, ranging from that one difficult resident to misguided boards of directors and even from natural to human-made disasters. Regardless of the obstacle or its source, the goal of a strong community is worth our continued efforts.

In the quest to build strong communities, obstacles are inevitable. A common one in many communities is that one resident who seems to thrive on criticizing any attempts to make the community a better place. Overcoming that difficult resident's challenge requires patience, listening, and determination. That effort may be multiplied when dealing with a subset of residents intent on fighting any change in the community.

The challenge of dealing with difficult residents and rebellious factions can be overcome with a commitment to listening, communicating, and a continued focus on the bigger picture. Finding common ground is an important part of the process, as is resolving disputes.

When the challenge comes from the board itself, overcoming it may seem like a herculean task. Reflecting on the board's role in a community association and on factors that contribute to the development of a rogue board can mitigate the risk of one emerging.

Overcoming apathy helps the community build greater cohesion and a deeper bench of future community leaders. Ultimately, overcoming the challenge of a rogue board requires collective action by residents, whose role is to hold their elected representatives accountable.

Finally, a community can have all internal governance and operations aligned, only to be literally blown away by an unexpected natural or human-made disaster. Ensuring a strong, vibrant community also requires awareness of such risks to its welfare, stability, and safety. While not all disasters are preventable, the risk to the integrity of the community can be mitigated through a sober assessment of risks and investments in planning for any that might occur.

Part III focuses on the challenges most commonly faced by community associations, namely, challenging residents and boards, as well as natural and human-made disasters. As they do, they would do well to remember and apply the timeless words of Churchill: Our success is not permanent, but, thankfully, our missteps are not fatal. It is the process of having the courage to continue that inevitably leads to success.

## CHAPTER 7

# Dealing with Challenging Residents

Ask yourself a question: Will this matter one year from now?

—RICHARD CARLSON,

American Author, *Don't Sweat the Small Stuff*

## CHAPTER INTRODUCTION

Dealing with angry residents or rebellious factions is an inevitable part of community management. Experienced boards can probably share many stories about a perpetually angry resident. Similarly, boards frequently deal with rebellious factions, a group of residents united in opposition to some aspect of the board's leadership. At Associa, we refer to them as "challenging" because we make every effort to understand their needs and interests, to communicate and collaborate with them, and to transform them into our partners in building a better community.

The confrontational nature of these challenges sometimes drains the time and energy of board members and community managers, impacting overall community morale and participation. With patience, understanding, and empathy, however, these leaders can mitigate disruptive influences and even promote more constructive behaviors. This can help the board put matters into perspective so they do not have to sweat the small stuff and, as Richard Carlson suggests, determine if the issue is a passing tempest or something that may matter a year from now.

Community conflicts can cause division, hinder operations, and undermine productivity. Board members have a duty to resolve them while fostering a cooperative spirit within the community association. A commitment to peace and harmony requires taking time to understand the details of the dispute and the driving force of those who are upset.

When coping with challenging residents, it is important to remember that not all who are initially difficult will remain so permanently. An effective board can mitigate their impact by adopting a structured and empathetic approach. This involves not only identifying their characteristics, but also employing strategies that address their concerns constructively. By understanding the underlying issues and responding patiently and respectfully, boards can navigate these challenging interactions and maintain a harmonious community environment.

Like the angry resident, a rebellious faction can be a wrench in the gears for ongoing operations and community harmony. A faction is not inherently troublesome, but when the group is united in opposition to community progress and does not feel heard, the equation can change. Defining the faction, taking steps to mitigate the emergence of factions, and exploring how to engage an emerging faction positively can help a board keep its focus on building community now.

Finally, resolving disputes within a community association is rarely straightforward. No universal formula can address the variety of variables involved. Previous chapters have provided boards with communication tools and techniques for gauging community preferences, but even the most diligent among them will encounter conflicts that require more nuanced approaches. Regardless of the source of the dispute, it is helpful to explore a variety of strategies for resolving it. By leveraging procedural consistency, engaging in collaborative efforts, and utilizing professional resources when necessary, boards can navigate and resolve conflicts effectively, fostering a harmonious community environment.

## RESPONDING TO THAT ONE CHALLENGING RESIDENT

Almost every community association, board of directors, and community manager has dealt with that one consistently challenging resident. Never seeing things like the rest of the community, these persons see everything as a conspiracy: They insist their boards are out to get them or somehow believe the rules simply do not apply to them. They approach each encounter with board members with metaphorical guns blazing, and no response seems to please them.

Fortunately, most residents are reasonable and can work within the structure of a community association. Some, however, seem to thrive on creating controversy. Their presence can be a drain on the board's and manager's time and negatively impact participation in community meetings. The good news is that, for most, the role of angry resident may not be a permanent state. An effective board or manager can help mitigate their impact by taking a methodical approach. They can also check their initial emotional responses by asking Richard Carlson's question with which we opened this chapter: Will this matter a year from now?

It is helpful to begin by identifying the proverbial challenging resident. We do not use this term in reference to someone who simply disagrees with some or most of the community association's work. Board members address many issues, and it is impossible for them to please all of the residents all of the time. A challenging resident, rather, is one who habitually does not abide by community rules, disregards community processes, and treats others disrespectfully.

Responding to this type of resident does not have to be a complicated process. Knowing the path to take when an interaction becomes heated or the parties are at loggerheads can help defuse tense situations. Board members versed in their governing documents and internal processes and who focus on process can prevail. This requires patience and a reminder to prioritize the bigger picture over the personalities involved.

While many challenging resident situations can be resolved, sometimes other factors may work against finding a solution. In such cases, boards can avail themselves of professional assistance from their managers, association counsels, or even first responders.

## Defining the Challenging Resident

The ability to disagree without being disagreeable may require patience, but it is a real asset in dealing with negative personalities. Too many persons believe, however, that others should align with their views 100 percent to be worthy of friendship, kindness, or camaraderie. That view is unfortunate and contributes to the challenges boards face when interacting with challenging residents.

By way of reminder, we do not use "challenging" in reference to someone who simply may disagree with a board action, but, rather, to a resident who consistently is at odds with the community or with neighbors and as a result, consumes an undue portion of the community's time. There is no perfect list of the characteristics of challenging residents, but a few distinguishing features stand out. These include their being angry, disrespectful, blameless, and threatening.

### Angry

As the term suggests, challenging residents are driven by emotions, typically anger, causing them to overreact. This can cloud their abilities to be open to resolutions and can heighten the emotions of the persons on their receiving ends.

Instead of simply objecting to, asking questions about, or responsibly discussing policies or rule enforcement measures adopted by their boards, for example, they may lash out furiously, often using insulting language and instantly creating hostile environments that make discussion difficult. Equally important—and just as damaging to their causes—their tirades and outbursts may cause listeners to respond emotionally while losing focus on whether angry persons are right and what the appropriate, responsive courses of action may be.

## Disrespectful

One of the distinguishing features of challenging residents is that they are consistently disrespectful. They demean board members, managers, and neighbors. They act as if their perspectives allegedly are so obvious that those who do not see or share them have serious mental defects. Name-calling is a common trait.

Perhaps the worst part about such disrespect is its potential for breeding it in others. Like good manners, this negativity can be contagious, especially within factions. Ladies and gentlemen who otherwise would be polite can find themselves wrapped up in a common cause and become as disrespectful as the bad example who influenced them.

## Blameless

Regardless of the underlying issues that trigger challenging residents, they never accept blame. A friendly reminder to comply with rules that prohibit bikes or other personal property on balconies, for example, can infuriate them. Such irate residents typically blame their boards or managers, the policies or processes, or their neighbors as they search for all possible reasons to deny responsibility, even when confronted with photographic evidence. In such cases, I'm reminded of the scene in *Duck Soup* in which Chico Marx responds to a valid accusation, "Well, who ya gonna believe, me or your own (lying) eyes?"

Amazingly, classic projection typically comes into play for these challenging residents. This can include blaming the governing documents for being vague or outdated, the board or manager for not communicating timely or effectively, or even their own children or staff for whom they deny responsibility.

## Threatening

Another hallmark of challenging residents is their use of threats. Typically, these take the form of threatening to take legal action or to alert the media. When boards and managers act within the scope of their authority, these threats usually are inconsequential, but if they are ignored, they can develop into time-consuming problems.

## Responding to Challenging Residents

Responding to challenging residents can be heartening if approached with an open mind and initial assumption of good intent.

Living in a community association has benefits and challenges. Among these is the reality that for many, the initial interaction with the manager or board of directors typically begins with a violation notice. Today's busy and stressful lifestyles can leave many with little or no patience. Pairing that with the consequences of resenting being told what to do or that something was done wrong is a recipe for confrontation.

Such ostensibly minor disagreements can evolve into seemingly major problems if they gain public attention. Some local media love to run stories that portray community associations in a negative light. This underscores the importance of board members following defined processes related to a dispute and focusing on the issue, not the person. If the media gets involved, the management company and association counsel may be able to help. At our company, for example, we employ industry public relations specialists to assist our clients when necessary.

In formulating an approach to a challenging resident, the focus should be on the process, not the person. Working through the resolution process set by the community's governing documents is the fairest and most consistent way to address a challenging resident. Using that process with a dash of patience and a lot of listening is most likely to de-escalate the situation and open the door to resolution. Our teams have learned through experience that a process that includes respectfully listening, empathizing, sharing the "why," building rapport, restoring trust, and following up works well in tough situations.

## Listening

Listening effectively is the first step in dealing with challenging residents. Let them talk—and talk and talk and talk, if necessary. Do not interrupt, especially to deny or rebut. They want to be heard—so hear them.

Letting challenging residents articulate their frustrations allows them to vent and helps listeners understand why they are so upset. Such listening sessions allow disgruntled residents to work through their emotions while listeners get a sense of what else is driving their intensity. Often, their underlying frustrations are a mélange of personal or professional issues combined with those experienced within the community association. This supercharges the intensity and clouds the ability to focus on the core issue.

Listening actively entails asking clarifying questions at the appropriate time—and listening further by considering the answers while working toward resolution. Listeners should use sincere body language to their advantage, making and holding eye contact to indicate attentiveness, nodding when in agreement or to demonstrate understanding, taking notes to reflect engagement, and summarizing complaints to confirm understanding.

At the risk of sounding academic, I recommend listeners employ a communication power tool from Associa's continuing education program for community managers, namely, the Aristotelian Appeals of ethos/logos/pathos. It entails listening while separating the speaker's ethical, logical, and emotional appeals, respectively. Remember: Just because someone is angry, disrespectful, and even vulgar does not mean he or she is wrong. Listening analytically empowers the listener to ask, "What if he is right?"—and act accordingly.

Listening is a far cry from simply waiting for a turn to speak, to deny, or to rebut. It means focusing on the information articulated and the context in which it is provided. It also means gaining insight into the perspectives expressed and determining how to develop resolutions through which everyone wins rather than declaring winners and losers. When most effective, it should result in participants learning each other's perspectives and then collaborating toward mutually acceptable resolutions.

**Empathizing**

While sympathy means feeling concerned about others, empathy means sharing or embracing their concerns. A communication specialist explained the difference this way: "A passenger on a ship was seasick and throwing up. His sympathetic friend told him he was sorry he was not feeling well. His empathetic friend put his arm around him and threw up with him!" Clearly, the latter "felt his pain." That is empathy.

In de-escalating situations with challenging residents, board members and managers should put themselves in their shoes. They can ask themselves, "If our roles were reversed and I were the disgruntled resident, how would I want to be treated? What would make me happy?" Then, they should act accordingly.

Empathetic board members and managers must be not only kind, respectful, patient, and understanding, but also inquisitive and responsive. The following steps can be a helpful reminder of how to treat unhappy residents with empathy:

- Acknowledge their frustrations: "I understand how you feel and the inconvenience you are experiencing."
- Thank them for taking the time to explain the matter and to ensure others do not experience similar frustrations: "Thank you for taking the time to bring this matter to our attention. By allowing us to resolve this situation, you are helping us preclude it from happening to other residents."

- Express commitment to resolve the situation: "You have my word that I will do my best to get to the bottom of this and to try to make things right."

- The bottom line is that after hearing residents out, taking a moment to acknowledge their state of mind can further lay the groundwork for the steps that follow. Remember: No matter how angry they are, they might be right.

## Sharing the "Why"

Working with challenging residents can result in positive outcomes only if participants eventually engage in resolving the situation to everyone's satisfaction. Board members can neither cower to forceful demands, nor favor one hostile resident at the expense of others. Their success will be facilitated if the disgruntled party can be persuaded to consider why the situation evolved and how it can be resolved fairly and consistently within the parameters defined by the association's governing documents.

After the challenging resident has expressed concerns, it is appropriate to engage in a conversation about the underlying issue. A brief explanation of the association rules or policies that are the subject of the dispute can help the resident understand the "why" behind the actions. This also can be an inflection point to engage the resident regarding possible ways to resolve the matter or to provide information about how to appeal the matter with the board if such action is appropriate. If frustration begins to re-emerge, it can be helpful to remind the resident that the board or manager and the resident share the same goal of resolving the issue.

## Building Rapport

Empathy and mutual understanding are the foundation from which to build rapport with challenging residents and to transform them into constructive members of the association. If their frustrations stemmed from their perceptions of a previous lack of responsiveness, now is the time to assure them that, going forward, the relationship will be improved based on their newly established mutual understanding and commitment to interaction.

Events or perceived actions that occurred in the past cannot be changed, but their results can be motivators for moving forward together in peace and harmony. Sometimes, it helps to focus on the positive by avoiding unnecessary references to the negativity of the past and underscoring the positivity of the emerging consensus as a foundation from which to build trust.

## Restoring Trust

Right or wrong, challenging residents often have lost faith in the processes and persons perceived as being able to resolve their issues. The success of building rapport based on listening actively and empathetically depends on working hard on both sides to preclude additional problems, redirect any resolutions that have gone off course, and enhance trust and confidence in a mutually productive relationship going forward.

Restoring trust, if possible, is key to achieving long-term resolution of problems. It strengthens over time only if the interactions are more positive than in the past and if everyone makes a concerted effort to succeed together.

## Following Up

The process of responding to challenging residents and transforming them into constructive neighbors never ends. Its ongoing nature means a newly improved relationship continually can ascend to higher levels of success or, alternatively, can descend into the old ways of negativity and frustration. Success depends on following up to ensure the resolution process is on track and any bumps in the road are smoothed as quickly as possible.

Setting a time to follow up on progress, for example, heartens doubters who worry whether a problem truly was resolved. If challenged residents complained about never knowing what the board was doing, for example, board members could set times to follow up with them and to evaluate their success in communicating more regularly and effectively, being responsive to public comments expressed at board meetings, promoting interaction via websites and in-person, etc.

This creates a promise made/promise delivered scenario that can build trust by following up.

## When Nothing Seems to Work

Despite the best efforts of the most experienced boards of directors and community managers, there are times when no approach makes progress with challenging residents. Although this is rare, it happens. The residents in question continue to create toxicity that impacts the board, the manager, and other residents. The ongoing issue may be related to a grudge held by a challenging resident or to a personal crisis happening to that person. When traditional approaches to resident engagement fail to yield positive results, other options become viable. These include asking the disgruntled to communicate in writing, whether by email, text, or other means; engaging local resources; consulting legal counsel; and attempting other strategies that are respectful to all concerned.

### Communicate in Writing

When challenging residents reject efforts to find a resolution and continue to badger, berate, and otherwise denigrate the board or manager, they create an even more toxic environment that impacts the board's ability to govern and absorbs a disproportionate amount of the manager's time. In such circumstances, it is appropriate to direct the resident to communicate in writing via email, text, or other means. This can be helpful in two ways. First, communicating in writing requires authors to put their concerns into words. This could help them sort through the whirlwind of unrelated emotions that may exacerbate their frustrations but have nothing to do with the issue. Second, it creates a paper trail to show residents they have been heard and that progress is being made regarding their concerns.

### Engage Local Resources

Sometimes, the underlying issue causing hostility and/or repeated violations of community standards is the resident's mental or physical condition. Community associations are microcosms of society. They face the same challenges as other entities: Aging residents, for example, may be living alone, dealing with dementia, experiencing a mental health crisis, and/or hoarding. In such cases, the board should consult with counsel about reaching out to local municipal, county, or state agencies that can help.

Most jurisdictions have resources that can provide mental health intervention, assistance to aging residents, and other means of helping impacted residents. Many associations, for example, successfully worked with county or municipal health departments to navigate the many unknowns of dealing with the COVID-19 pandemic.

### Consult Legal Counsel

For most interactions with challenging residents, opportunities for them to be heard and engaged are gateways to resolving their issues. Occasionally, however, boards and managers deal with irate residents who refuse to be assuaged, regardless of the number of attempts or strategies employed. Fortunately, these instances are not the norm; unfortunately, they occur.

At times like this, the board and manager may have no recourse but to engage the community association's law firm. Counsel can advise the board about legal measures the association can take to resolve underlying issues or to further direct challenging residents into more constructive pathways.

## Respect Residents

Even with the most challenging of angry residents, board members and managers should be respectful. This admittedly may require inordinate patience and self-control, especially for those not used to tolerating rudeness at work or at home. A longtime friend of mine who has been described as having "old world manners" and whose courtesy and patience are legendary often says, "Patience is a virtue *I do not have!*" You would never know it from her demeanor, just as residents never should detect impatience on the part of board members and managers.

This is especially true when dealing with the impact of factors such as aging, mental health, or debilitating illness. Board members should prioritize the health and safety of residents, whether they are causing the problem or suffering the consequences of those who are. They should always respect the privacy of everyone involved and consult with their legal counsel before turning to municipal, county, or state resources to help resolve matters. It should go without saying that information about underlying issues or perceptions of their causes should be kept confidential.

## Interacting with Rebellious Factions

A community association's mission is to set community standards, enhance property values, provide amenities, and create connections among its residents. Because each community association is representative of society at large, it should come as no surprise that diverse interests within it can give rise to factions.

For purposes of this discussion, we define "faction" as a group of residents with a shared interest or perspective. They can be a positive influence by engaging residents and identifying community interests. On the other hand, they can also be a source of conflict and create obstacles to implementing community goals. Understanding the nature of factions, ways to mitigate negative impacts, and methods for resolving factional disputes can help the community association function efficiently and minimize conflict.

### Defining Rebellious Factions

Having a group of residents united and engaged in the affairs of the community can be a great asset to a community association. Conversely, that same group, united in its opposition to the board's actions, can be a detriment.

As with the angry resident, occasionally, a rebellious faction can emerge in a community association. As a group, they can counter the board's efforts, and in some cases, may lay claim to the true will of the residents.

Factions come in all shapes and sizes but tend to exhibit traits such as being rebellious, united, organized, and empowered. Understanding those traits empowers board members with the insight they need to mitigate their negative impact.

**Rebellious.** As the label suggests, a rebellious faction is a group of community association residents who are ready to oppose board action or even the board itself. Such factions may emerge from disagreements about actions such as special assessments, personality clashes, board recalls, or other matters that stir their passions.

Rebellious factions typically form to counter the board's actions. Their hallmark is focusing on opposition rather than on proposing alternative solutions. Interestingly, they tend to show a lack of interest in running to be part of the community's governing body.

**United.** Unlike an angry resident who acts alone, a rebellious faction is a group of residents who are united in their intransigence to the direction of the board. Working in concert to oppose board actions, they express views that may be contrary to the board's vision. Together, they can be significantly more disruptive than a lone voice. A greater problem, however, is that such factions may form for a single purpose but then decide to carry their unity into the future, creating a voice of "common cause."

**Organized.** Rebellious factions tend to be organized—or try to be. Their organization can be accomplished easily by creating a social media presence to criticize the board or make accusations about board members' perceived motives. As they further their agenda by reaching out to other similar-minded residents, their organization may become bigger and stronger.

Such organizational effectiveness brings back early memories of a movie in which Tarzan said something like, "The weak must organize to oppose the strong." The question is, do organizers have a positive, constructive purpose, or, alternatively, do they seek to create havoc? Rebellious factions that fall into the latter category can pose significant challenges for association boards of directors.

Because they are organized and may have solicited opinions from a subset of residents, the group may believe its position represents a majority view of the community. This reminds me of the saying, "The plural of anecdotes is not 'data.'" That said, regardless of the percentage of residents for whom the group claims to speak, it is important to acknowledge concerns and welcome feedback.

**Empowered.** A rebellious faction can be described as empowered when it can influence board decisions. This empowerment can stem from sources such as a strong, unified membership base; effective leadership; the ability to communicate regularly and easily; and access to significant resources or information.

An empowered rebellious faction often demonstrates its power by leveraging community support to communicate its goals and grievances. Influenced by "mob mentality," those who otherwise would not act alone may feel comfortable being part of a group that speaks out against board decisions. Their empowerment is solidified if it can assert its influence consistently, leading to tangible changes that reflect its objectives and values. This can result in an outright challenge to the balance of power within the community association.


## Mitigating the Impact of Factions

Most community associations welcome the participation of groups interested in developing the community and furthering its best interests. That is not the perception (or history) of community association factions, however. Although not inherently bad, their impact can be negative if they work strictly in opposition to the board, creating obstacles without offering constructive direction for the issues at hand.

Effective boards can counter the negative influence of factions by creating opportunities for all voices in the community to feel heard and ensuring a governance process that welcomes participation from the community at large. This process can be achieved by focusing on internal processes, listening and observing, surveying, and engaging residents.

## Focusing on Internal Processes

Board members have a duty to remain focused on internal processes. A board that adheres to the policies and procedures outlined in the governing documents, consistently follows its internal processes, gathers facts before taking action, and applies community rules fairly and consistently is more likely to find acceptable solutions to challenges.

When dealing with angry residents or factions, board members should be clear: They welcome their engagement and feedback in finding solutions that are consistent with the internal processes that serve the best interest of the community. What is more, their suggestions will be considered as fairly and respectfully as those submitted by others who may not be angry, but who also want to be heard.

## Listening and Observing

Because the values and cultures of communities change over time, sometimes rules that were once widely supported may become outdated. When board members fail to recognize the need for change, factions can emerge.

An effective board goes beyond its responsibility to keep residents informed. It takes the time to listen to them and see them in action. If they observe, for example, a surge in violations of a specific rule, such as street parking, board members should consider listening to residents' opinions about its relevance and reviewing it for possible updating.

By keeping abreast of changing community preferences, board members not only fulfill their missions, but also remove points of contention that, if left unchecked, could lead to rebellious factions forming in the community.

## Surveying

Community associations have access to technology that enables them to take the pulse of residents at the push of a button. In addition to employing online survey tools to gain insight into community attitudes toward rules or board proposals, for example, boards of directors can design them to collect suggestions, observations, and feedback from residents. This can be done by way of the many free survey tools available on the internet or through community-wide applications such as TownSq, which Associa and other management companies offer to clients.

By keeping its finger on the pulse of the community, a board enhances its awareness of emerging community preferences and is more likely to take action that represents a majority of the community. Having hard data on hand can also help board members counter criticisms from factions who wrongly claim to represent the true opposing views of the community or who accuse the board of being out of touch.

## Engaging

Boards should welcome constructive criticism and opportunities to transform critics into allies. When a faction emerges, the board can create an opportunity for its members to present their concerns or ideas to them. Engaging the faction can be highly successful if its members are treated respectfully and professionally, if the ideas proposed are considered seriously and thoughtfully, and if the result is mutually satisfactory. The goal should be to achieve positive outcomes, precluding faction members from becoming increasingly hostile over futile attempts to make a difference and have an impact.

The board can use the engagement process to discuss the impact of the faction's ideas on the community, their potential success, and the reactions of other residents. Responding to the desire of a group to be heard and engaging its members in constructive dialogue can help find common ground and improve relationships that otherwise could worsen. The best-case scenario would be for their proposals to be helpful to the board's mission of serving the best interests of the community.

## Engaging Factions

Factions emerge in just about any organized human endeavor and can play a constructive or destructive role in governance. At its core, a faction is a group of people united around an idea or a concern with the goal of amplifying individual voices.

Working to understand factions is a critical initial step in building harmony. Approaching interactions with them as opportunities for reaching consensus and promoting harmony rather than as burdens that must be tolerated can turn a challenge into an asset.

A board can transform factional interests into a means of engagement with key community constituencies. This approach can be explored by finding common ground, engaging the faction to help in the community, or even using the faction as a focus group of a subset of interests in the community association.

### Finding Common Ground

Community association boards of directors can find common ground with rebellious factions by fostering open communication and demonstrating a genuine willingness to understand their concerns.

Providing a public comment period during which residents can voice their opinions during regular board meetings creates a platform for dialogue. Active listening can not only help board members understand the concerns expressed, but also show faction members their perspective is being heard and considered.

Such interaction should include exploring any potential compromises or solutions. By listening and demonstrating respect, empathy, and a commitment to mutual goals, the board can bridge divides and cultivate a more cohesive and cooperative community environment.

## Engaging

Community associations thrive on participation, especially because their boards of directors and community managers have countless tasks that can benefit from assistance or feedback, if not both. Engaging residents to serve on task forces or committees can open the governing process to wider involvement, bring more voices to the table, and help develop future members of the board. In the process, it creates increased opportunities for engagement and reduces or eliminates the need for factions to emerge to make their voices heard.

## Serving as Focus Groups

While a faction does not speak for the entirety of a community, it often represents an important collection of community interests. Boards can engage them as part of an effective strategy for obtaining feedback about specific community needs and preferences. If, for example, the faction is united around environmental interests, its members can be a good resource for ideas about improving the community's land, water, or air.

Factions can help board members gain insights into proposals that may be relevant or actionable. At the very least, as a subset of interests in the community association, factions can be sources of suggestions or feedback. Their engagement not only ensures their specific concerns are heard and addressed, but also fosters a sense of inclusion and empowerment. This approach helps board members make informed decisions.

## RESOLVING DISPUTES

Resolving disputes would be easy if there were a standard formula boards could apply. The reality is that many variables dictate the best approach to resolving them. Making every effort to communicate effectively and track community preferences are preventive measures. No matter how hard they try, however, even the most committed boards may need additional tools for resolving disputes with angry residents or rebellious factions.

Situational elements inevitably factor into disputes, and they can dictate the approach best suited for resolving them. Following the procedural guidelines outlined in the association's governing documents is required, and doing so ensures consistency and fairness.

When residents who previously felt unheard are engaged and experience cooperation and collaboration with board members, a pathway toward resolution may emerge. If those approaches fail, board members can turn to professionals who can lead parties in a dispute resolution process.

No one approach has, in my experience, proven most effective in resolving disputes, but the range outlined herein can help boards of directors determine which seems best suited for the challenge at hand. Generally, they fall into three categories, namely, process-oriented, collaboration, and outside resources.

### Process-Oriented Approaches

Process-oriented approaches to resolving disputes are opportunities to exchange information for the purpose of determining an outcome. They include using the association's due process, communicating effectively, and focusing on fairness and neutrality.

## Using the Association's Due Process

Perhaps the most common dispute resolution for community associations revolves around rule violations. Because they are required to provide due process to residents and define that due process in the association's governing documents, board members should prepare for this traditional form of process-oriented engagement by reviewing those documents.

From beginning to end, their actions must be consistent with the basic standards of fairness defined by due process, namely, giving the alleged violator advance notice of the violation and of the right to be heard regarding it, of how the board intends to resolve the situation, of possible consequences or outcomes, and of the resident's right to appeal if dissatisfied with the decision.

The policies and procedures for conflict resolution defined in the governing documents must be followed to the letter. Rules are in place to create a cohesive and functional community, and everyone must follow them, including board members.

The importance of clear, well-written governing documents cannot be overstated. Association members are more likely to accept the process of resolving conflicts when the rules are deemed necessary, clear, reasonable, and above all else, legal. Indeed, everyone benefits from a set of rules that guides board members in fulfilling their responsibilities more effectively and provides the standards of compliance for residents. Informed homeowners are more likely to comply voluntarily, which may lead to fewer issues in a happier, less stressful atmosphere.

## Communicating Effectively

Dealing with disputes does not always rise to the level of conflict resolution. Matters often can be dealt with through effective interpersonal communication that can result in a speedy solution to problems, minimize confusion, promote transparency, and build trust.

Relying on the process of communication to resolve disputes, however, must be consistent with the process and standards of fairness defined in the governing documents. If permitted, for example, board members and managers could approach rule violators via more informal, less confrontational methods of communication such as face-to-face conversations or telephone calls.

Many communities prefer to communicate by letter, often relying on templates that are prewritten and can be used verbatim or as starting points to be adapted for the purpose at hand. Template letters may allow boards and managers to respond quickly to violations and issues, but they can ring hollow, not capture the situation exactly, and annoy recipients. They also can detract from the authenticity of the board, resulting in misunderstandings and escalated tensions. Whether original or based on a template, letters should be respectful, provide complete information, define the response or action required, invite feedback and engagement, and provide an avenue for responding and working toward agreement.

The hallmarks of effective communication include targeting language for the intended readers or listeners. This typically means using words and terms that are understood easily, avoiding "inside lingo" that smacks of hiding behind community policy. Whether verbal or written, the message should be long enough to present complete information but short enough to keep the intended person's attention. There is no need to include more information than necessary, but the relevant guidelines outlined in the governing documents should be cited, as should any compelling reason regarding why the matter addressed is important to the community.

### Focusing on Fairness and Neutrality

Fairness and neutrality should be characteristic of board members and their actions. These standards should be evident daily, but especially when handling disputes and during any process of interacting with residents and representing them. They are critical not only in resolving conflicts, but also in avoiding them.

Being fair to all means board members must govern in the best interests of the community rather than of their own or of a select group. It also means no right or privilege should be extended to one resident that could not be extended to others under similar circumstances. Making an exception to give a grieving spouse or parent extended time to comply with a rule, for example, is typical of a consideration that would be given to others. Reasonable persons would not consider it special treatment.

## Collaboration

A more effective and efficient community association should be the goal of all members. Differences in opinions about how to achieve it can be the heart of disputes, particularly when both sides desire a well-functioning and vibrant community.

Under such circumstances, if the dispute is based on a structural shortcoming or even a blind spot the board may have, collaboration or a negotiated settlement seems a worthy course of action. This process can occur within the scope of the board's due process function, or it can be the result of a conscious decision to discuss the source of the dispute. Such a discussion can evolve into a collaborative effort to identify proposed changes.

The success of collaboration depends on communicating effectively and following up. What is more, it should be based on mutuality, that is, both sides striving toward a solution, rather than on the board or the resident insisting on the capitulation of the opposing party.

### Exploring Collaboration

Collaboration may sound easier than it is. To begin with, it takes two sides who are interested in reaching consensus instead of determining winners and losers. It pays to remember that those who adopt an "all or nothing" approach to conflicts sometimes get nothing. Constructive attitudes make collaboration worthy of exploration when disputes arise that are not at the level of the due process approach.

As in most cases of resolving disputes, the collaborative approach begins with identifying its root cause. Both parties can review the rules that apply to the violation in question and to the process for resolving conflicts, as well as other written materials or records. Given this context, they can focus their discussions on uncovering the issues causing the conflict. This opens the door to collaborating to get to the heart of the problem and reach an agreement.

Active listening throughout the exchange is essential, with each side allowing the other to speak and to ask and answer questions. Such healthy interactions help move matters forward as part of a collaborative process focused on finding common ground.

## Updating Residents

Reaching a resolution is not only a cause for relief—and sometimes celebration—but also a time for communication. To reinforce their success and preclude misunderstandings or conflicting memories about it, board members and managers should follow up to reiterate the agreement, communicate action items, update residents involved (and, if appropriate, the community at large), and provide contact information. By checking in, they ensure everyone is adhering to the agreed-upon terms and confirm everyone is on the same team.

Lessons learned from the process could be incorporated into the community's own best practices for dealing with similar issues or other conflicts. When those who disagree work in the best interest of their communities, everybody wins.

## Fostering Cooperation

Board members and formerly angry residents usually have something in common: They both recognize the importance of working together to find common ground and can attest that the community association process works.

Successful resolutions foster cooperation and can motivate former critics to become advocates for the community. Keeping lines of communication open can provide opportunities to engage them if similar matters arise in the future. Equally important, they can result in identifying potential committee members or even future board members.

## Outside Resources

Board members often overlook the outside resources that are readily available to help them resolve conflicts. They include their professional partners, including community managers and association attorneys.

The ecosystem of professional support a community association can call upon when needed should be a part of any board's arsenal for dispute resolution. This is especially true if the nature of the dispute is complex or involves legal matters. Fortunately, an effective board can lean on these professionals to help navigate the dispute resolution process. After working through the association's appeal process, if the party in dispute continues to make waves, it may be time for the board to call in reinforcements that can include the community manager or association counsel or consider engaging a mediator in the quest to resolve the matter.

### Community Manager

A community manager's function is to support board members in their duties, typically acting as their gatekeeper, collecting information, helping to resolve disputes, and assisting with other actionable matters. A good community manager can project a calm, professional, and informed demeanor even under the most trying circumstances.

Formal and continuing education, insightful perspective and extensive knowledge about community associations, effective communication, and a customer service focus are among the reasons for hiring community managers—and the reason they should be the first stop for any resident complaints.

## Association Counsel

A community association's counsel is an indispensable resource in resolving controversial or challenging disputes. This is especially true if the subject matter of the dispute is complex, involves money, or is rooted in a foreclosure action.

A board of directors generally is protected in its decision-making if it demonstrates sound judgment and fairness based on the policies and processes defined in the governing documents. The cornerstone of this concept is consulting with qualified counsel who can issue a legal opinion on which the board can rely. The attorney can analyze the dispute, apply the facts to relevant governing documents' provisions and laws, and advise the board on how to navigate the dispute in a manner that is ethically and legally appropriate. The cost of such consultation often is far less than any litigation that could arise from a dispute.

## Mediators or Arbitrators

Mediation or arbitration also can be an effective tool in resolving seemingly intractable disputes. It should not be a first-line option, but, rather, a means of finding a solution after consulting with association counsel to ensure it is within the scope of the board's authority and is the proper venue.

Mediation is typically nonbinding. It involves a neutral professional who hears both sides and tries to lead them to a mutually agreed solution. Its success depends on all parties being interested in negotiating to reach a consensus with the mediator as their "go-between."[1]

Arbitration, by comparison, can be binding or nonbinding and is conducted by a neutral professional who serves as an arbiter or arbitrator and hears both sides before rendering a solution, regardless of whether the parties reach a consensus. The difference is that the arbiter makes decisions based on rules of law or equity, while the arbitrator can use discretion and render decisions based on the presumed judgment of a reasonable person rather than on substantive law.[2] Both processes are intended to preclude litigation and require the advice of counsel.

Clearly, dealing with challenging residents and factions can result in positive outcomes when board members and managers use the tools and resources at their disposal. Doing so may require patience and effort, but the results are worth it.

## CONCLUSION

The diversity of opinions, backgrounds, and ideologies helps make our communities vibrant. Simultaneously, it can create friction and give rise to the proverbial angry resident or rebellious faction. Differences of opinion, however, do not have to be obstacles to progress but can be opportunities for better communication, collaboration, and cooperation. When confronted with seemingly intractable residents or groups, effective boards can mitigate negative impacts, regardless of the cause of the dispute.

In responding to angry residents, board members should remember their anger is not necessarily permanent. Resolving the negative impact of residents with axes to grind is less stressful when approached with a structured, empathetic, and process-focused response. By understanding the characteristics of challenging residents and deploying appropriate strategies to address their behaviors, boards can position themselves for success. Patience, practice, and process can help save the day.

Similarly, when confronted with rebellious factions, board members can employ strategies that help preserve community harmony and keep the operational gears moving. Taking the time to examine their triggers and finding ways to engage them constructively can move the scenario from obstruction to dialogue and progress. Perhaps more importantly, ensuring broad input into community decisions will help them mitigate the emergence of factions.

Equally important, it is helpful to understand that strategies for resolving disputes may vary depending on the circumstances. Individuals bring with them their experiences, biases, and fears that can foster frustration when events are perceived to go against their interests. Despite how the dispute began, boards can explore a variety of potential responses while keeping the best interests of the community in mind. When necessary, boards also can draw from the rich resources of professional expertise. With experience and time, they can evolve into community leaders who can effectively meet challenges that will inevitably emerge as part of their duties.

## QUESTIONS TO CONSIDER

1. What strategies does your board use to address angry residents who do not seem to respond to efforts to resolve their issues?

2. Has the board found a particular approach that is most helpful in addressing an angry resident or a rebellious faction? If so, why?

3. If your community has engaged a professional to help resolve a conflict, was the process helpful? If so, what were the lessons learned from the process?

4. What steps does your board take to ensure broad input or feedback about community decisions?

5. If a rebellious faction emerged in your community, what were its underlying issues of discontent? How did your board respond?

6. Has your board had to engage a faction in working toward conflict resolution? If so, was the process helpful in bringing the parties to a consensus?

7. How do your community documents address the handling of disputes or appeals of board decisions? How could the process be improved?

8. With what frequency does your board adjudicate disputes within your community? How can they be more successful in this process?

9. What are the unique elements of your community that shape how you approach handling conflict?

## CHAPTER 8

# Dealing with Challenging Boards of Directors

The government you elect is the government you deserve.

—THOMAS JEFFERSON,
Third President of the United States

## CHAPTER INTRODUCTION

Dealing with challenging boards of directors is less common than dealing with challenging residents, but when it does occur, it is an opportunity to make a significant difference for a community by helping its members do a better job. Ideally, all boards would meet the standards defined in chapter 4. They would apply community association rules fairly and consistently, continue to educate themselves and residents, and collaborate with each other as well as with homeowners and professional partners. When that is not the case, my team and I do our best to help them understand the issue at hand and what to do about it to represent their constituents more effectively. To paraphrase former President Jefferson, the board members we elect are the board members we deserve—but that underlines the importance of our helping them do a better job.

Comparable to our approach to challenging residents, we do not dismiss or generalize boards whose members may act inappropriately as simply "bad," "difficult," or "rogue," though individual and some of their collective actions may be. We use the term "challenging" for elected bodies that pose opportunities for us to help them improve, particularly through communication and continuing education programs. Similarly, we use "challenged boards" to refer to those dealing with members who are conducting themselves inappropriately and whose actions sometimes envelop the entire board. Finally, we use "bad boards" only for purposes of discussion pertinent to their collective characteristics that can prove damaging to communities. Above all, we remember: Nobody is perfect!

Because boards of directors are empowered to make decisions on behalf of their communities, when their success is plagued with internal problems, setting things right is not always easy. In most cases, understanding the cause of a problem can help define a strategy to enact change. What is more, it can serve as a preventive measure by sensitizing new and seasoned good board members to the kind of conduct they should avoid and can help correct in others.

Identifying the characteristics and negative impacts of challenging boards lays the foundation for improving them. In the end, working to redeem or change a board for the better means empowering members to fight for a more cooperative and transparent environment in which the community association will operate smoothly and in the best interests of all residents.

As the entity that leads a community association, a board of directors plays the key role in governance and wields significant influence over the community's operations and enjoyment. Boards are responsible for a range of responsibilities, from handling community finances and enforcing rules to building a sense of community. When they fail to fulfill their duties or—worse—abuse their powers, their negative impact can be far-reaching. It can lead to needlessly high assessments, legal disputes, and an overall deterioration of the quality of life in a community.

That is why such situations must be recognized, understood, and resolved. Understanding the dynamics of a challenging board begins with examining hallmarks that include financial mismanagement, arbitrary rule enforcement, and lack of transparency.

Similarly, the causes behind the emergence of difficult boards are varied. Most often, they emerge from inadequate homeowner participation, misunderstanding or not knowing rules and responsibilities defined in the governing documents, and lack of training or experience. Regardless of the causes, understanding them in context is essential to uncovering how communities can avoid or resolve them. Such strategies include putting a community back on track with the assistance of more active residents and a commitment to good governance and greater transparency. To help board members deal with such situations, this chapter focuses on the process of understanding challenging boards as the foundation for overcoming apathy in the community and overcoming bad boards when they emerge.

## UNDERSTANDING CHALLENGING BOARDS

Hardworking, effective community association board members who take their jobs seriously and do their work are the norm. From time to time, however, challenging boards of directors need assistance in ensuring all members are progressing together along the straight and narrow pathway to effectiveness.

The path to being a good board member begins with the understanding that a board of directors is empowered to govern a community association; its powers are enumerated in the community governing documents, state statutes, and precedents set by relevant court decisions; members are elected volunteers required to work in the best interests of their community associations; and decisions are made by majority votes, not by individuals.

Hundreds of thousands of residents volunteer their time to serve on their community association boards. When members shirk their duties, they can impact their communities negatively: Property values can fall, needed maintenance can be deferred, and a sense of community can be shattered by the lack of good leadership.

The presence of such boards is rare, but the emergence of one creates issues for residents. Understanding their characteristics, their causes, and their resulting impact on community associations can help prevent their emergence. Doing so is consistent with the adage, "An ounce of prevention is worth a pound of cure."

## Characteristics of Challenged Boards

First, the good news: So-called bad boards are incredibly rare. According to the Foundation for Community Association Research, more than 87 percent of community association residents believe their boards serve the best interests of their communities.[1] That is a remarkable statistic, especially considering that only 13 percent of Americans approve of the work of the U.S. Congress.[2] That said, a board whose members act badly can have a measurably negative impact on a community association. When those members have an undue influence on a board, the result is what can be stereotyped by others and in the media as a "bad board."

More objectively, a bad board is defined by its disregard for its duty to the community association and by exhibiting behaviors that demonstrate its lack of focus on the needs of the community. The result can undermine the mission of a community association to protect and enhance the value of homes, sow division among members, and alienate residents from participating in community governance.

Although not exclusive, the characteristics to be corrected include abusing power, mismanaging funds, arbitrarily enforcing rules, pursuing vendettas, lacking transparency, failing to meet, and ignoring feedback. Recognizing them is the first step toward correcting them.

## Abusing Power

The media stereotype of community association boards is that they are all-powerful. Given the sources of board authority, this is far from reality. Some board members, however, may internalize this stereotype and act like absolute monarchs while abusing their power. They may wrongly claim authority to undertake a variety of actions not supported by the community's governing documents, seemingly inventing rules to enforce while ignoring duly adopted rules or procedures.

## Mismanaging Funds

Most community associations are nonprofit corporations. Their budgets can range from tens of thousands to tens of millions of dollars. Managing their finances is a balancing act; mismanaging them can be perilous.

The board should strive to adopt budgets that are adequate to preserve and enhance the association while also setting aside funds for future repair and replacement of common elements.

Some board members, however, may ignore the reality of the community's financial needs by trying to keep assessments artificially low. This can cause deferred maintenance, which can negatively impact property values in the community. Worse, failing to keep budget balances at appropriate levels can result in future special assessments that strain residents' finances.

Beyond negligent budgeting, unscrupulous board members may engage in self-dealing, awarding lucrative contracts to friends, family, or entities in which they have undisclosed interests.

## Arbitrarily Enforcing Rules

Enforcing rules arbitrarily may be the most common characteristic of a bad board. This is exemplified by enforcing the governing documents inconsistently, depending on affinity for particular members. The worst examples include targeting residents for violations if they are perceived as insufficiently supporting the board or as being critical of board actions. Equally serious, it can manifest itself as the board ignoring rule violations of fellow board members, relatives, or friends.

## Pursuing Vendettas

Instead of focusing on the needs of the community, some board members may wrongly prioritize personal politics and pursue vendettas against their enemies. A bad board may take action or refuse to act in the community's best interest simply for political reasons or to get revenge on their political opponents. This includes unduly delaying the approval for a property improvement because of dislike for a resident or interpreting the rules more strictly for disliked residents in comparison to perceived allies.

## Lacking Transparency

While the best board members understand and support access to community information as required by state laws, their negative counterparts block transparency. Ignoring requirements of most states to make governing documents accessible to residents, for example, some board members persist in making them difficult to peruse. They shun the responsibility of communicating regularly to as large an audience as possible about the work the board has undertaken and, ideally, why they have taken particular actions. In every possible way, they seem to strive to keep residents in the dark, oblivious to the frustration and anger that lack of transparency can cause among homeowners who care and deserve to be kept informed.

## Failing to Meet

Despite the minimum number of public meetings typically required of community association boards of directors by governing documents and state statutes, some boards fail to meet regularly and/ or in the open. This is especially serious when the board continues to enforce rules and to collect assessments. Additionally, in certain circumstances, a board's failure to hold regular, required meetings can impact the validity of its actions.

**Ignoring Feedback**

The easiest way to alienate homeowners may be to ignore them. Instead of inviting their participation, welcoming and considering their feedback, and adapting to their articulated changing needs and interests, some board members shut residents out of the process. Acting in their own interests, they ignore feedback in countless ways. These include not listening to the concerns and preferences of the community, ignoring issues raised by residents at meetings, taking unilateral action without community input, and refusing to hear valid complaints or undertake requested changes. This type of behavior undermines the democratic process that is the foundation of community associations, often resulting in increased mistrust and greater frustration in the community.

## Why "Bad Boards" Happen

The adage that politics is not a spectator sport applies to community associations as well. Their impact on average families' biggest investments, their homes, should motivate many homeowners to run for election to their boards of directors—and many of them do.

The demands of today's world, however, leave many potential leaders little time for civic engagement, leaving many communities with a dearth of volunteers for board service. Few, if any, examples of constructive leadership that board members can emulate are included in the divisive daily coverage by the national media.

Truly, a rogue board does not evolve in a vacuum. Its causes are as diverse as the many types of community associations whose negative stereotypes can impact engagement. When "bad boards" happen, the problem typically begins with inadequate homeowner participation and negative perceptions of community associations, exacerbated by a lack of training for board members and even fewer leadership role models. Those are the causes discussed here.

## Inadequate Homeowner Participation

Some bad boards or board members start off on the right track but fall into a trap of entitlement. Board members who have served for many years only because there are no other options often develop a sense of entitlement. Unfortunately, a lack of candidates can translate into a lack of accountability. Running unopposed means they cannot be voted out of office. Feeling there is no interest in the board or what it does can atrophy the resolve of even the most dedicated board members. The result too often is an attitude that they have free reign in their communities because no one else cares.

## Negative Perceptions of Community Associations

Quick reviews of social media or viewings of certain local news programs too often will uncover untrue messages that community associations are terrible entities set up to torment their residents. The data do not support such negative claims. While bad boards exist, irrefutable data indicate residents find value in living in community associations and evaluate board members positively.

The negative portrayals of community associations in electronic and traditional media, however, can dissuade residents from volunteering in their associations. Likewise, a community that has experienced a bad board or board member may find it harder to recruit residents for leadership positions.

## Lack of Experience or Knowledge

Community association governance requires a level of knowledge about the community and its governing documents. Experience in management may be beneficial but is not required. While there are few prerequisites for serving on a community association board, a board member should at least be familiar with the concept of the board's role, as was discussed in more detail in chapter 4, and should have the experience or ability to participate effectively in board meetings.

Corruption in the courtroom has been attributed to ignorance of the law and incompetence regarding procedure. Similarly, if community association board members do not know the rules that govern them or how to implement the policies and procedures defined in the governing documents, they may be more likely to behave badly.

Bad boards can emerge if their members do not invest time and effort in understanding their roles or internalizing their community's governing documents. Without that experience and knowledge, they are prone to operate without a sense of their roles or duties to the community. Their resulting decisions are more likely to be arbitrary and to conflict with community rules. More importantly, they can enrage residents into turmoil.

**Scarcity of Leadership Role Models**

News programs and the internet are chock-a-block with divisiveness, selfishness, and outrageous behavior. They reflect the current national political environment that is rife with name-calling, misinformation, and false accusations. Similarly, many of the reality-based programs thrive on conflict. As a result, our society seems to grow increasingly tolerant of extreme behavior and language that would have made our parents blush. The sad result is the scarcity of leadership role models who exemplify servant leadership in popular culture. If the conduct and accomplishments of exemplary elected leaders were publicized better, community association board members could emulate them. Modeling such behavior would certainly benefit communities.

## Impact on Homeowners and Communities

Keeping everything operating smoothly in community associations requires dedication and hard work. While an effective board focuses on enhancing property values and connecting neighbors, a challenged or bad board tends to focus on itself. As a result, less attention is paid to fundamentals such as managing finances, protecting property values, building trust among residents, and enhancing the overall health of the community.

When board members are not focused on their duties, the result can be a parade of impacts that damage the community over time. They include increased fees and special assessments, decreased property value, erosion of trust, increased conflicts and legal disputes, and deterioration of quality of life.

**Increased Fees and Special Assessments**

A challenged or bad board can negatively impact community finances. Periodically, for example, news reports emerge about association boards that neglected their obligations to maintain their communities wisely and responsibly, leaving residents with special assessments in the tens of thousands of dollars or more.

When a board does not focus on its core duty to the community, the result can be increased fees and even special assessments for all residents. Often, this is because board members failed to keep assessments at a level needed to maintain the community, to set aside funds for future replacement costs, and to pay for required insurance policies.

**Decreased Property Value**

One of the benefits of living in a community association is relying on the board to preserve the aesthetics of the neighborhood. When the board fails to focus on fundamentals, it has a cascading detrimental effect on property values. This is typically the result of not maintaining common areas and amenities properly, leading to a decline in the community's desirability.

Property values can also decline when negligent financial management, particularly inadequately funding reserve accounts, causes costly special assessments that alienate potential buyers. A community with ongoing conflicts can develop a bad reputation, forcing potential residents to look for more attractive and stable communities.

## Erosion of Trust

The impact of a bad board can extend deep into the community, undermining faith in community associations as forms of self-governance. Many lessons were learned, for example, from the bad board that allegedly siphoned off more than $3 million while hiking association assessments. Because paying community association assessments is mandatory, such a misappropriation makes rebuilding trust in the system a herculean task.

## Increased Conflicts and Legal Disputes

Inevitably, the negativity of bad boards leads to increased conflicts and legal disputes. Perhaps the worst example occurred in one of the largest community associations in Florida. It accrued more than $2 million in legal and receivership fees to help the community recover from a bad board—approximately one-third of the association's annual budget![3] Although this example is extraordinary, it illustrates the cost a community can incur because of a bad board.

While the community continues to repair the damage caused by that board and much work lies ahead, efforts to date demonstrate that when residents work together, they can remove a bad board, even in a large community association.

## Deterioration of Quality of Life

Our home is supposed to be our refuge, a peaceful and harmonious place to relax with loved ones after a busy day of handling personal or professional obligations, preferably in an equally peaceful and harmonious neighborhood. A community in the grip of a bad board, however, can find itself fraught with discontent and conflict as its families experience a deterioration of their quality of life.

Caused by the detrimental leadership of a bad board, however, time otherwise devoted to enjoyment may be spent on internal politics, factions, and the latest gossip rather than on connecting with neighbors. More often than not, the board's lack of care for common elements and amenities due to its negligence undermines the very reason many people choose to live in community associations.

## OVERCOMING APATHY

When conflicts endure to the point they get exhausting or unbearable, many persons simply give up trying to deal with them. In behavioral science jargon, they selectively expose themselves to conflicting information, sometimes blocking it mentally and refusing to react to it. Such is the impact of bad board members whose egregious behavior cannot be overcome, so they are ignored. The result is apathy among residents. When they simply look the other way instead of engaging in corrective behavior, the negativity, unfortunately, can accelerate.

That is why we in the industry must do our best to help community associations overcome apathy in such circumstances. We can help by recommending strategies, including starting with positivity, promoting participation, and leading by example.

### Start with Positivity

A well-governed community association enhances the lives of its residents. Common areas, amenities, and their self-governing nature ordinarily facilitate developing relationships as residents engage with each other and with the community. When the condition of these attractions deteriorates because of neglect by bad boards, they are no longer frequented by residents. This, in turn, causes relationships to deteriorate or never develop.

This sad state of affairs is exacerbated when the first contact a resident has with a board is a violation letter. It sets the wrong tone for building community and reinforces negative perceptions, especially if rules are perceived to be enforced unfairly. Such poor introductions to community association living easily can transform newcomers' feelings from excitement and happiness to anger or apathy. Unless action is taken to the contrary, a vicious cycle can begin: Bad boards can cause apathy, and apathy can lead to increasingly bad boards.

My team and I believe the best way to fight apathy is to highlight the positives of community association life. This can be accomplished by proactively and positively engaging new residents from their first day in the community. Starting with positivity is the best way to start them on the right track and preclude negative first impressions about community associations. This strategy can include creating a welcome committee, distributing welcome packets, and mentoring new residents.

## Create a Welcome Committee

Creating a welcome committee whose members will greet new residents is an effective way to reinforce positive perceptions about community association living and dispel those shaped by unflattering public discourse. Because news coverage generally focuses on the negative, any resulting offensive stereotypes can be challenged from day one by friendly, purpose-minded members of the welcome committee.

Appointed by the board, these volunteers can introduce themselves to new residents, offer best wishes and a warm welcome, provide a short orientation to the community, and invite them to attend community events or meetings. An in-person welcome and the opportunity to ask questions while learning about the community will ensure a positive start for new residents.

## Distribute Welcome Packets

It is common knowledge that everyone gets only one opportunity to make a first impression. Rather than risk new residents' first encounters with their boards relating to violation letters, board members and managers can welcome them with a helpful, informal, and user-friendly welcome packet.

The packet should include a welcome letter and information about amenities, association and resident responsibilities, key contact numbers, and answers to frequently asked questions. The quality and appearance of the packet can set the tone for new residents' positive relationships with their community associations. It can also clarify any confusion about the role of the association.

Additionally, many associations reach out to local businesses to include coupons or certificates for their products or services. Like the welcome wagon of years past, this is an easy way to win over new residents.

## Mentor New Residents

A great way to demonstrate the positive aspects of community associations is to provide mentors for new residents, perhaps recruiting volunteers from members of the welcome committee. Assigned to interact with designated new residents and their families during their first few months in the neighborhood, mentors could facilitate their transition by sharing their experiences, introducing them at community functions or board meetings, answering questions, and serving as resources about subjects as varied as the governing documents and nearby shopping. Based on their insights and relationships, they could help their mentees make new friends by introducing them to residents with shared interests in hobbies or professions and those in the same age group or with children of similar ages.

An added benefit of providing mentors is that they can enhance positive first impressions made about the community and minimize or eliminate any negative impressions that might have been made.

## Promote Participation

While some persons are energetic, enthusiastic leaders or at least volunteers by nature, others are more reserved. Instead of simply relying on the former, board members can make a concerted effort to invite all residents to participate in community association activities. By building an environment that provides every resident with myriad opportunities to get involved, they can strengthen relationships, enhance morale, and reap the benefits of cumulative positive attitudes among those working for the greater good.

Proactive programs to engage residents can fortify communities and build benches of future leaders. Not every resident may have the resources to participate extensively, but some might find a way to do so, at least on a limited basis, if the invitation to participate is compelling and manageable. This could include serving on temporary or standing committees, supporting holiday or other special events, or suggesting subjects for surveys or movie nights.

Bringing more residents into the community governance process highlights the ability of community associations to connect their residents. Inviting everyone to participate is a viable way to expand involvement and fight apathy in a community. If it is true that bad boards emerge from apathy, then the converse should be true: Good boards emerge from engaged, enthusiastic residents who participate in building the community.

Boards can easily invite everyone to participate by creating committees, hosting social events, and providing an open environment.

### Create Committees

Creating committees is one of the most effective means of engaging residents and building future community leaders. The board can establish a variety of ad hoc/special and standing committees to assist it in fulfilling its duties to the community. The difference between them is that ad hoc or special committees address a single issue (such as planning the winter holiday party) on a short-term basis and are dissolved when their purpose is accomplished. Standing committees, by comparison, meet regularly and address ongoing responsibilities (such as landscaping) over the long term.

After ensuring that their creation, membership, and mission would comply with governing document directives, board members could announce them and invite participation. Following are the most commonly appointed community association committees:

- **Welcome Committee.** Helps new residents transition into association living and feel as if they are part of the community. Sometimes serves as a source of mentors for new residents.

- **Social Committee.** Organizes fun-filled social events at which residents can strengthen relationships with their neighbors.

- **Education Committee.** Provides resources and learning opportunities to help residents understand community operations.

- **Landscaping Committee.** Helps the board develop and implement decisions related to the look and feel of common spaces.

- **Architectural Review Committee.** Helps the board ensure proposed home improvements or other construction projects comply with the association's architectural standards and governing documents.

Using targeted efforts to engage residents in committee work can expand their participation in the community and transform apathetic residents into active participants. Clearly, such engagement is the best way to combat apathy.

## Host Social Events

Who doesn't love a party or festive gathering? Social events ranging from holiday and anniversary celebrations to movie nights and adopt-a-street projects bring residents together in a positive atmosphere—creating the perfect antidote for apathy. Such social events facilitate neighbors feeling connected to each other and their communities as a whole.

Under the leadership of special event planning or standing social committees appointed by the board, the community can schedule and fund activities that promote interaction. By attracting residents with shared interests and demographics, they simultaneously foster diversity and inclusivity.

By hosting social functions regularly, the board can nurture a higher level of resident engagement, enhance social cohesion, and demonstrate its value beyond mere rule enforcement. What a fun way to overcome apathy!

## Provide an Open Environment

Many states such as California,[4] Nevada,[5] and Virginia[6] mandate open forums be part of regular community association board of directors meetings. These forums can be the heart of open environments provided to combat apathy while encouraging residents' participation. They provide residents a platform from which to voice their concerns, share ideas, and ask questions in a structured setting.

Especially for larger communities, it makes sense to set time limits for speakers and to enforce them fairly so everyone has equal access to the forum, board members, and other attendees. Doing so motivates speakers to use their time efficiently and precludes their having to wait for their turns seemingly forever while early speakers rant uninterrupted for as long as they want. This benefit to them should be explained to the public when time limits are set.

Wise board members enforce time limits not only fairly, but also efficiently. Their practices include using a timekeeping device that gives a one-minute warning and then buzzes when time expires; prohibiting interruptions during a speaker's allotted time, except to clarify something that might have been misstated or was not heard; and accepting written statements from speakers and others.

The impact of open forums can be augmented by installing community suggestion boxes and providing response mechanisms. The latter can be a response section in a community newsletter or a report presented at a regular board meeting.

Apathy will be overcome, however, only if those who speak out are actually heard, if their suggestions are considered, and if there is a follow-up process that assures them their time and effort were worthwhile.

## Lead by Example

We began this chapter with Thomas Jefferson's observation that we deserve the government we elect. A corollary to his wise words is that those who are elected and those who elected them have the power to create the government they desire. For community association board members, this includes leading by example. Their doing so can motivate others to participate and to excel—eliminating or at least diminishing apathy in the process.

Building a constructive, engaging environment that highlights the positives of community association living is not an aspirational goal, but, rather, a matter of choice for boards of directors. It begins with the board leading by example. A board that presents itself professionally and proactively engages residents sets the tone for appropriate behavior in a community association. Such leadership also focuses on building community, which helps engage residents and mitigates apathy that can lead to the emergence of a bad board. Board members lead by example when they set a professional tone, create an open environment, and prepare for meetings.

## Set the Tone

Board members set the tone for the community and should be held responsible for keeping it positive, even when others are negative. This begins with treating fellow board members respectfully, focusing on the community and its processes while avoiding personal politics and engaging residents in the full spectrum of community activities.

If confronted by angry or disrespectful residents, it is imperative that board members respond professionally, calmly, and respectfully—never mirroring rudeness, hatefulness, or emotional tirades. Such exemplary reactions can not only reduce the emotional impact of residents' anger, but they also set examples that can be modeled by observers.

When board members respond negatively to irate residents, situations can escalate to unpleasant exchanges that can discourage future participation by others, thereby exacerbating apathy. Conversely, constructive exchanges facilitated by board members who set appropriate tones can promote engagement and combat apathy.

## Create an Open Environment

Creating an open environment in all aspects of community association living encourages engagement and discourages apathy. Integrating into a new community association can be intimidating. New residents are more likely to feel comfortable and respected if they are welcomed by enthusiastic volunteers who invite them to participate at meetings, attend a variety of activities, and meet new friends.

Community does not happen; it requires proactive participants. Effective boards are instrumental in this process as they create an open environment in which new or existing residents can easily become part of the fabric of the community through engagement.

## Prepare for Meetings

Attendance is a popular metric for successful events. It improves when attendees have justifiable expectations that hosts, organizers, and presenters will prepare thoroughly, including by reviewing materials in advance, crafting pertinent questions, being able to deal with unforeseen circumstances, and allowing public comments. Residents and board members are more likely to attend association board meetings when participants are prepared to present and engage effectively. Ensuring a quorum must be a top priority, especially because no business can be conducted in its absence.

On the rare occasion that board members and managers develop a reputation for being unprepared, starting late, wasting time, and perhaps not being able to take action for lack of a quorum, attendance suffers and apathy blossoms. Such lack of professionalism can undermine faith in the board's competence, especially if establishing a quorum evolves into a regular problem.

The board should take time to ensure it can establish a quorum and is organized and ready for any community meetings. This helps ensure the meeting runs efficiently and does not stretch into the wee hours of the morning. An organized board presents itself as knowledgeable and invested in the community's success. Conversely, a disorganized board creates the impression of disinterest and perhaps even of incompetence.

Well-prepared board members and managers are the cornerstone of well-run meetings and activities, which, in turn, foster participation. They are essential to overcoming apathy.

## OVERCOMING BAD BOARDS

Pushing back against an overreaching or bad board can be daunting but can be put into perspective by understanding the process of effectively challenging a bad board or bad board members. The starting point for any effort to improve governance should focus on the well-being of the community.

Homeowners justifiably become frustrated with board members who mismanage funds, enforce rules unfairly and inconsistently, shun transparency and accountability, or commit other transgressions. Because even the worst imaginable boards, however, hold the reins of power, when necessary, residents need practical strategies and a vision for securing alternate community leadership. They can begin by organizing, developing ideas, looking at recall provisions, maintaining positive messaging, and, when necessary, hiring legal action as a last resort. These steps for overcoming bad boards are not necessarily successive, but they can be discussed in three categories, namely, engaging the process, mounting a campaign, and seeking legal recourse.

## Engage the Process

Community association boards are elected. To remain in their positions, board members must be responsive to those who elect them, namely, residents. Sometimes, boards or their members seem unresponsive, but they simply may be unaware of the concerns they allegedly are ignoring. If they do not know about them, how can they respond? This is especially true when the concerned persons have not expressed themselves at board meetings or otherwise brought those concerns to the attention of the board.

If the problem is that simple, so is the solution. That is why a point of departure for countering such seemingly bad, unresponsive boards is to articulate concerns while engaging in the community governing process. Concerned residents can begin by expressing their issues at board meetings, making a record about the situation at hand, and reaching out to neighbors.

### Express Concerns at Board Meetings

A popular Spanish *dicho*, or aphorism, in Texas is *hablando se entiende la gente*. Figuratively, that translates to "through communication, we understand each other." That is why the first step in dealing with seemingly or truly unresponsive boards is to attend board meetings and community events to express concerns during open forums.

Wise residents committed to resolving the situation by causing board members to be responsive always frame issues in terms of the good of the community. They refrain from criticizing the personalities or perceived agendas of board members and focus on the issues. Equally important, they speak sincerely, respectfully, and professionally. Cognizant of time restrictions, they prepare talking points that can be articulated within those limits. If they have much more information to share, they make their key points, including statements that obviously invite questions from listeners, and supplement their oral presentations with documents or other materials to be included in the records of the meeting.

## Make a Record about Concerns

Speaking at public forums is not the only way to make a record of concerns. Residents can petition their boards via letters signed by individuals or groups. This is an easy way to enumerate concerns, ask for a response, and offer suggestions for desired changes.

Letter writers should follow the same guidelines offered for public speakers, including being respectful, framing issues in the context of what is best for the community, and refraining from making personal attacks or name-calling.

## Reach Out to Neighbors

There is strength in numbers. Change often occurs more easily when like-minded residents work together to achieve a goal. The more of them who share the same point of view, the more likely they are to achieve change. It is smart to begin the process by chatting with neighbors to determine who and how many share concerns. If the numbers are low, so is the likelihood of change. If they are high, it should be easier to open the door for collaboration or to change the leadership.

## Mount a Campaign

Change does not happen in a vacuum. In any form of elected leadership, engagement and participation are required. When residents try every possible way to work with a board constructively but fail, they may have no option other than to accept the reality of having a bad board that cannot be rehabilitated and therefore has to be replaced.

Fighting back against a bad board requires organization and creation of a positive message that outlines a new path for the community. Implementing lessons learned from Thomas Jefferson's words that we get the government we deserve requires taking responsibility for the direction of the community. This means organizing like-minded neighbors, developing a positive agenda, determining the need to organize a recall (and if so, how), and finally, assembling a slate of candidates to run in the next community election. Indeed, change can happen when residents work together.

### Organize

As a form of democratic governance, effective change in a community association requires organized efforts to build consensus and a coalition to vote for change. This does not happen without effort. The process begins by sharing concerns with friends and neighbors in the community, including expressing frustrations with the current direction and exploring potential solutions to the current state of affairs.

Although it is natural and easy to express frustration with the weaknesses (or perceived evils!) of individual board members and their leadership styles, it is more effective to organize around the idea of making the community better. Keeping the focus on promoting positive change is an effective way to attract residents to the cause.

### Develop a Positive Agenda

Developing a positive agenda that serves the needs and interests of the community is essential to overcoming a bad board. Sometimes, accentuating the positive is the best means of causing others to notice the negatives of the status quo or of the alternative.

One of the biggest mistakes homeowners make when confronting a bad board is focusing on personalities. This approach only fuels division in the community. Rather than engaging in name-calling and accusations, it is better to build a campaign that stresses how electing new leaders would result in a more productive and harmonious community. This can include a list of objectives, goals, and aspirations the community could achieve if residents made a leadership change.

As always, leaders for change should refrain from making anonymous attacks on existing board members. Instead, they should have the confidence to stand by their public comments, always making only fact-based statements that can be substantiated. By focusing on ways to improve the community, advocates for change can highlight current leadership deficits by contrasting their proposed agendas with the lack of focus of the current bad board. Generally, then, building a coalition for change is easier and more sustainable when it is about implementing a positive agenda rather than about merely listing grievances.

## Petition for a Recall

Most persons dissatisfied with their governing boards are content to wait for the next election, confident they can elect better successors. Sometimes, however, residents may be passionate about effectuating change sooner. If so, they should determine any options defined by their governing documents or state statutes.

Many governing documents and some states allow residents of a community association to initiate a recall election against bad board members, but only under certain circumstances. Nevada, for example, allows recall elections if 10 percent of an association's voting members or a lower percentage provided in the governing documents petition the current board.[7] Arizona,[8] California,[9] Florida,[10]

North Carolina,[11] Virginia,[12] and other states also allow for the removal of board members. This is typically done by a majority vote of the membership but can vary by state and by governing documents. Additionally, if the governing documents are silent, provisions allowing board member recalls may exist in either the state's relevant statutes for homeowners or condominium associations, corporate codes, or nonprofit corporation codes. It is always appropriate (and advisable) to obtain a legal opinion about the requirements applicable to your community.

## Recruit Board Candidates

I recall an interview with a reporter for a major publication who asked questions about fighting a bad board. What was interesting is that she had experience dealing with a bad member of her condominium board. She and her neighbors organized, developed a positive agenda, and recruited a candidate for the next election. Their actions illustrate effective strategies to promote change on the community's board. She described their success as follows:

> *Eventually, a group of us decided to organize. We collectively chose a candidate who would run in the next HOA election to replace the problematic board member. We reached out to everyone we knew in the building, collected proxy votes, and texted each other reminders about the upcoming election—and we won.*[13]

When neighbors form a coalition to fight a bad board member, they need to find a qualified and passionate volunteer to run as an opposition candidate. The group promoting change can unite around this candidate to secure the support and the number of votes needed to get elected through the association's annual voting or recall process. In best-case scenarios, the bad board member reads the handwriting on the wall and steps down during a current term or decides not to run for re-election.

The key to winning such elections is to recruit qualified candidates who have the time, energy, and interest needed to run, to win, and to serve significantly better than the offending incumbent. Above all, remember: You cannot beat somebody with nobody. Only an opponent can defeat an incumbent.

## Seek Legal Recourse

Lawsuits to counter a bad board are costly, slow, and can further divide a community. If a bad board has pushed the community into dire straits, however, seeking legal recourse may be the option of last resort to catalyze change. Prior to starting down this typically long, often difficult, and usually expensive road, residents should engage in the process and mount a campaign to elect new leadership. If that process fails or is thwarted by the bad board, then engaging counsel may be appropriate. This can include engaging state agencies, consulting counsel, and considering litigation.

### Engage State Agencies

State agency personnel can be helpful when residents complain that their boards of directors are acting beyond their governing documents or counter to state statutes. Although most states do not have an agency that oversees community associations, they have agencies, departments, or designated persons who deal with their issues. Residents can reach out to the state's attorney general, the state's secretary of state, or to an agency that oversees nonprofit entities.

The process begins with identifying the right entity and designated person within that entity to contact. Then the concerned parties should draft an appropriately addressed letter that outlines community concerns and includes supporting information. The situation should not be exaggerated, but should be framed clearly, succinctly, and factually. The state might not intervene, but personnel will typically contact the board to request written responses to allegations.

This effectively puts the board on notice and may be enough to trigger self-reflection and change.

For other North American jurisdictions, like Canada, the province may have a government entity to oversee or assist regarding community association matters. Condominiums in Ontario, Canada, for example, are regulated by the Condominium Authority, which also manages the provincial Condominium Authority Tribunal.[14] The tribunal is a venue for residents to file disputes with their community associations.

## Consult Counsel

Litigation is costly and time-consuming. Before taking legal action against the board, residents should consult qualified counsel with expertise in community associations. Their attorneys can advise them whether they have standing to take legal action, the likelihood of success, the time it may take to find resolution, and the likely cost.

In some cases, a lawyer might identify actions short of a lawsuit that could bring about desired changes. The expense of litigation can be an obstacle not only for the concerned residents, but also for the community association. This in itself could motivate collaboration and resolution. Consulting counsel, however, is the only way to get a road map that provides viable options and the cost of achieving change.

## Consider Litigation

The cost and complexity of litigation often make it the option of last resort when pursuing a bad board. The burden of legal expenses falls on the party challenging the board, which means the group seeking legal redress will have to fund its legal efforts. If the underlying issues are of a nature that puts the community in jeopardy and all other options have been exhausted, however, such action can be effective. If the community is at its breaking point, the group seeking legal recourse can consult counsel for options and then build an action plan that includes raising funds.

## CONCLUSION

In the final analysis, dealing with challenging boards requires a multifaceted approach that is built on a foundation of understanding, strategic planning, and legal prudence. It can be daunting and certainly will require collaboration and cooperation among the residents impacted. Working through the community association's governance system, running a slate of candidates to replace a bad board, or even resorting to legal action are viable options.

If there is a common denominator in countering a bad member or board, it is that almost every approach requires a need for collective action by like-minded neighbors. Patience is needed to build a case for change and then to unite residents in a common cause. In enduring this arduous process, however, a community can emerge more united. In the end, the goal for any community should be to foster a sense of cohesion and to engage with each other.

---

### QUESTIONS TO CONSIDER

1. Has your community experienced a difficult board or board members? If so, what aspects of their leadership created problems?

2. How would you evaluate participation in your community? What programs are designed to increase interest in working with your community association?

3. If your community has experienced bad board leadership, how did it impact your community operations?

4. Does your community have programs to welcome new residents or encourage community involvement? If so, how do these programs work?

5. How does your board exhibit leadership by example?

6.  How frequently does your community association hold social events? What type of events are they? How can attendance be improved?

7.  Has your community ever had to recall a board member? If so, what were the reasons for the recall, and what was the outcome?

8.  Have you or your neighbors ever considered running for your community association board? What were the most compelling reasons for running?

9.  Has your community ever had to undertake litigation to address board dysfunction? If so, how did the process commence, and was it successful?

## CHAPTER 9

# Dealing with Disasters

Be Prepared.

—ROBERT BADEN-POWELL,
British Author, *Scouting for Boys*

## CHAPTER INTRODUCTION

Natural and human-made disasters pose a challenge to community associations. They not only lead to material loss, but can also damage the sense of belonging that communities provide.

Robert Baden-Powell's motto for Boy Scouts, "Be Prepared," is a good mantra for any organization, including a community association. It is especially appropriate for association board members and community managers who must deal with disasters. The importance of their harnessing the talent and energy of their association in preparing for them cannot be overstated.

Creating, building, and executing a disaster plan is the embodiment of the role of the community's leadership in protecting and enhancing community assets. The plan should be a structured approach to what a community needs to do before, during, and after a disaster. It can help reduce lengthy recovery times and support residents as they deal with the inevitable emotional turmoil associated with experiencing catastrophic losses.

Preparing for natural and human-made disasters begins with a risk analysis, which is the basis for setting goals. Board members or their designees can examine the disaster risks that may impact their communities. Depending on their geography, natural disaster risks can include hurricanes and tornadoes, wildfires, floods, or earthquakes. Human-made disasters can also include threats to public safety and to health.

The process of assessing their likelihood should help the planning process focus on and prioritize the greatest risks. After identifying disaster risks, any potential risk factors can be prioritized by their frequency of occurrence in their neighborhoods.

The best way to draft a disaster plan is to engage the diverse talent within an association. Board members can draft plans or appoint committees to research and draft them for the board's consideration. An effective plan should consider a range of issues, including insurance coverage, emergency communication, restoration contractors, and other factors critical to facilitating recovery.

As the plan takes shape, it should specify actions that can be taken before, during, and after a disaster. At each step of the process, communicating timely and effectively with residents is essential to meriting their trust and strengthening their confidence.

When a community has been restored, it is wise to look back on and to evaluate the efficacy of the plan and then to apply lessons learned to plans for dealing with future natural and human-made disasters, beginning with preparation.

## PREPARING FOR DISASTERS

Disasters happen. Regardless of where a community association is located, its elected leaders should recognize and be prepared for the inherent risks of natural or human-made disasters that can impact their communities. While it may be impossible to prevent a disaster, community associations can mitigate their impact by being prepared.

The best time to prepare for a potential natural disaster is before it strikes. Waiting until a hurricane, wildfire, or flood is imminent does not give a community adequate time or focus to develop and put a plan into motion. Similarly, the best way to prepare for a human-made disaster is to be keenly attuned to current events and challenges from the local to the international levels. When disasters strike, community association residents may be impacted and unable to focus on anything beyond their own families' recovery.

Having supported many client communities through disasters, I learned long ago that those who have invested time in preparing disaster plans are in the best positions to begin recovery processes after the dangers have passed. Even with a plan in place, disaster recovery can be traumatic, so any steps that can reduce the burden of the disaster will be welcomed by residents. To successfully prepare for a disaster, a community should assess risks, prioritize risks, share the plan, and update and test the plan.

## Assess Risks

Preparing for natural and human-made disasters is as challenging as it is important. The many unknowns include the disasters for which communities should prepare, elements on which the board should focus, and how best to engage residents when disasters loom. Every journey begins with the first step, and the starting point for formulating disaster response plans is to assess the risk of a given disaster happening in a community.

For U.S. communities on the East Coast and along the Gulf of Mexico, for example, hurricanes are the most likely potential natural disaster, while those on the West Coast are more likely to have to deal with wildfires or earthquakes. Human-made disasters, such as civil unrest or mass violence, on the other hand, may be sparked by controversy or entail "copycat" situations of crimes against society.

Whatever their location, association board members and managers should begin by identifying their communities' most likely natural and human-made disaster risks and then building plans that address them.

## Natural Disaster Risks

The risk of a given natural disaster will vary according to location, and its impact, whether minor or extensive, will vary according to its severity. Understanding the types of risks and their likelihood at any given time and place is essential to preparing a response plan and educating residents about the risks, recovery, and steps they can take to mitigate impact.

One element of disaster preparedness that gets overlooked is that the recovery process can take from months to years. Most of us have experienced a bad storm or a minor flood that impacted us for a week or two. A major disaster, by comparison, can impact a community for months and even years.

In assessing risks, it helps to review the major disasters that affect communities and their potential impact. Disasters include hurricanes, wildfires, floods, and earthquakes.

**Hurricanes.** Hurricanes can have a devasting impact on a community. Unlike other disasters, they are typically preceded by at least a few days of notice, giving families time to evacuate and to take steps to protect their homes. A major hurricane can devastate a community association; impact a large area; and complicate recovery, sometimes extending it for months or even years. In 2018, for example, Hurricane Michael, a Category 5 hurricane, came ashore in the Florida Panhandle. It impacted several of Associa's client communities and our local branch office. There was little left of many beachfront properties, at times only a cement slab.

**Wildfires.** Longer fire seasons in the Western United States are the result of increasing summer heat and droughts. Like a hurricane, the impact of a wildfire can be catastrophic, having a long-term impact on a community and requiring a lengthy recovery. One need only remember the Camp Fire in 2018 that destroyed the town of Paradise in a matter of hours or the heartbreaking destruction of Hawaii's historically significant town of Lahaina, which was devastated in 2023. During that same fire disaster, Associa lost one of our own corporate offices.

**Floods.** Floods can impact entire communities or only parts of them. They are treated differently from other disasters for insurance purposes, and recovery from them can take months or years. To prepare thoroughly, board members and managers should research whether their community associations or parts of it lie in a flood plain. This lesson was learned the hard way by a large community association in Houston during Hurricane Harvey: It was built inside a reservoir designed to hold water in the event of a flood! After floodwaters receded, the community recovered over several months, but the residents gained the knowledge of ongoing flood risk and realized the reality of higher insurance premiums.

**Earthquakes.** Unlike hurricanes, wildfires, and even flooding, earthquakes typically strike without warning. Their sudden nature makes it imperative to have a community plan in place so a response can be initiated as soon as possible. Like other major disasters, earthquakes can impact larger areas, which can complicate recovery efforts.

## Human-Made Disaster Risks

Preparing for human-made disasters can be more challenging because of the unpredictability of human nature. They can occur within community associations or beyond their boundaries, thereby impacting them differently. Whether deliberate or accidental, human-made disasters can impact communities significantly, whether short-term or long-term, physically and/or psychologically. They include deliberate challenges to public safety, including civil unrest and mass violence; accidental situations related to construction; challenges to public health such as outbreaks, epidemics, or pandemics; and environmental issues such as water contamination or toxins released during industrial or oil and gas production. The dividing line for these human-made disasters is often whether they are deliberate or accidental.

**Public safety.** Challenges to public safety can include senseless crimes such as mass shootings at malls, churches, or schools. As if they were not sufficiently dangerous in and of themselves, they unfortunately often lead to "copycat" replications in similar or worse proportions. Other public safety disaster risks are transportation- and construction-related, resulting in communities being impacted by deaths and injuries from dangerous roads or bridges and inadequately constructed buildings. Association-sponsored festivities can also turn into disaster, for example, if fireworks exhibits are not executed properly or if carnival rides collapse. Boards should be aware of potential risks and consult counsel and their insurance agents to mitigate potential risks.

**Public health.** Before 2019, no community association I know of would have found it necessary to plan for a disease outbreak or epidemic, much less a pandemic. The worldwide impact of COVID-19, which was first identified in China in 2019 and mercilessly plagued our globe through early 2023, continues to be a threat.[1] It simultaneously impacted every aspect of community association life. Board members and managers suddenly faced challenges, including limited access to each other and to residents, how to handle infected residents in condominium associations, and how to handle widespread delinquencies resulting from so many residents losing their jobs. The many unknowns faced by communities during this time demonstrated the benefit of collaborating as a board to respond to unprecedented challenges in which new information became available during the crisis itself.

**Environmental issues.** Environmental issues can be controversial because they are typically perceived from different perspectives—industrialists versus environmentalists, conservatives versus liberals, etc. They also garner attention based on their locale, which gives rise to Not in My Back Yard (NIMBY) opponents versus those not impacted and therefore, perhaps not interested.

Communities can be affected by environmental issues and disasters as varied as oil spills; derailments of trains carrying hazardous materials; pollutants or toxic chemicals released into the air by businesses; contaminated air, water, or land; and problems at waste disposal sites. Preparation for dealing with such possible human-made disasters, which are typically accidental, begins with monitoring the news and actions taken by local, state, and federal agencies and legislative bodies.

### Other Possible Disasters

Board members can think outside the box to identify and prepare for possible disasters that might occur because of proximity or other reasons. Communities that are near airports or other transportation centers, major malls, criminal justice institutions, and other facilities must be prepared to deal with a variety of human-made disasters. In such cases, residents would welcome having a plan to secure the neighborhood or condominium tower by limiting access from the outside and protecting residents.

## Prioritize Risks

After the potential risks of disasters for community associations are reviewed, they need to be prioritized. In doing so, board members should consider not only news and weather reports, but also lessons learned from experience. They are most likely to formulate an effective disaster preparedness plan when they collaborate with residents and focus on specific hazards most likely to impact their communities.

While Gulf Coast communities should prioritize hurricane responses and those in the West should focus on wildfires, board members also need to prioritize human-made disasters possibly sparked by current events in the news. If the community faces more than one potential disaster risk, using historical data can help determine which risk should be the first point of focus for any plan. By identifying the most likely disaster and its potential impact, the board can allocate its resources more effectively. This ensures the most pressing risks are examined first.

When prioritizing likely disasters, board members can also consider characteristics that may be unique for their communities. Such an examination should include the age, design, and current condition of existing infrastructure. Looking beyond infrastructure, they should consider community demographics, availability of emergency services, and any nearby evacuation routes. In a community association consisting of mostly retired residents, for example, acknowledging that some may require evacuation assistance can ensure the plan considers these unique community aspects.

**Establish Objectives and Deadlines**

Before preparing a disaster plan, board members should establish its specific objectives and their related deadlines. This helps maintain a sense of urgency and accountability for its developers.

Deadlines motivate participants to work at the appropriate pace needed to complete critical steps as timely and as efficiently as possible. Specific objectives foster focus and collaboration among team members working on the plan. Truly, a structured, goal-oriented approach builds confidence in the board members' leadership and demonstrates they are proactively mitigating potential risks faced by their communities.

**Craft a Disaster Plan**

While many variables impact the process of preparing, responding to, and recovering from a disaster, having a plan will help identify and sequence actions that need to be taken. Crafting the plan before any disaster strikes provides time to review and analyze community needs and allows a rational approach rather than an ad hoc response in the face of peril.

Putting together a disaster plan is also an excellent opportunity to engage residents. The process can begin by recruiting residents to serve on a task force or committee to help draft the plan for the board's review and approval. As part of that process, committee members can examine budget issues, identify important factors to include, and then begin putting the plan together. In doing so, they should identify processes or assets important to the community and highlight the role of the community association in preserving and protecting property values in the neighborhood.

**Establish a Committee**

The diversity of residents' experiences is a strength community associations can find helpful in developing a disaster plan. When done right, work groups established by boards for this purpose can strengthen community engagement and morale and formulate better products. The process looks like this:

- Adopt a board resolution that charges the committee with developing a disaster preparation and response plan that includes the following elements:
  - Number of members and method of appointment
  - Presiding officers and any other officers deemed necessary, including a recording secretary
  - Terms of office
  - Board's liaison to the committee
  - Available resources, including budget
  - Frequency of mandated and/or called meetings
  - Timeline, including milestones and targeted completion date

- Quorum requirements for holding meetings, taking action
- Voting thresholds for adopting proposals and reports
- Specific objectives
- Required progress and final reports
- Presentation to board of directors for consideration
- Any other charges or directives

Board members can begin by announcing the project and recruiting volunteers with diverse backgrounds to develop it. Engaging residents to keep the community association safe benefits not only the families who expect safe neighborhoods under all circumstances, but also board members who are responsible for their safety.

## Adopt a Budget

Developing a disaster plan is not free. Researching vendors, producing documentation, and printing and distributing plans have cost components. Board members should adopt a budget and provide resources such as access to printers to enable the disaster planning committee to complete its work.

## Review Pertinent Factors

Many factors should be considered as part of a disaster preparedness plan. Depending on the risk assessment, the board or committee can research and include information about a variety of topics. All plans, for example, should include insurance information, a catalog of community assets, important points of contact, and factors pertinent to the disasters posing the greatest risk to a community. Although not exhaustive, the factors discussed are an excellent starting point. They include reviewing insurance coverage, documenting community assets, considering a disaster recovery service, identifying important contacts, assigning staff responsibilities, communicating with residents, and identifying utility shut-off locations.

**Review insurance coverage.** Reviewing insurance policies to ensure they are appropriate and will not impact the community unduly is a critical element of any disaster planning process. This is especially important because many community associations recently have been hit by astronomical increases in insurance rates. Premium increases are often paired with a percentage deductible, that is, a requirement to pay a percentage of the claimed loss, rather than a fixed deductible amount.

When disaster strikes, residents may have to move to alternative housing. While this cost is often covered by homeowners' policies, the period covered is typically far less than the time to rebuild the community.

Wise board members ensure funding is available to cover deductibles after major losses. The consequences of not having these funds on hand could require them to impose special assessments. This could compound a disaster's impact by requiring homeowners to make additional payments while incurring the costs of alternate housing.

Planners should remember that even if a community has been impacted by a major disaster, residents are obligated to pay assessments and mortgage payments. If insurance coverage is inadequate or deductibles are too high, the impact of the disaster will be exacerbated.

**Document community assets.** Advance preparation of photographic or video documentation of components at highest risk of damage provides a point of reference for claims. Because insurance companies usually require documentation of damage when claims are filed, having a record of the predisaster condition of assets can help the claims process proceed more quickly and efficiently.

**Consider a disaster recovery service.** Many disaster recovery companies offer opportunities for community associations to contract for disaster recovery services before disasters hit. This is most common in regions subject to hurricanes.

Our management company's disaster recovery affiliate, LHR, for example, offers such programs. These services can help communities begin disaster recovery processes more quickly because the business partners have been pre-vetted, precluding boards from having to vet potential partners in the harried days after a loss.

**Identify important contacts.** Having contact information handy during any emergency saves time, especially in getting help and disseminating information. That is why disaster plans should include a list of important contacts, including the following:

- Emergency personnel, including first responders for natural and human-made disasters
- Insurance representatives
- Restoration contractors
- Community association board members and community manager
- Local elected officials
- Local authorities responsible for disaster response, waste removal, and permitting
- Residents most likely to need assistance

The contact list should be stored in a safe space, with copies kept off-site or in the Cloud. Storing it with the photographic or video documentation of community assets will facilitate processing claims that result from the disaster.

Assisting residents who are elderly or have disabilities is a hallmark of good neighbors in community associations. Their contact and relevant information should be given to first responders when appropriate so they can get them to safety. Implementing a buddy system is an easy strategy. What is more, timely assistance during outages could save the lives of residents whose health care requires electricity.

## Categorize Essential Actions

A well-thought-out disaster plan categorizes essential actions that can be taken before, during, and after the event and who can initiate them. Hurricanes and wildfires, for example, may give responders time to take specific actions before the disaster strikes. Building on advance preparations, however, disasters such as mass shootings offer no advance warnings, forcing responders to take action during and after the event.

The key benefit of categorizing action into checklists to follow before, during, and after events is that those required to act are identified and aware of their duties. When a hurricane is expected, for example, the plan should identify responsible personnel and define a process for securing buildings and furnishings, communicating with residents, and taking steps to reduce damage during the event. Actions specified may include offering temporary shelters, implementing safety measures, and updating residents. Finally, post-event actions could include inspecting and securing the community, communicating with residents, and notifying the insurance company.

**Assign staff and leadership responsibilities.** When disasters are imminent, community association staff must swing into action. They should not only know exactly what to do, but also be ready to adapt to circumstances as necessary. A disaster response plan should assign responsibilities to them. Although tasks will vary depending on the nature of the community, they include ensuring duplicate copies of insurance policies, activating emergency notices to send to residents, securing access to the community, and readying common elements for the approaching event.

It is also important to identify which leader or leaders are authorized to put a disaster plan in motion. The board president is a likely contender, as are other board members. Alternatively, the plan can include benchmarks for initiating action.

Our company, for example, has a corporate disaster response team that works with our branches and clients. As soon as the forecast cone of probability for a hurricane includes one of our branches, the plan is initiated. Alternatively, any branch leader or member of our corporate response team can initiate the process when conditions warrant. Defining clear responsibilities means action can be taken timely in the face of danger.

**Communicate with residents.** The planning committee should determine how the community association can communicate with residents before, during, and after a disaster, especially if they are no longer at their primary locations. This may have been challenging in the past, but the advent of mobile phones and management company-based applications facilitates disseminating notices simultaneously to wide audiences.

Cognizant that many interested residents may not have the time or interest to read the entire document, the committee can facilitate communicating with them by including an executive summary and a list of answers to frequently asked questions.

Clearly, communication before, during, and after a disaster is a critical element of any plan. In the hours and days after an event, residents most likely are emotionally and physically exhausted. They may interpret lack of information as a lack of action or concern on the part of the board. That is why it is essential for plans to include communication channels and messages intended to assuage their anxieties related to the unknown and to empower them to do what is best for their families.

Plans must forecast how to communicate with residents not only by using the best available technology, but also when electricity and internet connectivity are lost. On the technology side, a community's resident application such as TownSq can be used to disseminate information to residents. This can be particularly useful as a community braces for a hurricane or other known approaching event.

When traditional lines of communication fail, implementing an alternate plan for disseminating information is essential. Effective backup means of communicating under such circumstances include posting updates at centralized locations and calling upon preidentified block or floor captains to distribute updates to their sections of the community.

**Locate utility shut-off locations.** Disaster plans should list the location of shut-off valves and switches for utilities that serve the common areas. This information should be known or at least easily accessible to those most likely to act should it be necessary to shut off services during emergencies. Alternatively, if the shut-off locations are secure and owned by a utility company, the emergency point of contact should be documented and available.

### Submit Progress and Final Report

To promote accountability and transparency, the disaster plan should establish expectations for reporting progress and final recommendations to residents and to the board of directors. It should clarify that the final report will be submitted to the board for its consideration.

## Share the Plan

Crafting disaster preparedness plans may be challenging, but its authors may soon realize the greater challenges are responding to the feedback it generates and implementing it.

### Organize the Plan

To facilitate sharing the plan, it should be organized and made accessible in a manner that works best for a community's culture. Many communities organize the information in a tabbed binder, categorizing content by topic and type of disaster.

### Prepare a Plan Summary

Once board members have reviewed and approved a disaster plan, they should prepare a separate plan summary. This is typically a one-page document to share with the community at large. It should include emergency contact information, actions for which residents are responsible, and the most frequently asked questions. Equally important, it should specify where the complete plan can be accessed.

For condominium associations, differentiating the responsibility of the association from those of homeowners can facilitate preparation and recovery actions.

**Communicate the Plan**

A well-developed plan demonstrates the board's commitment to its community, but it will not be appreciated or helpful if it is not communicated. The document, or at least shorter versions or sections relevant to residents, should be communicated as widely as possible. The following are a few suggestions for accomplishing this goal:

- Distribute the plan's one-page summary.
- Reproduce the plan in a small handbook.
- Post the plan online and publicize links to it.
- Host in-person or web-based presentations.
- Produce videos to show at a board meeting and to post online.

## Update and Test the Plan

To maintain readiness and adaptability, a community association periodically should test and update its disaster plan. Scheduling an annual review facilitates its remaining relevant and effective. It also provides the opportunity to incorporate new information, lessons learned, and changing factors within and beyond the community.

Reviewing it regularly also allows the community association to address any gaps or areas overlooked and to update it with any best practices of emergency management standards. Incorporating feedback from homeowners and local first responders can not only improve the plan's effectiveness, but also assure residents their needs and interests are considered. What is more, engaging the community in reviewing and testing the plan creates a sense of ownership among homeowners and reinforces the board's commitment to their sense of well-being.

Many of us can easily recall the blaring beeps that accompany the emergency management system tests that pop up occasionally on our televisions or radios. They are reminders that testing lines of communication is another essential aspect of maintaining an effective disaster plan. Because traditional lines of communication can be disrupted during a crisis, having a reliable alternative communication method is imperative.

Periodically testing the tools the board anticipates using will increase the likelihood that information can be distributed quickly and accurately during emergencies. Additionally, it affords another opportunity to incorporate community feedback and to train those responsible for using the communication tools. Cumulatively, this proactive approach builds confidence in the process and enhances the community's preparedness to disseminate information to residents during disasters.

## RESPONDING TO A DISASTER

A disaster plan can help the community take on the critical responses needed in the hours following a disaster. As the process moves forward, the response gives way to long-term recovery efforts. Acting as soon as it is safe to do so is crucial. The first twenty-four to forty-eight hours following a disaster set the stage for how the community's leadership will be perceived by the residents. Ironically, this period is also the time during which vital information is most likely not available because of the impact of the disaster and the need for overwhelmed first responders to prioritize their responses.

These challenges make having a disaster plan even more valuable. The plan will keep the community focused on the strategic steps that require immediate action. Although unexpected circumstances and challenges often arise, it is far better to adopt and implement a plan that was thought out carefully in advance than to have to improvise with collective off-the-top-of-the-head thinking.

The immediate aftermath of a disaster is the time to prioritize communication, assess damage, contact recovery partners, and engage with government disaster response agencies. Effective communication is the backbone of any crisis, partly because it fills the vacuum created by not knowing what to do or what is going on and is the means of coordinating response efforts. The advanced investment in building lines of communication will come to fruition, as activating these channels will facilitate keeping residents informed and distributing important directives. This minimizes confusion during such a critical period.

Assessing damage to the community's common elements is an ongoing part of every step in the process. It requires contacting the association's insurance provider to schedule an adjuster to inspect the property. As part of this step or after it, engaging a restoration company can accelerate the recovery process. These two steps undoubtedly will generate information to share in periodic community updates. To the extent that any emergency recovery commences before the adjuster arrives, we advise recovery teams to photograph or video the scenes of damage in the mitigation work being done while being cautious to avoid injury.

Local, state, and federal disaster agencies can play significant roles in the response process. Because there is a chain of command built into their collaboration, local agencies should be contacted first. Its representatives then likely will take charge of dealing with state and federal authorities appropriately, completing the required forms, providing the necessary information, and reporting that thresholds for assistance are met.

Texas is among the states that has a division of emergency management that coordinates with local and federal counterparts to lessen the impact of emergencies and disasters. The Federal Emergency Management Agency (FEMA) can help with debris removal and otherwise assist the community and its residents. Similarly, the Red Cross, Small Business Administration (SBA), and local charities can provide resources. Coordinating the response process with these agencies is essential to accessing resources needed to meet short-term and long-term recovery goals.

## Contract Disaster Response Partners

Assessing the damage to the community association should begin as soon as it is safe to do so. This is important not only to ensure repairs and to benefit from insurance and assistance coverage, but also to inform residents about any inherent dangers posed by the damage.

Executing the response elements of a community's disaster plan includes engaging insurance companies, completing damage inspections, and activating the community's restoration partners. It is wise to have the documentation of the previous and current conditions of a community's assets on hand in case they are requested by insurance adjusters or emergency assistance personnel. The critical elements of this step are to evaluate damage, assess coverage, and begin to identify estimated timelines for rebuilding and repair—although initial timelines typically will change over time. These steps, usually required by insurance policies, are likely to generate much-needed information about the potential timeline for recovery.

### Engage Insurance Company

One of the most critical steps in a community's initial response to a disaster is contacting the insurance company. This is easier to accomplish if the contact information is included in the disaster plan and if hard copies are made available in case of a loss of power. Contacting the insurance provider begins the process of scheduling an adjuster to visit the community and of completing a damage assessment.

## Complete Damage Assessment

Logically, insurance policies require providers or their designees to inspect the covered elements of a property. This inspection allows their experts to evaluate any damage and to prepare an estimate of their restoration costs. The estimated coverage amount will be presented to board members, who then will have a better idea about the cost of the recovery process and how much of that expense will be covered by the policy. Armed with the estimated costs of damages and the related resources that will be available to rebuild, the board can engage restoration partners.

## Activate Restoration Partners

Informing residents that community restoration partners are engaged builds hope and confidence that repairs will be made and that a better day lies ahead. In the aftermath of many hurricanes, however, sometimes that positivity is foiled by ill-intentioned contractors who sign up communities or individuals, take payments, and do poor-quality work or no work at all.

Having a prearranged agreement with a restoration partner can help the board avoid this situation. To assist our clients, for example, our association management company has a restoration affiliate that works with them to restore their communities after disasters. Because they partner with our management company, their relationship with the community is ongoing, so doing a good job is essential to their customer service. This knowledge enables homeowners to work with a known, trusted, and bonded entity while maintaining their optimism about the future.

Restoration partners should provide timely information about the availability of supplies and initial estimated timelines for the restoration process. Homeowners may not always like what they hear, but it is far better for them to know, plan, and cope accordingly than to be left in the dark to grow increasingly frustrated about the unknown.

## Prioritize Communication

Communication can make or break confidence in boards of directors, especially when tensions and anxieties are high after a natural or human-made disaster. Almost all of us have experienced the frustration of waiting for power and/or water to be restored or for snow to be removed from our streets. Not knowing when we will get relief compounds the negativity.

The reality is that in the hours and even days following a major disaster, information can be scarce. For community association residents, the lack of information is frustrating and often perceived incorrectly as a lack of action on the board's part. Even when the information is unfavorable, communication is essential. Residents should be informed that board members and community managers are doing their best to keep them informed. This includes explaining the steps that must be taken before securing a preliminary timeline for the recovery process, setting honest and realistic expectations, and scheduling regular updates.

As part of their customer service, board members may not only acknowledge frustration, but also express empathy as their communities move forward.

### Set Expectations

While most of us have experienced a bad storm or other event that causes minor inconvenience, a disaster is different. It is traumatic. As such, it is critical to set homeowners' expectations that the process may take time, that there are many initial unknowns, and that regular communiques will provide as much as possible of the information residents desire.

The expectations for the process that is to follow should be set in the initial communication. It should include an overview of the actions the board is taking and a preview of the steps that will follow. Residents should know, for example, that the insurance adjuster needs to prepare an estimate of the damage, which could take a few days. Following is a sample initial communique:

> *Our community association's insurance provider is prioritizing an assessment of the damage to our community. We hope this can be completed in the next two or three days. Once that estimate is ready, the board will engage a contractor to help with our recovery efforts. As this process moves forward, we will keep you updated by providing information, including about next steps and timelines, as it becomes available.*

In the case of disaster response, communication is about both conveying information and educating residents. Most persons are not familiar with the disaster recovery process, so communicating timely, thoroughly, and effectively can help set expectations and allow residents to understand how the process will unfold.

## Communicate Regularly

Effective communication is especially important during the initial hours and days following a disaster. Those impacted are eager for information about when the recovery process will begin—and, more importantly, when it will be completed. Because this is when information is least available—but most desired—board members should immediately implement the communication strategy defined in their plans. The best documents include an assuring initial communication followed by regular updates, whether via traditional or alternative channels required by lack of power.

Board members may be waiting to receive inspection reports from insurance adjusters before they can hire restoration contractors, but residents cannot wait. They want to know *now* when their power, water, or other utilities will be restored and other repairs made. Scheduling regular times to disseminate information or post hard-copy updates will remove some of the uncertainty surrounding the response process.

Updates can convey that the board is still awaiting to hear from emergency response authorities, insurance agents, or other key sources of information. The point is to share relevant information with homeowners, reminding them about pending actions and projected completion dates, and assuring them board members are working with all due diligence.

**Express Empathy and Acknowledge Frustration**

Anyone who has been through a power outage understands the frustration of waiting for power to be restored. If it takes more than twenty-four hours, it seems as if the regular order of life has broken down. During and after a major disaster, power and other conveniences may be out of service for days, weeks, or even longer. Combine dealing with those inconveniences with dealing with major damages or loss of homes, and it is easy to understand how frustration can build.

Communiques sent after major disasters should acknowledge justifiable frustration, express empathy, and remind residents that the community association board members and staff have been impacted the same way. Apologies are not necessary because natural disasters are not under the control of the board, but reminders that the community is in this together can help mitigate frustration and remind residents the board is engaged proactively.

## Engage Support Agencies

One of the most heartening aspects of disaster recovery is the response that can come from community, state, and even national organizations. Americans are known for our outpouring of recovery assistance not only within our states, but also in others—and in other countries. Numerous local authorities and state emergency management divisions play significant parts in the disaster recovery process. Federal entities such as the Federal Emergency Management Agency (FEMA) can also help communities and residents when certain thresholds are met.

Finally, national and local disaster response charities can provide additional resources for residents and their communities. As part of the initial response to a disaster, sharing information about these resources helps residents obtain financial and material support and demonstrates board members' leadership for their communities.

### Contact Local and State Emergency Agencies

Local and state disaster response agencies are an important resource for community associations, especially during the initial days after a disaster. They provide expertise, services, and equipment necessary to help execute responses to large-scale disasters. Their support can include search and rescue operations, logistical support, debris removal, and public health care.

Establishing and maintaining lines of communication with agency contacts is another means through which community associations can access them easily when they are needed and obtain timely information about restoring critical services.

### Engage FEMA

Administered through the U.S. Department of Homeland Security, FEMA is the primary federal entity charged with responding to disasters. Its website notes its history is "rooted in the story of a nation committed to finding strength in the face of unpredictable and devastating disasters."[2]

FEMA can provide resources to help communities recover from major disasters. Working through local elected officials or reaching out to it directly, the board and community can identify how its resources can assist recovery efforts. The agency is also empowered to assist displaced residents find shelter and can help clear debris to open roads, which is essential to allow people and supplies to move more freely.

**Reach Out to Charities**

Local and national charities also play a part in disaster response. The Red Cross is the most notable: Following a disaster, it can provide a host of resources, including food, water, shelter, resources to help victims get back on their feet, and other support.

A rich variety of charities also exist for the sole purpose of helping survivors. Our community association management team, for example, operates the largest charity in the industry, Associa Cares, which has distributed more than $5 million in assistance globally since its founding in 2007. Through it, we provide direct financial assistance to those impacted by natural or human-made disasters. Our public charity finds great joy in aiding those impacted, regardless of whether they live in a community we manage.

Providing information about resources available to residents is a constructive way the board can demonstrate leadership.

## RECOVERING FROM A DISASTER

What distinguishes a major disaster from a less severe one is the extent of the damage to the community and the time it will take for the community to recover. Having worked with many community associations that have experienced floods, hurricanes, wildfires, structural fires, and other disasters, I recognize elements of the recovery process that appear consistently, regardless of the type of major disaster. As communities work toward long-term recovery during the weeks and months following initial disaster responses, they may benefit from these common observations shared herein.

Communication is highlighted frequently throughout this book.

There is a reason for this. The importance of communicating diligently in the wake of a disaster cannot be overemphasized. As order and services are restored, communication demonstrates the power and impact of residents supporting each other.

Celebrating small wins in the community or helping those less fortunate inspires residents to do even more for their neighbors. As with any major project or event, at the appropriate time, the board and community can look back at their response process to evaluate its effectiveness and determine how it can be improved.

## Communicate!

Communicating regularly can help mitigate information vacuums that come on the heels of a disaster. When residents do not receive communication from the board, it is easy for them to wrongly assume the board is not working in the community's interest. The board can mitigate this problem by prioritizing communication throughout the recovery process. This can be accomplished by celebrating small wins, reiterating progress made to date, and updating timelines.

### Celebrate Small Wins

Each step forward in the recovery process is an opportunity to celebrate. Restoration of electricity, engaging a restoration contractor, or opening a damaged clubhouse are only some of the benchmarks worth noting. The initial list of things to do can seem endless. Taking time to acknowledge progress creates a sense of momentum in what often is a frustratingly lengthy process.

### Reiterate Progress

Like celebrating wins, it is beneficial to reiterate recovery progress in community communication. The overwhelming work it takes to recover fully and our tendency to focus on what we do not have contribute to frustrations. Using regular community updates or even creating a chart to demonstrate milestones visually reminds everyone that progress is being made. They underscore the work the board is doing to help things get back to normal as soon as possible.

**Provide Updated Timelines**

Any recovery process must cope with a plethora of unknowns. One of the biggest is pinning down a date when everything will be back to normal. With all the variables in the recovery process, providing updates to timelines helps set or reset expectations.

Updates can be provided in writing or by visual aids. Years ago, for example, we had a client condominium tower that experienced a massive fire. The recovery process was long. The age of the building and the materials used in its construction required additional mediation on top of the restoration process. This included inspecting the hundreds of units in the building. The board and restoration company posted a simplified building diagram they updated daily. Residents could check the chart to see how the project was proceeding and get a clearer idea of when their units would be reached. This helped the community work through the uncertainty and variability common in a major restoration.

## Demonstrate the Power of Community

It can be difficult to imagine the challenges faced by those who suffer great material loss in a disaster. Their fears, anxieties, and inconveniences can be compounded by the reality that recovery, both on an individual level and a community scale, can be lengthy. The feeling of loss, disruption of daily routines, and absence of conveniences previously taken for granted can linger for months.

During this time, those impacted can benefit from restoring a sense of community and mutual support. Even small actions in this space can be helpful. To help restore that feeling of unity and let others know they are not alone, neighbors can work together. This can be achieved by taking actions such as thanking first responders, recognizing the good works and heroic efforts of community residents, and finding ways to help those most impacted.

### Thank First Responders

In the weeks following a disaster, many of those impacted understandably will be focused on their losses. That is a good time to boost their spirits with moments of gratitude and hope. Expressions of gratitude and acknowledgment to first responders or others who have helped the community, for example, strengthen a sense of community.

Taking that advice to heart, for example, a few months after a major fire, residents of an impacted community signed a large thank-you card and delivered it to the local fire department. This action was welcomed by the first responders and provided the community a moment to focus on gratitude, countering the months of feelings of loss they experienced.

### Recognize Heroic Residents

Good neighbors are a blessing. Exemplary neighbors who selflessly and heroically helped others after a disaster should be recognized. My favorite examples include a resident who helped evacuate a mobility-impaired resident from a fire and a family who opened their home to provide temporary lodging for someone who had lost his. These acts of good neighborliness often are overlooked. Recognizing them brings a bright spot to a difficult time and strengthens the sense of community.

### Help Those Worse Off

Part of the impact of a natural or human-made disaster is a feeling of helplessness and the realization that some are always impacted worse than others. Helping those who are suffering most can help restore peace of mind and provide a sense of control. Finding ways to help them and give back to the community helps residents put their losses into perspective. This could be as simple as volunteering to help clean up an underserved community; clear a public park; or donate time, supplies, or money to local relief agencies.

## Review Response for Lessons Learned

As the recovery process comes to an end, reviewing a disaster plan and its efficacy is a necessary step to ensure the community learns from the experience. As its strengths and weaknesses are analyzed and evaluated, information gleaned from this process can be used to fortify the existing disaster plan and incorporate updates based on its actual performance. This positions the community to respond more effectively if faced with future disasters or challenges.

The process can begin by examining the plan's efficacy, including the support of response partners such as insurance providers and emergency personnel. It can conclude by updating the community's disaster plan for the future.

### Analyze Plan Efficacy

No community can prepare for all the unknowns that accompany a major disaster. When one strikes, a community's plan is put to the test. Afterward, it is a worthy endeavor to review its effectiveness, including by assessing its overall worthiness and the adequacy of the elements that comprise it. Identifying what worked and what did not—and why—is the best way to benefit from lessons learned going forward. Acknowledging suboptimal performance is important, not to assign blame for planning or execution deficiencies, but rather, for better planning ahead.

An important step in this analysis is collecting and considering feedback from community residents. This is essential in understanding the perspectives of those whom the plan is intended to serve. Also important is examining restoration timelines and looking for any obstacles that may have slowed the recovery process. Findings generated by this process can be used to update and improve the plan to strengthen community resilience in the face of future challenges.

## Evaluate Partner Response

As the recovery process closes, it provides an opportunity for the board to review the response of key partners, including its insurance provider, management company, and restoration contractor. By reviewing the work and services expected versus the work and services completed, board members can determine whether the value anticipated was delivered. They also should evaluate whether their partners' responses facilitated or hindered the recovery process. In the end, only they can decide if the community benefited from the essential services these partners provided or if it is time to search for new partners.

## Update Disaster Plan

The passage of time tends to soften our memories. That is why community associations should immediately evaluate and update their disaster plans. It is best to make notes as the process evolves and to employ them as the basis for updating the plan as soon as possible after the recovery process is completed. Completing this task timely helps fortify the plan by incorporating lessons learned while they are still fresh in everyone's mind. Dealing with a major disaster is unfortunate, but harnessing the experience to ensure improved responses in the event of future challenges can turn lemons into lemonade.

## CONCLUSION

In the final analysis, disaster preparedness and response benefit from an organized and well-thought-out response plan. A good plan begins with the identification of potential risks faced by the community association. Those risks become the basis for setting goals, including those related to deadlines and key benchmarks. Board members should appoint residents to help shape the plan. The greater the collaboration with interested parties, the more likely the final product will reflect a community's true needs.

As the plan takes shape, critical components that will impact the response and recovery process should be developed. First among these are insurance coverage and any deductibles the community must meet. Identifying and cataloging community assets can accelerate post-disaster insurance inspections. A robust communication plan is another element critical to success.

Disaster recovery can be a long process. As the community restores itself to a predisaster state, board members should celebrate wins and keep the community informed about progress. This is the time to recognize residents who helped others during and after the disaster. Celebrating their actions provides a much-needed dose of positivity during the long and often frustrating rebuilding process.

Finally, implementing a disaster plan should be followed by thorough reviews and updates. Incorporating feedback from all stakeholders, including residents and response partners, ensures the plan evolves to meet new challenges effectively. By learning from each experience and continually improving, communities can turn the lessons learned from past adversities into opportunities for growth and preparedness, thereby transforming potential vulnerabilities into strengths.

## QUESTIONS TO CONSIDER

1. What types of disaster risks does your community face? Does your association have a disaster response plan? If so, does it plan effectively for those risks?

2. In the event of a disaster, how would your association communicate with residents? How would you improve that plan, especially when there is no power?

3.  Does your association have enough funding to cover insurance deductibles for damages caused during disasters? If not, how would you obtain the needed funds?

4.  What is the condition of your community's common areas and assets? Does your association inventory them and their status periodically, and is that information handy in case of disaster? How would you improve this system?

5.  Has your community experienced a disaster? If so, how would you evaluate your association's response and recovery process based on the impact on your community and fellow residents?

6.  Ineffective communication can create or exacerbate problems in a disaster response. Has your community ever experienced challenges due to poor communication from the board or management? If so, how was this resolved?

7.  How does your association recognize the contributions of its residents, especially those who engage in projects such as developing disaster response plans? Do you have suggestions for accomplishing this?

8.  How would you evaluate your community's plan for a potential natural or human-made disaster? How would you improve it?

PART IV

# ALTERNATIVE OUTCOMES

Life is filled with difficult decisions,
and the winners are those who make them.

—DAN BROWN,
American Writer

## PART IV INTRODUCTION

Unlocking the power of a community association is a choice. It requires a decision by its leaders to strive to make use of the full potential of the association to improve the lives of its residents. As author Dan Brown notes, the winners are those willing to make tough decisions. It is not a tough decision to want to find alternative outcomes that maximize the benefits of community, but it is a deliberate decision, and the benefits await those who make that choice. By making a conscious decision to maximize community, we can change the narrative, engage residents, and plan for the future. We do this by making news, engaging the community, and measuring success. These are the focus of Part IV.

One can start with the story of community associations. The data tell us they meet the needs of their residents. As noted in chapter 2, more than 89 percent of residents express satisfaction with their community associations. Because no one would get this impression from local news, it is important to change the narrative through positive actions and by sharing a community's story, especially its successes.

In a news environment in which community associations have a perception challenge, this can be daunting. With an understanding of traditional media and by leveraging social media, communities can highlight their successes and share their perspectives when the media calls.

In addition to protecting and enhancing the value of properties, a community association is about connecting neighbors. It is not a difficult decision to operate an association in the same way it has been done for years, focusing on basics such as rule enforcement and assessment collection. Successful communities exceed minimum expectations to expand the governance model with increased participation, greater transparency, and more content residents.

Understanding, connection, and trust are built through engagement. Improving connections among residents, the association, and the municipality should be a goal of every community association. By understanding community engagement, boards set the stage for planning successful events and enhancing the bonds among neighbors.

When it comes to decisions, it is also critical to remember that success is not spontaneous. It is the result of planning, goal setting, and measuring progress. Even the most successful communities will need to change over time. With a strong base of engaged residents, communities can create a strategic plan to address future needs or current deficiencies. The planning process is one that can have benefits beyond the goals set. Assessing the community's needs and setting priorities and goals provide an opportunity to unite residents in pursuing a common goal.

It is remarkable what we can achieve alone or with our community when we decide to pursue an alternate outcome. As Brown suggests, this leads to victory for the community and its residents.

## CHAPTER 10

# Making News

All I know is what I read in the papers.

—WILL ROGERS,
American Actor, Humorist

## CHAPTER INTRODUCTION

Some people believe everything they learn through the media, and unfortunately, sometimes the coverage is as disheartening as it is inaccurate. If, like Will Rogers, they believe what they read in the papers, then community association boards of directors and managers must try their best to help reporters publish and broadcast the truth. They also must interact with media representatives confidently and be armed with facts, figures, and examples about the community association lifestyle.

Many can identify with the portrayal by one of my favorite comedians, Martin Short, of a particularly memorable character in a 1980s skit on a popular comedy show. His hyperbolic spoof of investigative news shows aired during widespread news coverage about the adverse health effects of smoking. Short played Nathan Thurm, an attorney being interviewed relentlessly about tobacco issues as he chain-smoked, sweated, and stammered his way through. His exaggerated nervous tics and weak denials added to the hilarity.

It is understandable if community board members and managers feel a bit like Thurm when they are interviewed by hostile reporters, especially those unjustifiably negative about community associations. It does not have to be that way. Foresight and planning, coupled with forthrightness and professionalism, are the keys to more positive and constructive interactions with the media.

Will Rogers' witty statement makes a good point. For most people, perceptions and opinions are shaped by news. If all they know is what they "read in the papers," this can be problematic for community associations. News coverage typically reinforces negative stereotypes about them, regardless of how positive the news should be.

Over the years, however, survey data consistently have indicated that residents in community associations overwhelmingly report positive experiences and appreciate the work their boards do for their communities. Residents and board members should be proud of their work. When it comes to making news, they should consider sharing their stories and statistics. Doing so can counter negative coverage and, at the very least provide information to better balance news coverage about community associations.

Gone are the days, however, when board members dealt only with traditional media typically organized as print and electronic media that included newspapers and magazines versus radio and broadcast television, respectively. Today's board members also deal with new media, which are digital channels that include social media and can be accessed easily via cell phones.[1]

For purposes of simplicity, I use "media" to refer to all of the above. I often use "traditional media" as before, but differentiate it from "social media," via which users frequently post information from other forms of news media, such as news banners on digital versions of newspapers.

The best way to avoid negative coverage of community associations in traditional or social media is for board members to carry out their duties consistently and fairly. Knowing how to engage with media representatives can position them better to use media to their advantage and be ready when interviews are requested.

The subject is broad and affords countless opportunities for developing insight and expertise about these avenues of communication. Accordingly, it behooves board members to include it in their continuing education programs. For purposes of this book, however, we will focus on the aspects of it that board members are most likely to contend with.

Developing, understanding, and implementing strategies for interacting with traditional media, knowing how to respond to media inquiries, and making the best use of social media can allow board members to share their positive stories about the accomplishments and benefits of their community associations.

## INTERACTING WITH TRADITIONAL MEDIA

The reality of interacting with traditional media is that most journalists are committed to covering both sides of a story. That means that if they receive negative information about a community association, they are likely to reach out to association board members or community managers for comment. On the other hand, if a community association broaches a subject in a press release or press conference, reporters will likely give opponents or detractors opportunities to comment or disagree.

Sometimes, the parties call press conferences to express their points of view, not realizing that journalists almost inevitably will contact the other side for comment. Interestingly, in the midst of controversies, both sides often believe the other side got better coverage and that their own coverage was unfair. This inevitably results in someone saying, "If everybody is unhappy, the reporter must have been fair." That, of course, is not necessarily true.

The last twenty years have seen an incredible shift in the consumption of news. Those of us old enough can recall when there were only three major television networks and morning and evening newspapers. The landscape today is very different, with twenty-four-hour news channels, social media applications, online influencers, and a host of other ways to distribute messages around the clock.

Even with the advent of news media channels, traditional media such as television news and local newspapers still play an important role in keeping us informed about important developments. For those regular consumers of traditional media, it is evident that most of the stories published are generally negative. As discussed earlier, this does not reflect the reality of community association living. Rather, it serves as a reminder to strive for good association governance, assuming an association does not want to be the subject of another negative story.

Those who volunteer to serve on community association boards of directors know the effort they put into making their communities vibrant. Community associations have a positive story to tell. Being aware that traditional media likes to cover negative aspects of community association life can motivate board members as they craft strategies for positive engagement with the local press. This can be especially important for larger community associations that may be home to hundreds if not thousands of residents. When it comes to interacting with traditional media, there are strategies that can help ensure boards have positive impacts. These strategies for engagement include developing a media relations policy and engaging the media.

## Developing a Media Relations Policy

Most community associations may never face media scrutiny. The larger the community association and the greater the role it plays in the local housing market, the more likely it is to attract unwanted attention. If a situation or dispute attracts the attention of the local news, having a plan in place describing how the board will respond can minimize stress and help ensure an appropriate response.

As the board is a collective entity, establishing a process to study and evaluate the issues at hand and their impact, approve actions, and respond in unity can establish clear lines of authority. This will allow the board to address community matters with one voice.

The plan does not need to be complicated. It should establish the plan's purpose, outline approval processes, designate spokespersons, and explore media training.

## Defining a Statement of Purpose

A solid media plan begins with a statement of purpose. As the elected body to govern the community association, the board is authorized to act on behalf of the community association. As we have discussed in previous chapters, this authority includes executing contracts with third parties, making decisions on behalf of the community association, and enforcing rules. Similarly, the board can speak on behalf of the community association.

The statement of purpose for the media plan should be stated clearly. A simple statement such as the following will suffice: "Because community associations are frequent targets of media stories, this plan outlines the elected board of directors' strategy for responding timely and appropriately to media matters related to our community."

The purpose statement can also cite governing document provisions that empower the board to act on behalf of the community association. It should be limited in scope, defining a process for the board to speak on behalf of the community when the subject of the media inquiry is the community itself.

## Outlining Approval Processes

The policy should spell out the process for reviewing and approving any statement made on behalf of the community to a media outlet. As the board operates as a collective, it speaks or acts when there is an aligned majority. Accordingly, board members should participate in vetting and approving potential statements. Simultaneously, however, often there is a short turnaround time to formulate and approve a response. The policy should provide a mechanism for the board to review and approve action, and it should also have an element of flexibility to allow for a critical response when most of the board is unresponsive or unreachable.

## Designating a Spokesperson

Adopting a policy for media relations has the benefit of defining ownership when a matter comes to the fore. Designating a spokesperson or spokespersons allows the board to know with certainty whose responsibility it is to respond to a media inquiry—and under what circumstances. This prompts the board to select a board member or designee with the background best suited to the task.

The designation of spokespersons should be clear in its directive that the spokesperson speaks on behalf of the community only when the action is approved by the board and consistent with the method specified in the media relations policy.

## Exploring Media Training

Effective board members welcome opportunities to improve their skill sets. Media training is a topic that should be on all boards' education goals. While many community associations may never have to deal with a media inquiry or media crisis, when they do, their related news coverage can impact the public's perception of a community association. This is especially true for larger community associations or higher-profile condominium buildings. We do not advocate obtaining a degree in marketing or communication, but a one- or two-hour online course covering the basics about media relations can give the board a foundation for handling these matters.

## Engaging the Media

The media play a critical role in our democracy. The constitutional right of freedom of the press empowers news organizations to investigate, report, and document instances of both good and bad actors. Community associations often make news, but not always for the right reasons. Stories typically focus on aggressive or misinformed boards overstepping their authority. It can be frustrating.

The best way to preclude negative news coverage is for boards of directors to govern the community effectively with an attitude of service to homeowners and consideration of their needs, interests, and perspectives. The best way to increase the likelihood of positive news coverage is to deserve it. This means consistently disseminating the good news about community associations and their residents, being prepared to reshape the narrative when necessary, such as when the media have been misinformed, and welcoming opportunities to tell "our side of the story."

Too many people make the mistake of avoiding reporters when the subject is uncomfortable. They should bear in mind that the story is going to run anyway, with or without their comments. It is better to provide their perspectives and to rebut or explain negatives than to risk only the other side being presented. Relatedly, research indicates that unrebutted negatives are believed, so smart board members arm themselves with facts and figures and take the opportunity to rebut negativity when possible.

Boards of directors should recognize the public's interest in community associations. We live in an increasingly transparent society in which traditional media keeps us informed about our communities. Because they impact most people's biggest investments, their homes, community associations are a topic of interest.

This does not mean board members or community associations should be courting news coverage, but rather they should position themselves to be able to respond, advocate for, and defend their communities in the event of media attention.

In previous chapters, we outlined how investing time in understanding the board's authority or preparing for a disaster can have a positive impact on the community. Likewise, when it comes to engaging with the media, developing a process to respond can support the board's effort to serve the community well. This process begins with recognizing the value of relationships, using press releases to communicate positive news about communities, and helping shape opinions about community associations by well-placed letters to the editor.

## Building Relationships

Relationships are a powerful tool to help share a community's story. When it comes to developing news stories, positioning the board or its representatives as credible sources for information about community associations can be beneficial. Because most reporters are not experts on the subject, informing them about how associations operate and benefit their residents and sharing information about community events can soften their perspectives.

The first step is to identify reporters who regularly cover local community association stories. Most news sites have links to reporters' email addresses or provide an address for submitting stories. This information can be the basis for building a list of contacts who can be engaged through regular communication or invitations to community events. This can not only highlight resident engagement in the community, but also help establish an open line of communication and build trust. By fostering these connections, community associations can support more accurate and favorable media coverage, helping to influence perceptions of community associations positively.

## Crafting Press Releases

A press release is an official statement sent to selected media that is timely, intended for and worthy of public attention, suitable for the audiences of the media to whom it is sent, and provides relevant contact information about the sender. A useful tool for engaging traditional media, it sometimes causes recipients to follow up and instead write an alternate story from their medium's perspective.

Generally, a press release should be one page but no longer than two pages and preferably have an attached photograph(s) or other visual related to the subject. It should convey the story in simple, concise language, avoiding hyperbole. Appropriate subjects for community associations are events or activities that highlight the association's role in bringing together residents or activities to support the larger community. The latter can range from supporting local conservation and recycling efforts to assisting those in need after natural or human-made disasters.

A sample press release can be seen in Appendix B. Generally, however, it should include the following elements, which are expanded upon immediately thereafter:

- Header with basic information about the company, contact person, and release date
- Headline
- Dateline
- Lead paragraph summarizing the journalistic 5Ws + H
- Supporting paragraphs written in descending order of importance
- End notation
- Boilerplate
- Social media links

**Header.** Press releases can be printed on the company's letterhead or on special forms that identify their purpose with information such as "NEWS FROM XYZ COMMUNITY ASSOCIATION." The header should also include the name, email address, telephone number, and title of the designated contact person who can answer questions or provide additional information.

To maintain credibility with the media, the contact person should be knowledgeable about the subject of the release, have the trust and confidence of the board of directors to speak for the association, and have at least a knack (if not training) for dealing with the media.

Finally, the header should include the release date and other guidelines such as "For immediate release" or "For release (date/time)."

**Headline.** The headline is an attention-getter that reflects the gist of the story in the fewest words possible. Its preferred length is one line, but it can be two or even three lines if necessary.

**Dateline.** The dateline begins with the name of the city or town in which the community association is located, followed by the intended date for disseminating the information in the release. It is placed at the beginning of the lead paragraph of the release, separated by a dash.

The name of the state is added only if necessary, for example, if the press release is being sent to locales in which the city is not known or if it could be confused with a city by the same name in another state. In most cases, stories that are published will include the name of the city in the dateline but will omit the date.

If the release is issued for immediate release, the date in the dateline should be the same as the date on which the release is sent. If it is held for release on a future date, that future date should be in the dateline.

**Lead paragraph.** The journalistic 5Ws + H that should comprise the lead paragraph of a news story are the Who, What, Where, When, Why, and How of the story. It is that simple—nothing more and nothing less. The rest of the information will follow in the supporting paragraphs of the story.

**Supporting paragraphs.** Written in an "inverted pyramid" style, that is, in descending order of importance, the supporting paragraphs should develop the information in the headline and in the lead paragraph. It is smart to include at least two quotes, perhaps one from a board member or manager and a second one from a resident or an event organizer.

Paragraphs should be short and never split across pages. If the release is longer than one page, write "more" at the bottom center of each page that is numbered.

When news articles are longer than the available space, they usually are cut from the bottom, with little or no thought typically given to content. That is why it is imperative to include the most important information in the lead paragraph. Word of warning: Avoid placing the contact, ticket purchase, or other important information in the last paragraphs because they very well could be deleted before publication.

**End notation.** At the end of the press release, add three hatchet signs (###) or "-30-" to indicate the end.

**Boilerplate.** The boilerplate is a short paragraph at the end of the press release that conveys standard background information about the organization issuing the release, much like a short "About Us" statement on a company website. Although the same information is typically used for all press releases, it should be updated periodically to reflect changes in the community association. At our company, for example, we update our boilerplate two to three times per year to ensure the summary is an accurate description of our evolving organization.

**Social media links.** Many press releases include links to the organization's social media accounts. Intended to provide additional information about an organization or community association, these can include links to Facebook, X (formerly Twitter), Instagram, and/or other publicly accessible sites.

Once a press release is finalized, it can be sent electronically or by standard mail to known local news contacts and posted to community social media channels. If it addresses an issue of urgent importance, it can be delivered by someone who is prepared to be interviewed or to answer questions.

### Drafting Letters to the Editor

A letter to the editor is a traditionally useful tool to engage with public forums like newspapers and other print publications to provide additional perspective about relevant stories. It can be based on a timely subject that impacts the community or one covered in a press release or reported in the media. When published or shared as a follow-up to a press release, it can help disseminate information to a wider audience.

Before writing a letter to the editor, check the publication's guidelines. They usually address topics such as length, method of delivery, prohibition of profane language, and required contact information. To increase the likelihood of their publication, they should be short; begin with compelling language that will gain the reader's attention; and be respectful, relevant, and timely.

A well-written letter to the editor can engage residents, local officials, and policymakers who are interested in the subject matter of the story. It can also provide additional perspectives about the subject by sharing information overlooked or misreported in the original story.

When a letter is supported by facts and shares the perspectives and experiences of community association residents, it enhances the credibility of and counters negative perceptions about community associations. Even if the letter is not published, it alerts media representatives that there is another side to the story. What is more, by sharing it with homeowners, the board demonstrates its action to defend the community or the community association model against critics.

The board of directors should be cognizant of its role when drafting letters to the editor and adopt a policy outlining steps that should be taken and conditions that should be met before a letter is drafted on its behalf. This should include the votes required to send and approve a letter, the need to speak with one voice without board members speaking publicly in disagreement, and limitations regarding appropriate purposes or subjects.

Letters to the editor issued by board members should be limited to sharing experiences or information about the community association or countering inaccurate information about their community association or community associations in general. For topics beyond these subjects, the board should refrain from public engagement, especially avoiding entering political debates or other divisive matters.

## HANDLING MEDIA INQUIRIES

Traditional media has an interest in reporting stories about community associations. Such stories typically arise when residents have problems or disagreements with their respective community associations, believe their concerns have not been addressed adequately, and hope media attention will pressure decision-makers into being more responsive. For regular readers of newspapers and viewers of local news, negative coverage about a community association is not uncommon.

Responding to a media inquiry is an opportunity to help balance a story, provide updated and accurate information, demonstrate that the underlying issue has been handled—effectively making the coverage moot—and, sometimes, to turn a negative story into a positive one. This is easier to accomplish when the board has a structured approach to ensure correct information is provided in a timely manner.

Because of the high interest in local stories about community associations, understanding the basics of responding to media inquiries and inquiries about pending legal matters can best position the board to evaluate the need to respond. Responding with a concise written statement can ensure the board's point of view is expressed without having to be interviewed in person or over the telephone.

## Responding to Media Inquiries

Generally, reporters researching stories about community associations are responding to complaints by residents and will have their sides of the story before calling. Obtaining responses from community associations is typically one of the last actions taken before stories are published.

Most reporters reach out to the community association's main line but might call a clubhouse or the community manager. Whoever is contacted should inform the board immediately so members can begin the process of determining whether and how to respond. They should recognize the opportunity to respond to the information in the story but should not feel pressured to respond immediately to the caller.

This is the time to implement the board's media policy discussed earlier. It begins with the designated point person, either a board member or the community manager, fielding the call. Board members then can then follow the step-by-step process developed to ensure appropriate and accurate responses. Alternatively, the board can respond with "no comment," but such a response may result in painting the board and the association in a negative light.

Board members should think long and hard before deciding to ignore reporters' calls. The ease and convenience of not responding should be balanced against the time available for a response, the comfort with the reporter, the underlying facts of the story as presented, and the opportunity to present an alternate perspective in a unified voice.

Wise board members take the time to investigate the matter before issuing a response. This can be achieved by the following process that comprises obtaining contact information, requesting deadlines, documenting requests, not engaging immediately, escalating requests, evaluating and preparing responses, and following up.

**Obtain Contact Information**

The board policy should be clear: Responding to media inquiries is a matter for the board of directors. When reporters call, association personnel should thank them for their calls, obtain deadlines and contact information for them and for the media outlets they represent, and then immediately forward the information to the board. This will allow appropriate persons to respond with the appropriate messages approved by the board.

## Request Deadline

Personnel fielding media inquiries should also ask for deadlines for submitting information. If reporters are at the beginning stages of their investigation, they should be more flexible in their deadlines. In more common situations, however, reporters call a day or two before running their stories—sometimes as soon as later that day—so the deadline will be imminent. Regardless, deadlines impact the board's ability to respond and reply timely.

If board members cannot meet deadlines, they should say so. This sometimes results in extensions, or unfortunately, sometimes reporters annoyingly noting in their stories that board members were not available for comment or would not comment. That may not be fair, but it is reality.

## Document the Request

After assuring a reporter that the information will be forwarded to the board of director's designated person for a response, the staff member who receives the call should document the request by asking questions such as the following:

- How should I describe the purpose of your call?
- Is there specific information you want us to provide?
- Do you have questions that can be answered in writing?
- What is the best number and email address to use when responding?

The caller should be assured that someone will call back, even if it is only to say that a deadline cannot be met. What is important is for the reporter to know the call was received and acknowledged, even when requests for information or interviews are not granted. A polite exchange at this point could lay the foundation for a more positive and productive exchange if the reporter calls again or when the community association seeks coverage.

## Do Not Engage

The instant a reporter's call is answered, everything said by the person answering the call is on the record and can be quoted. That is why all staff members must be polite and avoid the instinct to answer questions or to "take the bait" of responding in kind to challenging or rude statements. They must not engage with callers, but rather must limit the interaction to collecting necessary information to route to the board or designated persons and to facilitate appropriate responses.

## Escalate Request

Escalating the request by immediately forwarding the information collected from a reporter to the board or designated person is imperative. Delays and "slow routing" are unacceptable, partly because they reduce the time available for studying the request, analyzing the situation at hand, confirming or disproving facts, determining whether to answer questions or accept an interview, and crafting a response.

## Evaluate and Prepare Response

As the best response to a reporter's call is being evaluated and prepared, it is helpful for decision-makers to have additional information about the reporter calling and the media outlet represented, including whether they have a history of positive, negative, or neutral coverage about community associations. Evaluators should consider this information and weigh the consequences of responding with complete information, declining the opportunity to respond, or simply not returning the call. The latter is not advised, simply because an aggressive reporter would call again (and again!) and perhaps grow frustrated, which could impact the article published.

Not all inquiries warrant a response, but if after reviewing the matter and exploring the facts, board members decide to craft a response, they should focus solely on the questions presented. Their first draft should be reviewed for appropriateness and accuracy while double-checking all facts and statements and ensuring the content will cast the community association and its residents in the best light possible.

If the inquiry relates to facts about a specific resident, it is advisable to respond with information about the process by which the community association handles the matter. If a local news reporter is calling about a complaint from a homeowner who was charged a fine, for example, the response should not focus on that resident. Instead, the response can outline the board's authority to issue fines and the process it follows, including offering appeal opportunities, before finalizing fines.

Unless a designated person with media training is available, it is often best to submit a written statement in response to an inquiry, although only if it has been reviewed and approved by legal counsel.

**Follow Up**

Once a response to a media inquiry has been vetted and approved, it can be transmitted to the reporter, usually by email. The statement can be included in the email body or attached as a PDF document, with a copy retained for future reference and as a resource for future inquiries.

Partly to enhance media relations, the designated person should follow up with a telephone call or email to ensure the statement was received. What is more, if the reporter used the drafted statement verbatim or wrote a fair or favorable article, the designated person should call and express gratitude. If necessary, however, the follow-up could be a letter to the editor that corrects facts, figures, or statements in the published article.

## Dealing with Legal Inquiries

Courts and the litigation process are important tools to resolve disputes when other methods prove unsuccessful. Our court system has developed rules over time to facilitate a dispute being presented, reviewed, and adjudicated by a dispassionate judge. When media inquiries focus on existing, pending, or possible litigation, qualified counsel should be contacted for advice before issuing a press statement about underlying issues. Making a statement regarding a pending legal matter risks prejudicing the proceedings and incurring the wrath of the judge presiding over the case. Accordingly, when a reporter's inquiry involves a legal matter, it is wise to seek counsel or decline to comment upon the advice of the association's attorney.

## Handling Ambush Interviews

A hallmark of early investigative journalism is the ambush interview pioneered by the late Mike Wallace of the highly regarded CBS "60 Minutes" program. The concept is simple: A reporter arrives at an office unexpectedly or waits outside a building, hidden from view. When the targeted persons appear, the reporter confronts them, peppering them with questions while a camera rolls.

This technique is rarely used, but it is always unsettling. No one who has been ambushed by a reporter ever considered it fair or professional, especially because the primary purpose of an ambush interview seems to be to get a reaction, not information to further the story.

It has been used in coverage of community association stories, much to the chagrin of those impacted. Should this happen to a representative of a community association, the following tips should be helpful in responding appropriately to this challenge: Respond positively, acknowledge the surprise, and ask the reporter to submit questions in writing.

### Respond Positively

Readers might react to this advice as "easier said than done," but it is worth mentioning. Cognizant that the purpose of an ambush interview is a reaction shot that conveys surprise, anger, anxiety, or all of the above, the best response is to react pleasantly, politely, and professionally. Instead of being defensive, taking the offensive, or speaking tersely, targeted persons should strive to take the high road, maintain composure, and convey confidence.

This is a good time to remember the communication truism, "It is not what you say; it is how you say it." It is also a good way to turn the table on the attacking reporter by denying the negative reaction sought and expected.

## Acknowledge Surprise

Responding positively to an ambush interview can yield even more positive results if its surprise nature is acknowledged with a subtle reference to its impropriety. Responding with a smile and a simple, "It is nice to see you. I wish you had told me you were coming. I would have been happy to discuss this matter with you . . ."

Responding to media inquiries accurately and appropriately while expressing the united voice of the board of directors is important. An ambush interview does not advance this goal but must be dealt with in the right way at the right time.

## Ask Reporter to Submit Questions

Denying a reporter an ambush interview does not mean the board is not interested in responding appropriately. It means, rather, that board members prefer to investigate the matter, evaluate related facts, and respond accurately. This is impossible to accomplish when the interview is a surprise.

Board members who are ambushed by reporters can end interactions by stressing that the board will investigate or evaluate matters and asking reporters to send questions to appropriate contacts. The reporter can then be thanked, and the target of the interview can exit the situation politely.

## ADAPTING TO SOCIAL MEDIA

In the late 1990s and early 2000s, the state of development of computer technology and network connections enabled the emergence of social media. Admittedly a broad term, "social media" generally encompasses sites and applications (apps) that connect people and allow interactive discourse. These connections can be familial, sports, hobbies, and other areas of focus that build communities of shared interests.

The estimated number of social media users in 2024 surpassed five billion.[2] Social media is remarkable because it allows individuals to connect with others within the same household or organization as easily as globally. In essence, it is as if everyone has been given a printing press, radio station, and television channel to communicate with the world.

As these channels evolved over the last twenty years, however, it became apparent they are both wonderful communication tools and a means by which rumors, innuendo, and misinformation can be distributed. Accordingly, understanding social media is essential for community association board members and managers who inevitably will have to deal with friends and foes who use them for good or ill. Relatedly, in the current communication environment, they are expected to choose the right social media and develop the right content to connect neighbors in the communities they manage. In addition to covering these subjects, it is my pleasure to share some tips based on my experiences.

### Understanding Social Media

Social media can be a valuable tool to engage residents, build a sense of community, and share community developments. Most of us are familiar with social media platforms, including Facebook, X (formerly Twitter), Threads, Instagram, and YouTube. The common element of these applications is that they allow the posting of updates, community events, and other news in real time. Additionally, they permit two-way communication and interaction, which allows users to respond to posts, provide feedback, or ask questions.

The combination of instantaneous posting and interactivity has allowed social media sites to emerge as a type of new digital public square. When used consistently and deliberately, social media can enhance community communication, create a participatory environment, and enhance connections.

Social media not only can enhance community association communication, but also has its downside. Its impersonal nature can foster a sense of "keyboard courage," allowing individuals to make accusations, spread rumors, or harass others. Because of this, a community association using social media should develop a strategy for sharing content, engaging residents, and dealing with users who leverage them for their own agendas. This includes developing content that benefits homeowners and using policies with guidelines for posting information on their sites.

## Developing a Social Media Strategy

Social media is a powerful communication tool that can create a sense of connection among residents and foster pride in the community. Its dynamic nature, however, requires a well-thought-out strategy for its use. A clear strategy should include the following elements:

**Goals.** A clear strategy begins with the board's goals for using these channels. They can include fostering residents' engagement, promoting community events, sharing information, and building a sense of community.

**Targeted audience.** At the risk of being obvious, board members should define their targeted audience as residents of their communities. This definition will impact their content, which would have to be broader if a broader audience were defined. They should be cognizant, however, that their posts can reach a secondary, unintended audience, including media representatives, competitors, and critics.

**Content.** Board members should consider the culture of the community to focus on sharing content that meets residents' expectations. They also should determine what services or areas of focus, if any, to exclude.

**Calendar.** Once the purposes and parameters are set, board members can develop a content calendar to ensure frequent and relevant postings.

**Style.** A community association should develop a style for its "voice" in addressing residents via social media. This means adopting a specific writing style, tone, and standards for responding to postings. This is essential for ensuring the community's social media presence is consistent and professional.

## Developing Content

The best use of a social media channel is to provide a regular stream of relevant information for its users. The responsibility for the channel or channels does not have to rest with the board. A better alternative—and an excellent way to engage residents—is for board members to appoint a committee to maintain the community's social media presence in line with its social media use policy and goals.

When it comes to community association social media postings, less is sometimes more. Posting too frequently or posting irrelevant information can make residents tune out. Social media posts should be interesting, engaging, and relevant, always focusing on timely events and efforts to enhance the neighborhood. These include general announcements, reminders of deadlines, event information, meeting schedules, polls, event photos, and recognitions of community residents.

Knowing what not to post is as important as knowing what to post. Social media may have ushered in an era of oversharing, but some residents may not want their names or photographs publicized because of privacy or security concerns. There may be a host of valid reasons to refrain from posting items via social media. Those to avoid include photos of children (without parental consent); association information about individual residents; confidential board business; and posts calling out an individual or that include rumors, defaming remarks, political views, or other inflammatory messages.

Equally important, social media is not the best venue for handling customer service issues. The public nature of postings, word limitations, and the challenge of conveying the appropriate tone all foster misunderstandings. When confronted with a complaint or customer service request, it is best to reply with an offer to arrange a time to discuss the matter in person or over the phone. Such a posting shows responsiveness and respects the individual's privacy while opening an avenue for resolving the matter in private.

## Adopting a Use Policy

A characteristic of social media is that a simple post can trigger negative responses that snowball into a community-wide disagreement. Careless postings can also escalate a situation with an unhappy homeowner or, at worst, create legal issues for the board.

The best way to mitigate issues and maintain a vibrant social media presence is by adopting a social media use policy that has been reviewed and approved by the association's legal counsel. Such a policy should comprise a written set of guidelines defining what is and what is not permitted to be posted to a community's official social media channel. Social media policies typically include the following elements:

- Rules for using the official channel
- Descriptions and examples of permitted and unacceptable uses
- Process for handling negativity
- Applicable laws and regulations

The rules should be published or shared with users prior to permitting them to post to the social media channel.

## Choosing the Right Channels

Only after defining their goals, audience, and guidelines for using social media in the community will board members be ready to decide which platforms best meet their needs. Because the wide variety of platforms have different focuses, types of content, and audiences, choosing the right platforms is essential to appropriate postings and reaching intended audiences. Utilizing the appropriate platform facilitates the board's posting timely updates, nurturing a sense of community, fostering discussion, and engaging residents in community activities.

Different platforms cater to different demographics and focus on specific types of media, such as photos, videos, or written communiques. Communication goals will be attained more easily after confirming the characteristics of a specific platform will support the board's goals and align with the community's culture to enhance outreach efforts.

While many of today's popular social media platforms have been active for some time, a quick review of their focus and utility is always worthwhile. The most commonly relied upon by community associations are X (formerly Twitter), Instagram, Threads, Facebook, YouTube, and private networks like TownSq.

### X (Formerly Twitter)

X is a popular social network used to communicate news, events, community stories, political opinions, and other information. Initially a microblogging site where posts were limited to 140 characters, it has evolved into a highly dynamic forum allowing longer posts, short videos, and other content. Although it can elicit strong opinions and debates, X can be a good forum to post community updates or event announcements. Note, however, that posts on X are public and can be viewed by a wide audience beyond the community.

## Instagram

Instagram is a social media platform that focuses on photos and imagery rather than text. It can be a great way to highlight community amenities, common spaces, and events showing residents gathering to enjoy each other's company. By way of fair warning, however, be sure to obtain written permission when posting photos of others, especially children, and not to post copyrighted photos or other content.

## Threads

Threads is Meta's (Facebook's parent company) competitor to X. Integrated with Instagram, it allows cross-posting to multiple sites. Like X, it accepts text and short videos. Postings can comprise up to 500 characters, and videos can run up to five minutes.

## Facebook

One of the most relied-upon social networks, Facebook often has a more personal connection. It is a good place to post news, events, community stories, polls, surveys, and more. Perhaps most important to community associations, it has the ability to organize interest groups and limit participation to specifically identified groups or "accepted friends," such as residents of community associations.

## YouTube

YouTube is an internet-based video service that accepts uploaded video programming. Generated by users, its content covers just about any topic imaginable. It is a great place to post longer-form content, including information about a community association or videos of community events. Although YouTube is a public forum, users can restrict who can view their content.

## Private Social Networks

A private social network operates very much like Facebook but restricts participation to a specific group. Many community association management firms, including ours, offer a private social network like TownSq that is exclusive to its members. Such networks typically require an invitation to join or request proof of residence in the community to be accepted. This helps preclude exposing internal community information to the public.

Some private networks offer additional services, such as allowing residents to access community documents, review their community association accounts, obtain architectural approvals, or make service requests.

## Tips for Using Community Social Media

One of the benefits of using social media is having the power to reach wide audiences. Essentially, it means we each have the power to turn our social media platforms into bespoke channels to promote our interests. Using social media thoughtfully enables community associations to define or refine our identities, highlight our positive elements, and engage residents.

Social media empowers boards to highlight and define their communities while using the medium as a tool to shine a light on what makes a community special. It also offers a venue for countering negative stereotypes about community associations and educating residents about the many benefits of living in an association.

The tips that follow are hardly exhaustive but are intended to help a community association get started or recharge current efforts. Generally, they underscore the importance of posting messages to define a community brand, recognize resident accomplishments, introduce new residents, promote social events, share visuals, get feedback, and highlight pets.

### Define Community Brand

The best part about using social media is creating a communication channel featuring preferred content. Posting useful information, community news, scheduled events, and photos of the community and its residents creates a sense of community. Board members can also promote transparency by sharing news about their activities and progress on community projects.

## Recognize Resident Accomplishments

For many avid consumers of news, social media has become the first stop to get the latest information about myriad topics. Community associations can use their own sites to post news about resident accomplishments, including job promotions, community service milestones, or simple acts of kindness or good neighborliness. News about positive behavior sets good examples for other residents.

## Introduce New Residents

Community association welcome committees will likely be delighted to make new residents feel welcome by introducing them to their neighbors via social media. A quick posting can provide their basic information, perhaps sharing their interests or reasons why they chose the community. This can help introduce them to the larger community while promoting resident connections.

Obtaining permission from new residents is critical, especially because they may be reluctant to share information via social media. Above all, their specific addresses should not be shared.

## Promote Social Events

Social media postings promoting community association events usually enhance attendance effectively, especially if they include attention-getting visuals or short videos. Facebook, Instagram, and X (formerly Twitter) offer instant communication with targeted audiences. Combined with traditional community communication channels, they publicize activities, often attracting attendees who otherwise would not have known about them.

Many social media channels allow residents to RSVP for events, which helps organizers and hosts plan for an appropriate number. Even if residents cannot attend, their simply knowing about events assures them the board is promoting community spirit.

Notices for board meetings will likely need to meet statutory notice requirements, such as traditional mailings, emails, or actual public postings. In these cases, especially, social media postings enhance traditional communications rather than replace them.

## Share Visuals

It is often said that a picture is worth a thousand words. Sharing visuals via social media is a great and easy way to engage residents. Thanks to smartphones, almost everyone has a camera handy—and knows how to use it. Even children can easily snap photographs or create videos that can highlight the visual appeal of a community and its people, places, and activities.

Think creatively and post images highlighting community amenities, events, and daily activities. Sharing photos is probably the best and easiest way to promote interaction, as residents are more likely to like, comment, and share posts highlighting the fun and interesting aspects of living in community associations.

## Get Feedback

Whether a community uses public social media or a private social media application, the resulting interactivity can be most constructive and beneficial if feedback is collected about timely issues and activities. Using polling features allows the board and community to take the pulse of resident sentiment throughout the year. These data can help board members focus on the issues most critical to the community and provide insights into how the board is perceived by the residents.

## Highlight Pets

Almost everyone loves a good pet picture almost as much as a cute baby photo. Social media facilitates sharing them and even creates contests to encourage residents to share photos of their fur babies. It is a lighthearted way for neighbors to share their interests in animals.

Posts can initiate conversations and help neighbors know each other better. Undeniably, dog lovers share a certain bond, as do cat lovers, and sometimes, the two groups enjoy friendly clashes over their preferences. (Those who live with both cats and dogs are in an entirely different category!)

Showcasing pets can convey a community's pet-friendly culture. It is a great way to enhance engagement, positivity, and camaraderie in a community.

## CONCLUSION

Every community association has positive stories to share. Thankfully, the ever-evolving landscape of traditional and social media provides an array of venues for sharing them. Effectively using both traditional and social media can enhance the perceptions and highlight the positive aspects of community association life.

For a savvy board of directors, this process begins by outlining a media relations policy to provide a clear process by which the board can engage or respond to media issues. It should begin with a clear statement of purpose and a process by which a board exercises its authority to review and approve media statements. Establishing this protocol in advance will reduce the stress and on-site decision-making that often results when the need emerges. By designating an appropriate spokesperson, the board can provide for consistent and appropriate engagement with media outlets.

Navigating the challenging media landscape is clarified by the understanding that some reporters or news outlets tend to focus on overzealous boards and sometimes overreact to a complaint by a resident that can be explained or rebutted. This is why community association boards of directors should employ traditional tools, such as press releases or letters to the editor, to showcase the benefits of community association living or provide a different perspective on an existing issue.

Becoming familiar with local reporters who cover community association issues can help designated spokespersons understand their focuses and areas of interest. Similarly, crafting press releases that highlight newsworthy community events can counterbalance negative perceptions about associations. Additionally, press releases can be cross-posted to internal community sites and social media, which can ensure positive stories get an audience.

Responding to a media inquiry can be challenging, but doing so is easier when boards of directors have plans, policies, and procedures in place. Board members can evaluate the benefit of responding based on the nature of the underlying issue being addressed. Answering questions accurately and fairly while highlighting the community's processes can provide a more balanced perspective to a story that is going to be published with or without the board's participation.

In responding to inquiries, however, a board should consider the risks, especially if the inquiry relates to pending litigation or is the result of a so-called ambush interview. In such cases, the board may wish to demur or touch base with legal counsel before answering.

With the rise of social media, boards are no longer limited to traditional print and electronic media channels to share their stories. Social media is a powerful tool for connecting with targeted audiences and sharing information. Developing a social media strategy and choosing appropriate social media applications can further enhance the board's effectiveness in communicating with homeowners.

Social media is not a passive communication tool. Because it depends on dynamic exchanges, it is used most effectively by boards that have a strategy and plan to manage a community's presence in social media spaces. Adopting social media policies and content plans empowers an association to do a better job of interacting with home-owners through the most appropriate social media channels.

Success is often the result of preparation and consistency. For most community associations, media inquiries may not be an issue, but understanding and engaging traditional and social media should be. Through advance planning, developing clear policies, and identifying ways to use traditional and social media wisely and appropriately, boards of directors can communicate and engage residents more effectively. Such efforts can help define communities to internal and external audiences, foster positive images, and instill pride in residents. Above all, doing so is essential to their success in operating and managing a community association.

---

## QUESTIONS TO CONSIDER

1. If the local media ever published or broadcast a favorable or unfavorable story about your community association, how well did your board members manage it? Do you have suggestions regarding how they could have responded better to secure more positive results?

2. How has your community interacted with traditional media outlets such as newspapers or local television stations? How have these interactions benefited or hurt your community association?

3. What qualities about your community do you wish the media would report? Would traditional or social media (or both) be the better choice for disseminating this information?

4. How would you improve your board's plan or policy for responding to inquiries from traditional media? Should different procedures be adopted for responding to traditional versus social media?

5.  How does your community association utilize traditional media or social media to its advantage? How would you improve the policies or procedures?

6.  If your community has a social media presence, what benefits have you seen, and what challenges have you encountered?

7.  How well does your community manage its social media presence? What changes should be made?

8.  What types of social media posts create the most interaction in your community? What social media channels are best for reaching your neighbors—Facebook, X, Instagram, etc.?

9.  Is there a social media channel your community prefers to use? What functionality makes it appealing to the community?

10.  Does your community use a private social media network such as TownSq? If so, has it had a positive impact on its communication? If not, how do you think it could?

## CHAPTER 11

# Engaging the Community

The greatness of a community is most accurately measured
by the compassionate actions of its members.

—CORETTA SCOTT KING,
American Civil Rights Leader

## CHAPTER INTRODUCTION

I began this book by defining community as a place where people live
in proximity, united by a common purpose and social norms. These
factors connect residents in a vibrant environment to enhance their
enjoyment of their homes and the fellowship of their neighbors.

When residents are connected and engage with each other, they
can unlock the power noted by Coretta Scott King when she said,
"The greatness of the community is most accurately measured by the
compassionate actions of its members." When residents feel connected, they foster a sense of common purpose and mutual support.
Their connection can be facilitated by creating opportunities for them
to engage with the association and with each other. The process begins
with residents electing their neighbors to govern the community, and
ideally, that governance reaches beyond community operations to foster active and compassionate neighbors.

For boards that want to cultivate community spirit, understanding the fundamentals of community engagement is critical. Engaging

residents goes beyond the traditional role of collecting assessments and enforcing rules to connecting neighbors. Community engagement depends on participation, creates a sense of belonging, and highlights the positive aspects of living in a community association.

Looking at traditional and enhanced ways to involve residents can help clarify the meaning of engagement. Traditionally, board service and committee participation have defined engagement in an association, but for creative boards, these are merely foundational forms of engagement. By broadening participation in the governance process and leveraging existing structures, boards can build engagement models that work best for their communities and are suitable for their cultures. The result is a culture of trust in the board and a sense of ownership in the community for residents. This can be the beginning of a virtuous cycle of connection leading to more engagement and better governance.

To succeed, board members must understand not only community engagement and how to enhance it, but also the role and purpose of successful community events. That is the focus of this chapter.

## UNDERSTANDING COMMUNITY ENGAGEMENT

Community associations are democracy in action. Residents elect a board of directors from among their neighbors to govern their community. When it comes to community engagement, however, many associations miss the opportunity to use the community association framework to connect residents. Ironically, for many residents, this means their first engagement with the board of directors is likely to be either a violation notice or even an assessment delinquency letter.

While collecting assessments and enforcing the rules are critical elements of association governance, a board focused solely on them misses opportunities to build a true sense of community. Some may feel the time-consuming responsibility of serving as volunteer board members limits their ability to foster community engagement, but engaging residents is a necessary component of their leadership in realizing the potential of community associations.

To maximize community engagement, we must start by understanding its parameters in the context of community associations. Working with residents, the board can define what types of engagement are most appealing and appropriate for them. Because of their actions, engagement can be expanded and the benefits of engagement can be realized. Finally, a look at obstacles to engagement can provide insights into how best to avoid challenges when connecting residents.

## Defining Engagement

In the context of community association living, engagement can mean different things to different people. Before examining methods for fostering engagement in community associations, it is helpful to define the term in this context.

At the foundational level, *engagement* means serving as a volunteer board leader. Boards of directors are required for every community association. As discussed in chapter 4, the board is the collective body that makes decisions for the community. Beyond that, boards often engage residents to serve on committees. These are the most common forms of engagement in a community association because they emerge logically from an association's governing documents. Successful community leadership, however, means reaching beyond or leveraging these traditional forms of engagement to connect residents more effectively with the association and with each other to highlight the value of living in a community association.

Fully defining community engagement means looking at traditional engagement models and bolstering them by encouraging participation in governance and at meetings. Sometimes, it entails appointing a lifestyle director.

## Traditional Engagement Models

The traditional engagement model for a community association is familiar to most of us. The board governs the community, and residents can engage by running for the board or attending regularly scheduled or annual meetings. This is community association engagement at its most basic.

One effective and beneficial way boards can expand traditional engagement is by creating, appointing, and working with committees for different purposes. Their doing so can benefit not only the appointees, but also the board and the community. Each committee should be charged with making recommendations to the board and meeting standards of transparency and accountability as they address the responsibilities delegated to it.

Regardless of the size of the community, engagement by committee has its benefits. Ultimately, as a community builds its own model for engagement, it will benefit from aligning it with its size, culture, and the needs of its residents.

## Participating in Governance

The board of directors is the essential element of community associations. Required by statute and defined in governing documents, elected boards are charged with making decisions and speaking on behalf of their associations. From an engagement standpoint, board service represents an engagement opportunity for all community associations and their residents. At its best, it promotes the quality of board members who always focus on the needs and interests of the community association and never lose sight of their mission.

Engagement is a valuable tool for developing future association leaders. Engaged residents are more likely to understand and espouse the value of living in a community association and of encouraging their neighbors to participate in both the governance and social aspects of the community. Those elected to the board are more likely to enjoy their service if their responsibilities are more than merely enforcing rules and assessing fees.

## Attending Meetings

Community associations are mini-democracies that function best when residents participate in the governing process by serving on the board or attending board meetings. Participation is a critical element of community engagement, but many residents find it difficult to attend as they struggle to meet the demands of work and family.

Board members can entice them with the promise of productive meetings during which relevant timely issues are addressed, meaningful decisions are made, and important actions are taken. Simultaneously, through their actions and demeanor, board members can reflect transparency and accountability while providing leadership examples to the community at large. If they think outside the box and include interesting items on the board agenda, they can facilitate greater meeting participation and perhaps attract future board members.

## Engaging a Lifestyle Director

For larger communities, such as master-planned associations, engagement may be directed by lifestyle directors who enhance the community experience for their residents. A lifestyle director engages residents in a variety of activities, maximizes the use of common elements to support that goal, and facilitates the administration of clubs within a community. Many popular active adult communities have literally hundreds of clubs to keep residents engaged by connecting them. In smaller communities, a social committee or a resident volunteer can assist in facilitating interest groups within the association.

## Leveraging Engagement

Communities interested in going beyond traditional participation models can use a little imagination to leverage their resources to foster greater resident engagement. This process engages more residents in the governance structure of the community association through committees, volunteer posts, and a general commitment to focus on resident engagement. In doing so, the board can not only enhance greater participation, but also build a deeper bench of residents capable of serving the community as future board members.

Engaging more residents in the governance process creates a more open environment in which residents feel they can impact the direction of the community. That success is reinforced when board members strive to expand governance, focus on building community, and recruit block captains.

**Expanding Governance**

The easiest and most beneficial way to expand governance is to create a structure of standing and ad hoc committees that can assist the board while serving the community. Board members can create and appoint a variety of committees that can focus on issues or activities and then make recommendations for the board's consideration. These can include a budget committee, architectural review committee, social committee, or others established to bring more residents into the community governance process.

Establishing committees and creating opportunities for residents to support the community help board members, as their appointees offer fresh perspectives and participate constructively. Their engagement lightens the burden of boards who often have more to do than time allows and creates a more open and responsive process. It also facilitates ready-made engagement, sparing residents the effort of determining how to contribute to the community. Offering ways to promote service creates a win-win situation for the community association and its members.

**Focusing on Community**

I never tire of stressing that a community whose sole focus is rule enforcement misses the opportunity to establish a truly connected neighborhood. By going beyond enforcing rules and collecting assessments, board members can focus on building their communities while helping neighbors connect and participate in the governance process.

Engagement means working within the community association while serving and representing its residents, including by celebrating their successes, accomplishments, and neighborly acts. With very little effort and likely great results, board members can and should recognize residents for their community-mindedness, pride reflected in their homes and landscaping, and support for neighbors in need.

## Recruiting Block Captains

One of the biggest misconceptions about recruiting community volunteers is that if residents have not stepped up, they are unlikely to do so. Sometimes, they simply need (and welcome) an invitation to be part of the community structure. When people commit to volunteering, they join a network through which they can build relationships and improve their community associations. This, in turn, can reinforce their positive attitudes about their chosen neighborhoods and lifestyles.

When recruiting volunteers, board members should set them up to succeed by confirming they have the time and interest to be effective regarding the subject or task at hand. Bad outcomes are often the result of broken commitments caused by lack of time or interest. Concurrently, volunteers engaged in interesting activities may develop a passion that leads to their even greater and more effective participation, including recruiting others to join the effort.

A great gateway engagement strategy is to establish a network of block captains who can share community information, collect feedback, and present a friendly face on behalf of an association. Because the responsibility should not be time-consuming, recruiting these volunteers should not be difficult. Their ability to communicate effectively will prove to be an important element in community engagement, especially as they supplement electronic and written communication with a human touch. Their effort goes a long way toward personalizing the association.

## Building an Engagement Model

There is no one-size-fits-all model for enhancing community engagement. By adapting suggestions presented herein to their insights and knowledge about their communities, however, board members can build one that suits their needs. Generally, those needs will depend on the diversity of residents and the size and culture of their neighborhoods.

Active adult communities, for example, are more likely to need more robust engagement because their residents have the time and desire for activities. A younger, more family-oriented community, by comparison, may need to find the right balance for residents who are juggling careers and bringing up young children. This reflects one of the unsung strengths of community associations: People can lead themselves and put in place programs that best meet needs based on the size of a community, the needs of its residents, and the general culture of the neighborhood.

To build a true sense of community, a board can and should adopt an engagement model suited to its community needs. Such a program can be humble, such as hosting an annual social event, or it can be more robust, such as a regular year-round program of movie and game nights, shopping trips to malls, tours of landmarks, and environmental projects. The bottom line is that to unlock the potential that exists in all community associations, such efforts need to be planned and intentional.

## Benefiting from Community Engagement

A community with engaged residents is one in which the members are more likely to realize the value of living in a community association.

The goal of any community is to provide a sense of belonging and connection among its residents. When this is done effectively, it enhances the living environment for everyone.

Effective, enjoyable engagement indirectly rebuts the unfair stereotypes of community association boards focusing solely on rule enforcement and continually being involved in petty political squabbles with residents. When widespread, it can fulfill the desire of residents to live in peaceful, connected neighborhoods.

Although there are many others, both tangible and intangible, the benefits of community engagement discussed here are a representative sample. They are familiarity, connectedness, greater feedback, increased volunteerism, improved communication, enhanced security, and better-satisfied homeowners.

## Familiarity

There is an old saying, "To know me is to like me," and this holds largely true when it comes to neighbors. Engaged communities provide opportunities to meet others. In doing so, they facilitate our understanding of what we have in common and remind us that we share the same goals. Knowing one's neighbors and board members affords insights into their motivations and removes speculation about actions taken in the community.

## Connectedness

Engaged residents feel a connectedness with their neighbors and their communities. This connection deepens their trust in relationships and actions by the board. Because they have shared experiences, they are in better positions to support one another.

Most persons find greater satisfaction when connected to causes larger than themselves. Being part of the community empowers them to work together toward a common goal. Connection has an add-on effect, as the more one feels connected to the community, the more one wants to participate and support its efforts.

## Greater Feedback

The more positive involvement in the community, the greater the opportunity for positive feedback. Engagement creates a culture of participation and mutual support. Involved residents feel a sense of ownership in the community, and with that ownership emerges a sense of responsibility for the community's well-being. That, in turn, prompts them to be more responsive to board requests for opinions, preferences, and participation. In effect, the more involved they become, the more feedback they provide. This is especially true when positive contributions and collaborative achievements are recognized and celebrated. Such recognition strengthens the positive feedback cycle by highlighting behaviors that serve as models for all residents. Acknowledging contributions sends a message that feedback is valued. This helps bolster community morale.

## Increased Volunteerism

A board that fosters engagement creates opportunities for increased volunteerism in support of the community. Engaging residents in an array of activities that include committee service, event support, neighborhood cleanups, and other activities brings more residents into the governance and operation of the community. This can dissipate the common "us versus them" mentality that emerges when there is a chasm between the board's governance and resident participation. A community that values, encourages, and facilitates participation will logically see more residents participate.

## Improved Communication

When residents engage frequently in community-based activities, they simultaneously engage in regular, open channels of dialogue between neighbors and between residents and the board of directors. This can be further enhanced when their engagement includes forums, meetings, or events that encourage socialization and sharing information.

Proactive engagement promotes conversations that allow residents to better know and understand each other, thereby reducing or eliminating bias or assumptions previously made when addressing community issues. The more residents get to know and understand each other, the more likely they are to share their unfiltered opinions and trust each other. This can support developing informal communication channels that enhance sharing information within the association.

Residents who are more comfortable sharing information also build greater transparency in the community, which, in turn, can facilitate addressing community concerns and reduce misunderstandings.

## Enhanced Security

The more individuals are involved in their community, the more aware they are of their neighbors and their surroundings. Knowing neighbors and the normal day-to-day flow of activities in the community makes it easier to identify suspicious persons or events that are beyond the normal range of activity in the neighborhood.

In short, engaged residents have greater situational awareness. Improved awareness, coupled with better communication and familiarity, allows easier identification and reporting of suspicious events or persons. Additionally, this sense of connectedness makes residents more likely to care about what happens in their community and to their neighbors, thus enhancing the security in the neighborhood.

## Better-Satisfied Homeowners

By involving a broader spectrum of the community in its activities and decision-making, board members give residents a sense of control and empowerment. Concurrently, as residents successfully voice their opinions and participate in addressing issues and planning events, they realize how they can impact their communities. The more satisfied they are that their perspectives are being considered seriously, the more satisfied they are likely to be with their boards, their communities, and their chosen lifestyles.

## Overcoming Obstacles to Community Engagement

"Where there is a will, there is a way" is a childhood lesson I state repeatedly, both at work and at home. Conversely, where there is no will, there is no way that something is likely to happen. These thoughts are applicable to community engagement. In spite of its benefits to all concerned, it is often stymied by obstacles including negative perceptions, lack of time, accessibility, and apathy. These are examined briefly for the purpose of identifying them so we can overcome them.

### Negative Perceptions

The reality is that some people have negative perceptions about community associations, even some who choose to reside in them. No matter how many times we cite data to the contrary, some naysayers continue to embrace their negativity about our way of life.

Unfortunately, this type of thinking sometimes causes residents to hesitate in engaging in their communities, preferring to stay off the association's radar. Such negative perceptions drive the need for greater resident engagement. They can be countered by creating events or opportunities to connect residents through positive social and educational activities and community governance.

### Lack of Time

Lack of time is the enemy of community engagement. Heavy schedules, countless school activities, seasonal vacations, and other responsibilities limit free time and make remaining time even more precious. We have all learned from the adage, however, that if you want something done, ask a busy person. Somehow, sometimes the busiest persons are the first to volunteer and respond—perhaps because they are gifted in time management or strong in their passion to get things done right. For a winning combination, we need to match them with their neighbors who have time on their hands but need to be motivated. The trick is to recruit them to collaborate, asking them to get engaged to the degree they can.

To engage residents whose time is limited, board members should avoid overwhelming them and ask them to help in small ways. If the community has not hosted many engagement events, they should be conservative in their number and timing, perhaps scheduling a few throughout the year.

Truly, tailoring engagement to the needs and preferences of the community is paramount. During or after events, they should collect feedback to ensure events are enjoyable and worthwhile to the residents and to determine how to adapt and evolve engagement opportunities to meet their needs, interests, and preferences.

## Accessibility

A few years ago, residents could complain legitimately that they could not participate in community meetings or events because they did not have transportation, they did not like crowds, or they had a medley of other reasons precluding their being physically present. Those excuses have been made irrelevant by technology, thanks to a wide array of low-cost or free products that make virtual attendance possible. Those who cannot participate in real time can watch the meetings or events later via social media, website links, YouTube, or through other arrangements made by organizers.

To overcome physical accessibility limitations when hosting educational or social events, organizers should arrange short videos, interviews of attendees, and streaming via the community's social media channels. Making community events accessible and visible facilitates participation.

## Apathy

Let us be frank: Apathy toward community engagement is often the consequence of negativity arising from the perspective that the board simply enforces rules, issues fines, and increases assessments. When board members determine to reach out to involve residents in shared governance and activities of mutual interest, they can dissolve that negativity. Their greatest challenges will be to prove the value of living in their communities and perhaps to make up for a history of not promoting engagement. Organizing robust, engaging events and opportunities for residents can dissipate negative perceptions that are the root causes of apathy.

## PLANNING SUCCESSFUL COMMUNITY EVENTS

A well-organized community event can lift community spirits, highlight the positive role of the community association, and build connections among residents. Whether attending a social, educational, or service event, everyone welcomes a fun, accessible opportunity to engage with others.

A community event is not difficult to organize, but it requires focus and planning to ensure all moving parts come together in just the right way. The best way to establish a process for sustainable events in a community is by investing the time and resources needed to formulate a solid plan. Successful communities can maintain a robust calendar of events by recruiting volunteers to serve on social committees. By combining their perspectives, preferences, experiences, and insights with those of their neighbors, volunteers can plan more interesting and relevant events that will encourage more widespread participation.

Their work extends beyond planning details such as setting the date and location, making physical arrangements, arranging food and beverages, and scheduling entertainment. They must consider safety issues, including mitigating any hazards at the event location and protecting the association by ensuring adequate insurance coverage.

If funding is not secured easily and cost is a factor, they can consider engaging business partners who work in the community to be part of and help fund the event. In the final analysis, planning wisely is essential to ensuring the event's success. Responsibilities are interrelated and should be considered by the social committee in the order that makes the most sense as the need dictates, not necessarily in the order in which the elements of a typical planning framework are discussed.

## Establish a Social Committee

All association committees are excellent ways to engage residents in community governance while developing potential future board members, but a social committee often attracts organizers who enjoy planning events and pleasing families. Its members can create a focal point for building or enhancing community engagement activities as they plan social, educational, and community service events. Their underlying mission is to enhance engagement while connecting members to build community spirit.

The responsibilities of social committees will vary depending on the preferences of communities. Before establishing it or any other committee, board members should review their governing documents for guidance regarding committee responsibilities, scope, and structure. Most social committees, however, focus on some or all of the following duties:

- Planning events
- Recruiting event volunteers
- Creating event budgets
- Establishing annual event calendars
- Executing event communication
- Securing event sponsors
- Collecting feedback from residents

## Plan Wisely

Carpenters and tailors often learn the hard way to measure twice and cut once. The same is true for hosting a community event. By planning wisely, social committee members can increase the likelihood of success. They need to plan for all possibilities related to expected versus actual turnout and its impact on physical arrangements, security, funding, safety, food, and beverages. As good stewards of association funds, they should stay within the bounds of their budgets, ensure safety standards are met, and be ready to cope with any unforeseen mishaps or accidents. Addressing these fundamentals will vary based on the nature of the event and the need to plan for contingencies and the event's aftermath.

**Social committee members should raise questions such as the following:**

- What is the weather forecast, and how will a change in weather impact the event?
- How will we cope if the turnout is significantly less or greater than expected?
- Who will clean up afterward—and how soon?
- What is Plan B if the speaker or entertainer cancels at the last minute?
- To whom can we donate decorations and leftover food and beverages?

## Secure Funding

How will we pay for this event? This pertinent question must be raised early, and every effort should be made to plan a successful, enjoyable, cost-effective event. The benefits of engagement make hosting a community event a worthwhile investment. As part of their annual budget process, board members should consider budgeting funds for community engagement and, more specifically, for events.

Social committees can propose a budget to the board or work with the one assigned to them by board members. If funding is a challenge, they can explore the possibility of securing sponsors or hosting a ticketed event and charging a small fee to cover expenses wholly or partially. Whether depending on a well-funded budget or making the best of available resources, committee members have numerous options for hosting engaging events.

## Review Insurance

It is always best to be prepared in case something goes wrong. Even at the most well-planned community events, accidents can occur. Reviewing the association's insurance policy can help determine if there is adequate coverage should an injury occur. If the policy is unclear or there are any questions, reaching out to the association's insurance agent can help clear up any uncertainty. If necessary, stand-alone policies for a community event can often be secured at reasonable rates.

When identifying possible risks, it is smart to seek additional input about risk management from the association's counsel and community manager.

## Make Arrangements

Making physical arrangements for events can cause great consternation among planners. If provisions are not made for RSVPs or ticket sales, for example, how can they plan for a specific number? One option is to use the association's private social media platform to collect attendance confirmation and to use resources, such as Facebook Events, to keep track of who plans to attend.

Nevertheless, committee members would be smart to have Plan B ready to implement in case the turnout is higher or lower than expected. They will have to make educated guesses based on available information as they decide on dates and venues, seating and decorations, food and beverages, scheduled entertainment, and engaging business partners.

**Dates and venues.** Giving residents lead time about when and where the event will be held promotes attendance. Planners should avoid times when many families go on vacations or when there are likely to be conflicting events, such as graduation ceremonies and proms in May and holiday celebrations and observations throughout the year.

For outdoor events, they can decide in advance what the protocol will be in case of inclement weather, whether moving to a predetermined indoor or covered venue or rescheduling on an alternate date.

**Seating and decorations.** Planners who arrange for RSVPs or ticket sales can determine the approximate number of attendees, but they cannot eliminate guesswork. Invariably, some who plan to attend will not at the last minute, while others who never responded to invitations will show up—unexpected, of course.

Knowing how many tables, chairs, centerpieces, and other decorations to arrange is always perplexing. Having many empty seats can reflect a failure in terms of turnout, but not having enough can be interpreted as poor planning. A seasoned host I know typically arranges tables and chairs for 10 percent fewer persons than the number who accepted the invitation or bought tickets, but leaves space and is prepared to set up additional seating quickly if more persons attend. When they do, she takes credit for a greater-than-expected turnout. "We had to add seating!" she exclaims.

To reuse decorations, the same host arranges for nearby hospital personnel to pick up floral centerpieces and deliver them to patients who do not have flowers. Other times, she has arranged centerpieces of teddy bears wrapped in cellophane and baskets of Beanie Babies and later delivered them to children's advocacy centers. These are excellent, thoughtful, generous ways to help or cheer others while building goodwill and enhancing cost-effectiveness.

**Food and beverages.** Food and beverages are expected at any social function and are likely to be the biggest part of an event budget. Planning appropriately is imperative, and hosts must be prepared to cope if the turnout is smaller or larger than expected. Social committees, especially those serving small communities or associations, should consider options such as potluck dinners or cooking competitions to entice residents to bring a dish or two. Relatedly, whether flatware, dinnerware, and drinkware are disposable, rented, or owned, they need to be available in sufficient quantities.

When significant quantities of food and beverages are left over, one option is to give them to a group that would appreciate them, assuming the gifted items are in pristine condition. This includes delivering them to facilities for children, first responders, food banks, and volunteers.

To encourage people to mingle, committees can consider setting up stations in different but conveniently located sites for appetizers, main courses, desserts, and beverages. This will encourage guests to move about and interact with others.

**Scheduled entertainment.** Entertainment tends to liven events, whether it occurs in the background, such as piano music, or demands the guests' undivided attention, such as a speaker or performer. If cost is a factor, invite budding musicians and other entertainers in the community to offer a complimentary performance. This includes student groups whose teachers welcome opportunities to perform and gain experience.

Because community events are intended to help residents connect and socialize, planners can consider a wide range of options. Outdoor games such as cornhole, bocce, or croquet can be set up in common areas; and indoor attractions could include bingo, lotería, card or board games, and movies.

Inviting well-known speakers to address timely issues typically draws crowds. Local governments, civic organizations, and many businesses have speakers' bureaus and welcome opportunities to provide them without charge. What is more, especially during election season, community events are a great opportunity to invite local officials and candidates, though always without taking sides and consistent with any stipulations in governing documents. They will learn about the community as they prepare their messages, and residents will get to know them better. A real win-win!

**Engage business partners.** Building community is about making connections. A community can enhance an engagement opportunity by incorporating its business partners or local businesses into planned events. Just as neighbors desire to connect with each other, so do local businesses and those that support the community association seek stronger connections to the association and perhaps to each other.

Planners should consider inviting business partners to participate as sponsors. They can help defray costs while providing connections to resources that residents may need. Involving reliable contractors, for example, is a win-win because they may meet future customers, while residents will benefit by connecting with vendors they may need to hire in the future.

Vendors who have a strong relationship with the community association have an added incentive to continue to do good work and should welcome opportunities to sponsor community events. Many, in fact, have budgets for this very purpose. As part of any sponsorship, planners should consider providing recognition to vendor partners through signage and logo placement in invitations and updates about the event.

Similarly, inviting local businesses to participate can foster potential future business opportunities while providing additional activities, food, or items to enhance the community engagement event. Such participation adds to the fun while allowing businesses to showcase their offerings in a relaxed and enjoyable environment. Participating businesses can serve as sponsors or host stalls to sell or demonstrate their products. By participating in community events, local businesses can connect with potential clients while the community positions itself as supporting small, family-owned businesses in the area. Another win-win!

At the end of the day, the ability to connect people to the community is what matters. That is why social committees search for ways to create engagement events that connect residents with each other and with the larger community in which the association is located. Such engagement results in more enjoyable events while highlighting the purpose and benefits of community association living.

## ENHANCING COMMUNITY ENGAGEMENT

Ever-increasing demands on our precious free time range from after-hours work- and education-related activities to sports, politics, family obligations, and traffic. On top of all that is a growing sense of isolation caused by changes in how we communicate and connect electronically. It makes one crave the so-called good old days when we had fewer distractions and seemingly more time to engage with others in face-to-face settings.

Cognizant that many people crave traditional in-person socialization, community association board members can adopt a goal of encouraging engagement. They can provide a framework for residents to connect by encouraging resident participation in association governance and by hosting social and educational or community service events. They can begin by removing barriers to participation in governance, thus allowing more attendees and more input at critical meetings, and by hosting social, educational, and community service events that bring residents together in relaxed and enjoyable environments.

## Increasing Meeting Participation

Board meetings are a necessary part of running a community association. They provide opportunities to discuss community issues in an open forum, obtain feedback from residents, and approve resolutions pertinent to the community's future. They are not "fun" in a traditional sense, however, and busy lifestyles preclude many residents from participating in regular or annual board meetings.

Increasing meeting participation is a worthy goal for board members who understand the value of enhancing residents' participation in governance. By taking advantage of witnessing and participating in democracy in action, homeowners can see firsthand the value of community association living.

Using a bit of imagination and the board's knowledge of local preferences, board members can increase participation by focusing on accessibility, recognizing resident contributions, and making a meeting into an event.

**Focusing on Accessibility**

To entice homeowners to spend some of their precious free time attending board meetings, board members can begin by making them more accessible. This includes scheduling them on days and times that are most convenient and likely conflicts are minimized. Online survey tools can gather related input from the residents, sending a message that board members focus on openness and transparency.

Consistent with governing documents and state statutes, board members can also explore adding a video-conferencing portal to allow virtual attendance. This type of accessibility was honed during the COVID-19 pandemic, mostly to conduct business efficiently and effectively when isolation and limited exposure to others were health standards. Many associations leveraged virtual meetings to great effect and continue to benefit from this method of facilitating residents' participation in governance.

**Recognizing Residents**

Recognizing residents at board meetings is a surefire way to increase attendance as honorees are joined by their friends, families, and neighbors. Board members can develop a framework and criteria that define contributions, accomplishments, or milestones that will be recognized. In doing so, they build community pride and demonstrate the wealth of talent that enriches the association.

The list of worthy recognitions seems endless. The most common ones are Yard of the Month, best holiday decorations, nicest neighbor, or other accolades that focus on community spirit and positive actions.

## Making It an Event

An easy way to promote attendance is to schedule social time before or after regular or annual board meetings, making them enjoyable, participatory events. This can add a bit of relaxation and fellowship to the routine. How this is executed will vary based on the specific culture of a community. Some boards invite local vendors to offer samples or tastings as part of the event. Other communities schedule musical performances that showcase resident talent or invite a local school band to perform a short program.

There are countless possibilities for this model. Its goal is to add a bit of time to relax and enjoy the company of neighbors as part of the meeting process. The result will be increased attendance and enhanced appreciation for community association living.

## Organizing Social Events

Social events help weave together the community while providing entertainment, fellowship, and other pleasantries. Well-organized social events engage residents and are the best way to highlight the values of living in a community association.

Depending on the neighborhood culture, the number of social events can vary, but they are a great way to highlight the uniqueness of the community and its residents. There truly is an endless list of social events boards could schedule, but my team and I have seen the greatest success in block parties, yard sales, holiday socials, holiday decoration competitions, cook-offs, hazardous waste collection, and home tours.

## Block Parties

Many of us have fond memories of attending block parties as we were growing up. Streets would be blocked off, picnic tables rolled out, and the air would be filled with the smell of barbeque or potluck dishes. Who does not love a good block party?

The road to a successful neighborhood block party begins with finding the best and most appropriate common area or convenient area or street in the community to temporarily block off. The planning committee can organize games and activities; and consider awards for best dish, best barbeque, or other categories. Depending on the availability and budget, food trucks can be arranged, and party favors (usually imprinted materials) can be distributed. The whole point is to create the festival-like feeling that is the hallmark of a good block party.

## Yard Sales

Everyone loves a good yard sale. A well-planned community-wide effort can be a great way for residents to socialize and the association to show off the community. One popular approach is to set an annual date on which residents host them. The association, perhaps through its social committee, can market the event inside and outside the community. Arrangements can include inviting vendors to set up refreshment stalls and food trucks to sell their treats in the common areas. These can be really fun-filled, cost-effective events and enormously successful.

One community association, for example, first hosted a community-wide yard sale on a lark. Fifteen years later, it is a noted annual social event that builds identity for the community and its residents and shows off the neighborhood to potential residents.

The local municipality provides a trolly to shuttle folks from nearby mass transit stops, and local vendors love the opportunity to market their wares.

## Holiday Socials

Holidays are a great excuse to bring people together. Conveniently distributed throughout the year, they provide opportunities to schedule events at times that best suit community needs and strike their celebratory moods. Fall trunk-or-treat festivities can be popular in communities with children and provide a safer alternative to traditional trick-or-treating. Likewise, summer holidays are great times for block parties, fireworks (where legal), or community cookouts.

## Holiday Decoration Competitions

Everyone likes a good spectacle, and hosting a holiday decorating contest can lift community spirits. Decorations also lighten the moods of, and get noticed by, residents and those living nearby. Although planners should focus on the civic aspects of holidays to be sensitive to the diversity of residents in the community, almost any national holiday or season can serve as the focus of an event.

Decoration competitions especially challenge misperceptions that community associations do not allow or support decorating one's house or yard. To help ensure such events do not conflict with community rules, planners should undertake a quick review of governing documents and share helpful decorating guidelines with residents. Whether events focus on Halloween, Independence Day, winter holidays, or other seasonal celebrations, they are a great way to unite the community in celebration.

## Cook-Offs

Cooking competition shows have been popular on television for some time, so why not bring out competitive spirits by hosting a community-wide cook-off? The event can be held in a common area with categories that fit the region and community. Dessert cook-offs, grilling challenges, and neighborhood bake-offs are easy to plan and do not require significant financial investments. They have the added benefit of sending many tasters home happy!

### Hazardous Waste Collection

Safe disposal of hazardous household waste is a great way to provide convenience to residents while doing right by the environment. It may be possible to reach out to local waste management officials to schedule a community hazardous waste collection event. Absent that ability, planners can contact one of many waste management companies that offer services to help safely dispose of herbicides, paint, petroleum products, used computers, and more.

### Home Tours

Communities that have distinctive architecture or want to promote the neighborhood to potential buyers can show off their neighborhood by hosting an annual parade of homes. Amazingly, it is relatively easy to find volunteers to open their homes to tours on a weekend and others to serve as docents. This is a great way to put the community on potential buyers' radar, show off the community's features, and build a sense of community pride.

## Hosting Educational or Community Service Events

Although many consider social events the most enjoyable way to build a sense of community, educational and community service-oriented events may be the most productive and rewarding. They can be designed to share information, consider new perspectives, learn new skills, or support those less fortunate—all while connecting with neighbors and building community.

In-person educational events allow interpersonal exchange of information by allowing residents to ask questions, discuss issues, and occasionally engage in healthy debates. Especially because they offer opportunities for self-improvement, they strengthen the association and its relationship to the community as a whole.

Community service events are also valuable tools for empowering residents to give back to their communities. Whether the activities are specific, such as volunteering to host a holiday gift-wrapping session, or broader in scope, such as organizing a free wellness clinic, they help participants feel positively about themselves and their communities. They are particularly important to organize when a natural or human-made disaster strikes.

Educational and community service events focus on collective action and demonstrate the power of neighbors working together for the good of their communities. The most popular include food drives, charity events, disaster preparation, public officials visits, National Night Out, and pet adoptions. These are highlighted here.

## Food Drives

During the height of the COVID-19 pandemic, news coverage focused on photographs and videos of food banks inundated with miles-long lines of people who needed food and water. Simultaneously, we learned about homebound persons whose access to food, water, medication, and other necessities was limited.

Those uncertain times were a challenge for us all, but the way communities stepped up to help others is unforgettable. Community associations across the country hosted food drives and supported local food banks and neighbors who had lost their jobs because of the pandemic.

Supporting those who are less fortunate or facing tough times, such as food deprivation (temporary or permanent), is an important, inspiring, and impressive service. It reminds us of the difference neighbors can make for each other when they unite in purpose through collaboration and collective action. Neighborhood food drives can unite communities in doing good work while directly impacting those in need.

## Charity Events

Many organizations devote themselves to worthy causes and make our communities and the world a better place. Community associations can further their goals by hosting charity events. One community our company manages stands out in its support of veterans. Each year, it takes great patriotic pride in hosting a fundraiser to pay for training a service animal to assist a veteran with disabilities.

Community associations can partner with local nonprofit organizations by providing volunteers for their activities or hosting events to support their causes. There is a wealth of local organizations that communities can support proudly, enthusiastically—and easily enough—by recruiting like-minded residents who will enjoy volunteering or otherwise contributing. Like food drives, these community service opportunities put the daily challenges faced by the less fortunate into perspective.

## Disaster Preparation

When a community has a heightened risk of natural disasters, such as hurricanes, hosting periodic or annual disaster preparedness seminars can help residents prepare for potential events. These education sessions are most helpful when they are scheduled at convenient times and when residents may be on high alert, such as during prehurricane season.

Disaster preparation seminars and workshops can be offered in person or virtually. They should cover subjects including how to prepare for and recover from a natural disaster, presentations and written materials from local disaster response officials who can answer questions, and responsibilities of residents and of the association regarding preparedness and recovery.

Capturing the session on video would enable other residents to view it at their leisure.

## Public Official Visits

Actions taken by local, state, and federal governments impact communities and their residents. Most public officials, whether elected or appointed, welcome opportunities to engage in community events to share information about their responsibilities and their impact on communities and the local economy, and to encourage participatory government. Elected officials such as members of the U.S. Congress or a state legislature, for example, could discuss new or potential laws and levels of funding for projects ranging from transportation and construction to the environment and community associations. Similarly, appointed officials such as an elections administrator or parks and recreation director could discuss current events and future activities. They, in turn, benefit from meeting constituents and receiving their questions and feedback.

Wise planners schedule visits from public officials responsible for the activities that most interest residents. One way to determine the scope and varied levels of interest is to conduct online surveys or install suggestion boxes at strategic locations and/or at regular and annual board meetings.

A word of warning: As nonprofit entities, community associations are typically prohibited from engaging or advocating for specific candidates, so hosting a candidate forum or other election-related activity may require advice from legal counsel and checking restrictions in governing documents. Inviting a duly elected official to address the community about nonpolitical issues, however, is allowed and builds important community connections.

## National Night Out

Organized by the National Association of Town Watch, National Night Out (NNO) is an annual nationwide event of which our firm, Associa, is a national sponsor. It builds relationships between communities and the law enforcement agencies that protect them. Any association interested in hosting an event can register through the NNO website, https://natw.org.[1]

Public safety is an important topic, and so is building trust and understanding between first responders and those they protect. Hosting an NNO event creates awareness about community safety and strengthens connections between the community and law enforcement.

## Pet Adoptions

Most people love pets, and hundreds of animals, especially cats and dogs, need loving homes. Community associations have hosted highly successful pet adoptions that create mutually beneficial relationships between people and pets and attract animal lovers interested in the cause.

The numerous benefits of pet companionship include a sense of partnership and responsibility, greater physical activity, satisfactory feelings of being needed and appreciated, and lower incidence of depression. The likelihood of success is heightened when associations or planning committees partner with local pet rescue organizations to host an adoption event in the community. It almost goes without saying that animals offered for adoption must be consistent with community rules and restrictions regarding size or breed.

## CONCLUSION

Achieving an engaged and connected community requires a commitment to the principles that define the concept of community. For boards that desire to unlock Coretta Scott King's promise of the "compassionate actions of its members," investing in engagement is essential. When board members create opportunities for engagement, they build environments that showcase the potential for connection and action that exists in all communities.

Engagement begins with board service but extends to finding ways to leverage the community association model to bring more residents into the community-building process. To do this, boards can adopt engagement models that work best for their community's demographics, size, and culture. Such engagement can create a sense of belonging when it incorporates engagement functions that include governance, social, educational, and community service opportunities.

In a time when technology and political differences drive neighbors apart, there is a need and desire for residents to engage with their communities in a positive and meaningful way. Because such engagement does not happen on its own, board members can prioritize engagement to convert routine interactions into events that showcase the benefits of community association living. It starts with a commitment, and it builds to a place where residents experience the full potential of the community association model. In the end, a focus on engagement supports a more enjoyable community with a higher quality of life.

## QUESTIONS TO CONSIDER

1. How does your community define engagement in the context of the association and its functions?

2. What types of community engagement events has your board undertaken over the last twelve months?

3. How would you evaluate your board of directors' success in organizing or planning community engagement events?

4. What social, educational, or community service events does your community host, and how can they be improved? Why are residents pleased or displeased with their frequency and diversity of focus?

5. How does your board of directors engage residents in the community association? How could this effort be expanded to involve more families?

6. How has your community association benefited from engaging residents in governance and activities?

7. What are your community's priorities and goals in planning engagement activities?

8. What are the obstacles to increasing engagement in your community association?

9. What are the most effective and enjoyable events your association has organized? What differentiated them from others?

10. Has your community engaged vendors or local businesses as sponsors or participants in community events? If so, how did they make a difference, either favorable or unfavorable, in terms of attendance and success?

## CHAPTER 12

# Measuring Success

The measure of success is not whether you have
a tough problem to deal with, but whether it
is the same problem you had last year.

—JOHN FOSTER DULLES,
Former U.S. Secretary of State

## CHAPTER INTRODUCTION

In business there is no better feeling than achieving a goal. Improving ourselves or the organizations to which we belong is rewarding and worthwhile. When it comes to community associations, continually striving to improve their governance and operations helps unlock the power of the community for all its residents. In essence, ensuring the association is focused on the future and not repeating past mistakes, as noted by former Secretary Dulles.

Measuring success assumes there is a goal or benchmark to be reached. As communities move through time, improvement and success do not just happen; they are the result of a directed approach to address specific needs. Through a thoughtful process of assessing the current state of the community, what it stands for, and what it would like to be, board members set a foundation upon which they can measure success.

This process begins with defining the community itself. Many organizations highlight their focus by creating vision, mission, and purpose statements. These statements establish a situational context within which they can measure where an organization is today, its short- and long-term aspirations for what it would like to become, and how it would like to reach that destination. Defining a community's vision, mission, and purpose is the first step in creating a framework to begin measuring progress.

Once these foundational statements have been created, they can serve as the basis to build a strategic plan for the community. One of the best aspects of community association living is that its governance and destiny reside with the residents. By working together to create a strategic road map for the future of the community, the association engages residents and demonstrates its role in serving their needs. The planning process also prepares the community for the future and assists in creating resilience to take on any challenges to come. More importantly, the process of evaluating goals creates an opportunity for residents to connect and find common ground for shaping their future as neighbors.

As the community's strategic plan takes shape, it provides a basis from which to set metrics and measure progress. This collective effort keeps the focus on the community and its needs. It also provides a recurring set of data points to show progress for the community's group efforts.

Investing in thinking about tomorrow, setting goals, and measuring the community's success ensures vitality well into the future. That is why, in this chapter, we focus first on defining a vision, mission, and purpose; then, we use these as the foundation from which to create a community strategic plan; and, finally, to implement the plan while measuring success.

# DEVELOPING A VISION, MISSION, AND PURPOSE

Looking to the future and improving a community creates exciting possibilities. Before that journey commences, it is helpful to know what defines the community today, what it aspires to be, and what guides its work. In other words, what are an organization's vision, mission, and purpose? Success is a measure of progress, and progress cannot be measured unless the starting line is established.

For many organizations, including community associations, defining their organizational visions, missions, and purposes helps establish who they are today, what they want to be tomorrow, and how they operate. Investing in developing such statements lays the foundation for measuring a community's success.

Doing so always makes sense, especially for community associations. After all, they govern the most valuable investments most families make, their homes. Establishing clear and concise statements about a community association's vision and mission can help residents understand its role in governance and provide a guiding statement for governing decisions. They can also provide direction to guide the community into the future, and a purpose statement can concisely convey its intent in its daily operations. These tools provide a foundation by which a community association can measure its success in its current state and what it aspires to become over time.

## Defining Vision, Mission, and Purpose Statements

Thanks to seventeenth-century mathematician René Descartes, we know that location is the product of identifying three coordinates, namely, $x$, $y$, and $z$. For organizations comprising individuals, it is not a stretch to define an organization by three similar descriptors. In the case of an organization, one could argue that the organization is defined by its vision, mission, and purpose. Collectively, these three descriptors define the organization in space and time for those whom it exists to serve. They provide information about what the organization aspires to be in the long run (vision), what it does and aspires to be in the short term (mission), and how it achieves its vision and mission (purpose).

Some strategic thinkers describe the vision as a reflection of where an organization aspires to be in the future, perhaps in ten to twenty years; the mission as where it wants to be in the near future, perhaps in two to five years; and the purpose as the means of realizing the vision and mission.

This terminology can be confusing because organizations use them differently, and some use "vision" and "mission" interchangeably. A *Forbes* newsletter article clarifies it by referencing the vision as the big picture, the mission as the road map for getting there, and the purpose as "the feeling that everyone, from the CEO to the janitor, has when you accomplish what you set out to do."[1] That clarification is consistent with my usage in this book, although we also use "mission" to refer to our status quo that evolves as we continually improve to serve our clients.

The process may seem somewhat corporate, but it is not. Having a concise statement about what the community is, what it wants to be, and how it operates provides a foundation upon which it can build for the future. It provides not only a focal point for governance, but also a statement that clarifies what the association does for those who make it their home. These statements serve as essential tools for communities committed to unlocking the potential that exists when good governance, engagement, and dedication meet.

## Defining a Vision Statement

As its name suggests, a vision statement encapsulates what an organization hopes to achieve in the future. Aspirational and motivational in nature, its goal is to guide the organization over time to a destination while focusing on the big picture. Although sometimes cited as the "finish line," in reality, an evolving organization periodically should review and revise its strategic plan, beginning with these core elements.

## Examples of Vision Statements

Listed here are the vision statements of three nationally known companies, followed by Associa's. Their mission statements are shown in the next section, simply to facilitate a comparison.

- **Ford Motor Company:** To become the world's most trusted company, designing smart vehicles for a smart world.
- **Starbucks:** To establish Starbucks as the premier purveyor of the finest coffee in the world while maintaining our uncompromising principles while we grow.
- **Tesla:** Create the most compelling car company of the twenty-first century while driving the world's transition to electric vehicles.
- **Associa:** Building the future of community.

## Defining a Mission Statement

For the purposes of measuring success, the mission statement is the point of departure for an organization, and the vision statement is the destination or finish line.

A mission statement is the ideal who, what, and why of an organization.[2] It is a simple statement (or brief summary) that expresses what the organization's purpose is, whom it serves, why it exists, and where it wants to be in the short term. If read by residents or potential residents, it should provide them with an overview of the community. Typically, a mission statement reflects the immediate goal of the organization; that is, it represents what the organization wants to be today and in the near future. When it comes to measuring progress or success, the mission statement is the point where the community begins its journey.

## Examples of Mission Statements

The mission statements of Ford, Starbucks, and Tesla offer insight into how some of the leading business organizations craft their goals for the near future. To reflect the community association management's perspectives, I again added Associa's.

- **Ford Motor Company:** We believe in the power of creating a world with fewer obstacles and limits, where people have the freedom to build a better life and pursue their dreams.
- **Starbucks:** Our mission, with every cup, with every conservation, with every community—we nurture the limitless possibilities of human connection.
- **Tesla:** Our mission is to accelerate the world's transition to sustainable energy.
- **Associa:** Our mission is to bring positive impact and meaningful value to every community.

## Defining a Purpose Statement

A purpose statement answers the question of how an organization intends to continue to meet its mission while pursuing its vision. Not every organization has one, but it is helpful as a broad statement that guides the day-to-day processes of an organization or community by explaining how it intends to operate and improve in the short- and long-term future. Of the three other companies whose vision and mission statements were referenced in the previous sections, for example, only Ford has such a statement.

A purpose statement has the benefit of being a concise guide for making decisions regarding governance and daily activities. It can also be a useful tool as a community measures its progress from its mission to achieving its vision.

## Examples of Purpose Statements

- **Ford Motor Company:** We believe in the power of creating a world with fewer obstacles and limits, where people have the freedom to build a better life and pursue their dreams.

- **Associa:** Serving others is our calling.

## Creating Vision, Mission, and Purpose Statements

Creating vision, mission, and purpose statements is the first step in the process of community goal-setting and measuring success. The statements provide a way to define and identify the big picture for a community association. They define a community, express its aspirations, and define its actions. These foundational statements distill the essence of the community and its vision into concise and understandable expressions. In doing so, they create a common understanding upon which to build for the future.

The process should begin with a review of the relevant elements of the governing documents. As noted before, reviewing them periodically helps the board understand its role and its limits. Board members should then use this knowledge to draft vision, mission, and purpose statements for their community association.

### Conceptualizing the Community

The next step is to develop the vision statement in terms that are broad enough to be aspirational but specific enough to be realistic. This is the loftiest element in the plan and defines the parameters within which the mission and purpose statements must be written.

Drafting vision, mission, and purpose statements provides an association an opportunity and process for defining itself and providing residents with concise statements about the association's aspirations and how it intends to realize them. Because each statement distills the many functions and goals of a community, it can be a bit like writing poetry, but the result is worth the effort.

In establishing a community's aspirations for the future, it sets the tone, standard, and boundaries within which the mission statement is drafted to define the who, what, and why of the organization. Finally, the process can focus on the purpose and how the community intends to evolve from achieving its vision by first realizing its mission.

### Considering Tips for Drafting Vision, Mission, and Purpose Statements

Drafting vision, mission, and purpose statements may be intimidating, but the process can be simplified. Wise planners understand that these statements are important guidelines but should be reviewed and refined as necessary over time.

Although best practices for strategic plans may call for establishing the number of years over which the vision, mission, and purpose will be achieved, many organizations write them in general terms without specifying their related periods. It seems logical, however, that measuring success will be easier if everyone agrees to incorporate deadlines in their plans.

Tips for crafting vision, mission, and purpose statements center on asking the right questions to garner the information that should be captured in the text. Examples follow:

**Vision statement**. Step one in crafting the vision statement is to establish the number of years over which the strategic plan will be implemented to the extent that its goals are realized. The largest corporations might plan for twenty or more years in the future, but community associations would be wise to plan for ten.

- How many years do we need to realize our dreams for the association?
- What general goals do we want to achieve in that number of years?
- Where do we visualize our association in ten (or any other number) years?

- What parameters should we set within which our
  shorter-term mission can be achieved and our purpose
  accomplished?

**Mission statement**. If the vision statement is written for ten years, the mission statement can be written for five or for increments culminating in that number. By comparison, the mission statement is the more flexible of the two because it can be revised more easily as progress is made. Nothing is more satisfactory than to report, "mission accomplished!" and update the statement accordingly, though always consistent with the association's vision.

- What exactly is our association?
- Whom do we serve?
- How do we serve?
- Why do we serve?
- How many years do we need to achieve our goals along the
  way toward realizing our vision over its defined period?
- What short-term goals should we define that are consistent
  with the aspiration defined in our vision statement?

**Purpose statement**. A purpose statement is an assertion of what an organization represents. A recent *Harvard Business Review* article notes a purpose statement should "accurately and honestly reflect the organization's true purpose."[3] In other words, it is a statement that illustrates the reason for the organization's existence. It can be a distillation of an organization's values, mission, and how it sees itself as part of the larger community. Equally important, it sets expectations for internal and external participants about what the organization is at its core.

An effective purpose statement should reflect the heart of the organization's purpose. For Associa, everything we do is to serve our clients and empower them to build the future of community. For us, a distillation of why we exist is to serve others. Based on that premise, our teams honed our purpose statement as follows: "Serving others is our calling." It is why we are here and what we aspire to do for each other and for our clients.

The key to drafting a purpose statement is to pinpoint the heart of why an organization exists and express it in a concise statement that expresses that sentiment authentically. The process of developing it is facilitated by answering the following questions:

- How do we operate?
- Whom do we serve?
- What are our standards?
- What is our organization's priority?

## Obtaining Feedback and Approval

Board members ultimately are responsible for approving strategic plans and their elements. Options for getting this done include working as a committee of the whole, appointing a board committee to work on it, or appointing a committee of residents with at least one board liaison member.

Regardless of the approach, the process should include collecting and incorporating feedback from residents. What is more, a period of public comment should be scheduled before the board considers adopting the plan. Engaging residents as stakeholders is a critical element. It makes the residents part of the process of building the future they want for their families and community.

To facilitate community involvement, however, the best approach is for the board to consider approving the vision, mission, and purpose statements early in the process of developing a strategic plan. The three would then serve as the framework for writing the plan as a whole.

To ensure buy-in from residents, board members can seek their feedback on the vision, mission, and purpose statements, which can be published in draft form on the association's website or through its private social media channels. They should also announce a comment period that is long enough for residents to provide thoughtful feedback, culminating with a public comment period at board meetings.

After the feedback from residents is collected, reviewed, and evaluated, the statements can be amended as needed. Their final versions can be adopted formally by board members at their next regular meeting.

By adopting vision, mission, and purpose statements, a community association creates important tools to measure its success over time. The vision statement defines the future of the organization, the mission statement provides the starting point, and the purpose statement clarifies how the association intends to move from mission to vision.

## CREATING AND IMPLEMENTING A COMMUNITY STRATEGIC PLAN

Successful communities do not just happen; they are the result of boards that are committed to maintaining the vibrancy of their communities. A goal without a plan to achieve it is merely an aspiration. A community with a vision and mission positions itself to plan for its future.

The planning process empowers a board to solicit resident feedback and use it to build a strategic plan for its community. In doing so, the board adds a layer of transparency by having a plan that defines the goals of the community association, what it does, and how it wants to improve. A community strategic plan is a road map for the association by prioritizing the association's work to preserve amenities, serve the community, and promote social engagement. It also helps set expectations for residents, provides common goals to unite them, and communicates the work and plans of the board.

Creating a community plan is more than a challenge. It is an opportunity for the board to set achievable goals to allocate resources in the best interest of the community. The process begins with defining the strategic plan in terms of its components, goals, and process. Building it requires laying a foundation from which to develop it. The last stage of creating the plan involves actually drafting it, collecting and considering feedback before finalizing it, and finally, securing board approval.

After investing time in gathering feedback, identifying priorities, and establishing goals, it is time to commence implementation. A well-thought-out strategic plan supports an organized approach that allows many of the participants involved and structures used in preparing the plan to engage in implementing it. It also allows for delegation of goals to help the board maintain momentum. This can include utilizing the internal structures initially created to set goals, for example, to gather feedback and measure progress. The process as a whole allows for weaving resident engagement into the future of the organization.

## Defining a Strategic Plan

A community association strategic plan is a blueprint that maps out the long-term goals and aspirations of the community. It allows the organization to focus on its long-range goals and is a result of introspection, resident feedback, and planning by the organization's leadership.

Most strategic plans focus on a future period that ranges from five to ten years, commence with vision and mission statements, and often include a purpose statement. The body of the strategic plan focuses on specific objectives, projects, and other actions the board and community aspire to achieve while preserving and enhancing the quality of life in the association. It also examines the resources needed, both in time and money, to complete projects associated with the plan. Through the process of establishing community goals, establishing benchmarks, and setting timelines, the community can unite around its collective effort to improve the lives of its residents.

## Components of a Strategic Plan

There are many ways to structure a strategic plan. Generally, most plans have a similar structure that comprises the following elements:

- An executive summary
- A reiteration of the organization's vision and mission statements
- An analysis of the organization's strengths, weaknesses, opportunities, and threats (SWOT)
- An identification of the organization's goals and priorities
- Additional information that can include a financial analysis, operational plan, or other components[4]

**Executive summary.** The executive summary, as its name suggests, is a high-level summary of the strategic plan. It can be framed with the rationale for creating the plan, along with the aspirations of the group who assembled it. Typically, it is a brief outline or short bulleted list of the plan's objectives and goals. In effect, it should allow a reader with no previous exposure to the plan to have a basic understanding of its purpose, goals, and objectives.

**Vision statement.** A vision statement is an aspirational statement that focuses on what the organization aspires to be or achieve in the specified long term. If the mission statement reflects the present, the vision statement focuses on the future but is rooted in the mission statement.

**Mission statement.** A mission statement expresses the organization's reason for being and how it serves its members. Consistent and aligned with the vision statement, it comprises shorter-term goals for realizing it.

**Purpose statement.** A purpose statement answers the question of how the organization intends to continue to meet its mission while pursuing its vision.

**SWOT analysis.** SWOT stands for Strengths, Weaknesses, Opportunities, and Threats. Its elements are used to establish an understanding of the organization's present status. They are useful tools for assessing what is working well and what areas can be improved while also identifying opportunities or dangers to the organization. A SWOT analysis can also assist in allocating resources to areas that may need more attention or improvement.

**Goals and priorities.** The goals and priorities are the heart of the strategic plan. These are the action items or objectives that the organization wants to achieve during the strategic plan's focus period. For community associations, this may include plans suggested in earlier chapters, such as community engagement goals or disaster response planning. Setting clearly articulated goals is critical to allowing current and future leaders to monitor progress toward expressed objectives.

**Additional components.** Depending on the organization's needs, additional components can be included in the plan. These can include financial analyses, environmental reviews, staffing plans, or operational plans that support the organization's current state and future goals.

## Tips for Goal Setting

Progress and success do not happen spontaneously. They are a product of focusing efforts to accomplish a task or goal. Articulating a goal can be a challenge, especially when the goal touches on subject matter that may not lend itself to easy measurement. When it comes to setting appropriate goals, businesses, community associations, and other organizations can benefit from research done by noted leaders such as George T. Doran. A municipal leader in Washington state, he was the first to articulate the concept of SMART Goals.[5]

His work provided a framework to better shape organizational goals. SMART stands for Specific, Measurable, Achievable, Relevant, and Time-based. Businesses, including my company, rely on this framework when establishing strategy and goals for our organizations. These tips can be helpful when engaging in the strategic planning process discussed in more detail herein.

**Specific.** The goal must be well-defined and specific. Everyone must have a clear understanding of the goal, know why it was set, who is involved, what should be accomplished, and what the proposed timeline is.

**Measurable.** A measurable goal helps track progress, correct the plan of action if needed, and demonstrate advancement to residents.

**Achievable.** Goals must be realistic and achievable within resources of time, effort, and money. Setting the bar too high might leave board members feeling defeated and frustrated and residents unhappy.

**Relevant.** Relevance can be established or tested by raising pertinent questions: Is the goal important to maintaining or improving the community? Will achieving it make a difference? Is it something most residents want?

**Time-based.** Setting deadlines is an imperative aspect of goal-setting and should reflect consideration of board members' availability and ability to devote themselves to meeting them in a timely manner. Long-term goals should be divided into phases with deadlines for each phase.

## The Plan as a Process

Even those who develop a deeply researched strategic plan cannot fully foresee future events or changes in values that may alter the desirability of goals they established. Although a well-written strategic plan is a road map, as with any journey, the destination or goal may change over time, or the route toward it may need adjustment. Accordingly, a strategic plan should be considered a living document capable of evolving with the needs of the community.

As progress toward goals is measured and additional feedback is generated, priorities can and will change. Adopting the view that the strategic plan can evolve will allow the board and community to continue to move toward their goals, even if the substance of the goal or its priority to the community changes.

## Building a Strategic Plan

Creating the vision, mission, and purpose statements and defining components and goals may be challenging, but they are only the initial steps of building a strategic plan for a community association. The next include laying the foundation, developing the plan, and, finally, actually creating it.

### Laying the Foundation

An association board of directors is responsible for governing the community association and charting its path to success presently and in the future. Developing a strategic plan is an effective means of ensuring the community and its volunteer resources are allocated appropriately. In the end, it will define the community's goals as the basis from which to allocate funds, efficiently govern the community, and measure success.

A worthwhile strategic plan provides a road map to the community's goals and the pathway for reaching them. In doing so, it provides the rationale for making decisions related to governance, thereby enhancing board transparency.

Before board members memorialize the elements of their strategic plan, it helps to engage in some preliminary work to lay the foundation for a robust plan. To help ensure its success, the plan should reflect goals that are within the board's authority, are financially achievable, consider external factors, reflect resident priorities, and build upon a realistic assessment of the community's status quo.

**Reviewing board authority.** A community association board has the authority to act only in areas delegated to it by the community governing documents and state statutes. Before laying out goals for the community strategic plan, the board should review the scope of its authority to ensure that any projects undertaken are within its purview. If the board members need additional assistance in interpreting those sources of authority, they should confer with qualified counsel. As a preliminary step, however, they should address only projects or goals for the community that are within their ability to effectuate.

**Assessing financial status.** Financial resources are the lifeblood of a community association, and a stable budget and finances are essential to start planning for the future. A community needs sufficient funding to cover expenses such as common area utilities, maintenance, landscaping, insurance, as well as professional services such as community management.

Before beginning the process of building a long-term plan, board members should have a shared understanding of the financial status of the community. This requires a review of current budgets, delinquencies, and any budget deviations in the recent past.

**Considering externalities.** Just like a family's budget, external forces can impact even the best-laid plans. To paraphrase Robert Burns, we must always be ready to adapt to the fact that "the best-laid plans of mice and men often go awry." As part of the planning process, the board should reflect on any current or potential externalities that could impact its long-term plan—and be ready to adapt accordingly.

Two areas that can impact community resources are insurance and reserve funding. Over the last few years, many community associations have seen increases in insurance premiums. Insurance is required to protect the community association and the common areas from damage and potential legal claims. Similarly, funds must be set aside for the future repair or replacement of common elements and amenities.

Any resources needed to implement elements of the community's strategic plan must be considered in light of the need to fund adequate insurance coverage and reserve funds. Considering these essential elements and their future costs is essential to realistically assessing the available resources for other projects.

**Reflecting on community input.** A criticism leveled against some community association boards is that they are not responsive to residents' needs. The process of establishing a community strategic plan is an excellent opportunity to engage residents in the goal-setting process and get an assessment of the board's priorities. This can be accomplished by surveying residents' priorities and then focusing the planning process on them. The result is a vivid demonstration of the board's responsiveness.

**Building on status quo.** The focus of any plan should build upon the status of the community. An assessment of how the community is operating, the state of any common elements and amenities, and any emergent issues within the community provides an excellent point of departure for the planning process. This sets up any resulting plan to be iterative of the community's status quo and to build upon elements and processes that are working well.

### Developing the Plan

Once the foundation for building the strategic plan has been laid, it is time to begin the process of developing the plan, which is the last step before actually creating it. Since the plan focuses on the long term, the process to develop it should be organized and thoughtful. Board members and volunteers should be willing to commit time to see the process through and allocate the resources to get it done. When advising clients about strategic planning, we typically suggest dividing the process into the following five categories:

- Reviewing vision and mission statements
- Adopting agenda
- Identifying priorities

- Selecting priorities
- Establishing measurable goals

Discussed here, these steps can be accomplished over time to allow for thoughtful consideration and exploration of the potential impact on the community.

**Reviewing vision and mission statements.** Success begins with reviewing the vision, mission, and purpose statements adopted earlier to ensure they still seem appropriate as reality sinks in throughout the strategic plan development process. Although the three are equally important, the focus at this point is on the first two because they are the basis for long- and short-term planning. Combined, they must be worthy of serving as the north star from which every aspect of the plan is aligned. If they are not, then revising them should be the first step of this part of the process.

**Adopting agenda.** After reviewing and affirming the community's vision and mission statements, it is time to begin building the agenda. This includes outlining the objectives of the long- and short-term plans, defining the goals and tasks the board wishes to achieve, and establishing a timeline that culminates with board adoption.

It may be helpful to appoint a board member or a community volunteer to coordinate these activities and facilitate discussions, track goal development, and ensure stakeholders are heard in the process.

**Identifying priorities.** The board should assemble a list of possible priorities that could serve as the basis for the strategic plan. Residents should be encouraged to share ideas and agree on priorities or projects they believe best define what the community would like to accomplish over the time frame of the plan.

As part of this process, each proposed priority should be analyzed and evaluated in terms of how much it would cost and how much time and effort it would take to achieve it. It also must fit somewhat neatly into the timeline developed for realizing the association's vision and mission.

Because brainstorming is encouraged, the board could assign a coordinator or engage a professional facilitator to ensure all residents are heard, and no ideas are rejected without proper consideration. The result should be a master list of proposals for the board to consider when selecting the best and most appropriate for the plan.

**Selecting priorities.** The better and more thorough the master list of priorities, the easier it will be for board members to review the proposals, consider their respective required time and financial commitments, and determine which best align with the community's needs. Those approved by a majority vote would be included in the master plan, while others could be kept on file for future reference.

The ultimate goal of this process is to identify and select the priorities that align with the community's needs and interests and are within the projected available financial resources.

**Establishing measurable goals.** Setting measurable goals is essential to measuring progress and declaring success. Because goal-setting is directly related to realizing a community's vision and mission, board members must define goals that are articulated clearly and set metrics to measure their progress or realization. Only then can they declare success.

What follows is an example of how to establish a measurable goal by setting a benchmark and a metric for measuring success:

- The board establishes a goal to increase resident engagement in community meetings by 10 percent.
- The next step is to set a benchmark, such as the current average attendance at community meetings.
- The measurable goal is set as the benchmark number plus 10 percent.

The key element of measuring success, then, is to establish a goal, a baseline, and a metric.

My hope is that this example illustrates how easy it is to measure success. Only by doing so can we gain insight and satisfaction into our progress or, alternatively, understand the areas in which we fall short and need to improve.

**Creating the Plan**

There are no shortcuts for laying the foundation for a strategic plan that is based on a long-term vision and short-term mission and for selecting the priorities to include in it. Neither are there shortcuts for the next step in the process, which is to create it. This includes drafting it, obtaining final feedback, finalizing it, and securing approval by the board.

**Drafting the plan.** The community's vision, mission, and plan priorities can now be incorporated into a written plan for the community. There are various ways to organize one. Many follow the sequence mentioned here:

- Begin with a purpose statement that outlines the reasons the plan was created and the goals it hopes to achieve, noting how they tie into the community's vision and support its mission.

- That can be followed by an executive summary or a high-level overview of the plan.

- The body of the document can include sections for the individual goals associated with the plan, budget information, and proposed timelines.

- Finally, an acknowledgments section should be included to recognize and thank the residents or volunteers who helped the board build the plan.

**Obtaining final feedback.** The draft plan should be made available for residents to review and provide feedback. It can be posted to the community website or shared on the association's private social network with an email address or other point of contact for submitting feedback. A comment period typically ranging from thirty to sixty days should be sufficient for this important step in the process.

**Finalizing the plan.** After considering the feedback and revising the plan as appropriate, board members should develop the draft they will consider adopting. Then, they should post it anew and give residents another opportunity to provide feedback during a second comment period and at a board meeting before they vote on it. After the plan, with any revisions, is completed, it can be reposted as the draft to be considered by the board, pending possible revisions based on final feedback.

**Approving the final plan.** After the board adopts the final strategic plan by majority vote in a regular open meeting, it becomes part of the record of the association. The board should announce and schedule periodic updates about progress in implementing the plan and in realizing the community's vision and mission.

## Implementing the Plan

Having set clear objectives, defined a process for measuring progress toward specific goals, and adopted a strategic plan, the board can commence execution. Successful plan implementation benefits from an organized and thoughtful process, such as the one used to assemble the plan. This helps convert the community's vision and mission into measurable results.

Ownership of goals is a key element of implementation. While the board is ultimately responsible for executing community initiatives, delegating projects to standing association committees or a temporary task force enhances engagement and can accelerate or at least facilitate progress.

To maintain momentum and keep residents informed, the implementation process should include periodic updates. These reports should be scheduled regularly to ensure progress is reported as accurately and thoroughly as appropriate. Such regular communication ensures residents know how the board is improving the community and how they are implementing the residents' desires. It also reassures them that their participation is as meaningful as it is appreciated and that it impacts the community positively.

Board members are most likely to succeed when they implement the strategic plan by delegating plan elements, establishing a reporting cadence, and adapting the plan based on their learning by experience.

## Delegating Plan Elements

Strategic plan execution requires ownership of the identified goals, which is impacted by the size of the community and the scope of the plan. Smaller community associations may delegate ownership of projects to board members, while larger ones can utilize standing or special purpose committees.

The objective of ownership of goals is to ensure that each has a person or persons driving the process, monitoring progress, and reporting to the board. To repeat: A project without ownership is merely an aspiration. What is more, using existing or new committees provides the ideal organizational structure for the board to oversee the entire project while delegating reporting requirements and authority to carry out the project elements.

## Establishing Reporting Cadence

Investing time, money, and effort in a strategic plan is wasteful if progress toward its goals is not reported adequately to stakeholders and those responsible for leading the project. An element of excitement abounds when a community completes its strategic plan and begins implementation: It is the excitement that comes with possibility. Establishing a reporting process and cadence will continue to move the plan forward.

Working with committees to address plan goals, including those related to community engagement or disaster planning, provides a ready-made framework for reporting. Committee reports are typically included on regular board meeting agendas, so progress reports about any delegated goals can be included in the regular committee report.

Having a regular reporting cadence ensures proper oversight and facilitates resolving any deviations or problems that may arise before they have a negative impact.

**Adapting the Plan**

As implementation moves forward, the board can monitor progress through the established reporting cadence. This should not be considered a rote process, but rather, an opportunity to review progress toward goals; assess consistency with budget and timelines; and deal with any perceived lack of progress or deviation from the original intent, level of funding, or adopted deadlines.

This is an excellent time for board members to review all available information and feedback and to determine whether to adapt any aspect of the plan, especially regarding costs and expected completion dates. Consistent monitoring is the key to ensuring any deviation from the expected timelines can be flagged and addressed before the process gets too far off course.

## MEASURING SUCCESS AND COMMUNICATING THE PLAN

Once the plan is in motion, the focus of efforts pivots to measuring success and communicating plan progress to residents. Establishing periodic reporting of goal metrics and reviewing progress ensures the plan continues to move forward. Gathering data, projecting outcomes, and making needed adjustments will move the community closer to achieving its goals, which is the main element of success. Residents will also benefit from clear communication, strengthened problem-solving skills, and a sense of empowerment that comes from unlocking the power of community. Communicating regularly not only keeps residents informed, but also maintains excitement about the projects and promotes transparency.

## Measuring Success

Success in realizing the goals of strategic plan goals can be measured qualitatively and quantitatively. Although the latter measurements are more consistent with business goals and traditional behavioral science measurements, the former are important because they capture how participants feel. Those findings are typical of persons whose attitudes are, "Do not confuse me with the facts. I have made up my mind." On a more positive note, it is a reminder of the belief that people may not remember what you said or wrote, but they will remember how you made them feel. My experience is that achieving goals makes everyone feel good. Generally, for most community associations, the qualitative aspect is more a byproduct experienced as quantitative measurements are ascertained and reported.

Academic studies that promote ways to measure goal performance are plentiful. My goal herein, however, is not to review them, but rather to provide a basic framework for a community association to measure progress regarding the elements of a strategic plan. Accordingly, I recommend the SMART goal method recommended earlier for developing measurable goals. Assuming the identified goals are specific, measurable, achievable, relevant, and time-bound, developing metrics for their measurement should be relatively easy. As the parameters for specific goals, they ensure progress is attainable by the specified deadline.

Goal measurement depends on constructing factors that will allow for a cadence of measurement and benchmarking. This is possible when goals are set with a metric in mind. The process then begins with the nature of the goal and establishing an appropriate metric to measure progress to its deadline set in the strategic plan.

Progress is augmented by setting periodic review sessions for the plan's stakeholders, giving them time for more in-depth assessments of movement toward goals and subsequent steps. Those reviews allow the measurement of progress to date and an opportunity to identify obstacles that were experienced or that may materialize.

Finally, synthesizing and evaluating data from committee reports and periodic reviews enables board members to convert the information into annual progress reports. Collectively, these steps help define means to measure success and keep stakeholders informed about the community's progress.

## Gathering Metric Data

Measuring progress toward goals requires gathering and reporting metrics. This part of the process begins with delegating ownership of a goal to a committee or task force and establishing a baseline metric from which to begin measuring. Data can be gathered on a periodic basis appropriate to the goal. If the goal, for example, is to reduce monthly assessment delinquencies, monthly data can be obtained from the association's financial reports. Similarly, if a goal is to increase resident attendance at quarterly social functions, data can be gathered at each event.

## Scheduling Reviews

The board or stakeholder group should schedule periodic strategic plan reviews to allow for studying goal progress made to date and identifying areas that may need additional support. As part of the process, data should be reviewed against related goals to determine what has been accomplished and assess if such progress has been sufficient to meet the goal timely. Ownership of goals can also be reviewed to assess whether the group responsible is working as intended or if changes are needed.

Scheduling periodic plan reviews facilitates focusing on the bigger picture, allows consistent evaluation of progress, and provides opportunities to adjust course as needed.

## Identifying Obstacles

A strategic plan helps a community realize its future goals, but no plan is clairvoyant. Obstacles to progress often emerge. When this happens, it is important to acknowledge the obstacle and explore the reasons for it. If a strategic goal, for example, is to reduce assessment delinquencies by 5 percent but delinquencies increase, the causes of the deviation must be examined and evaluated. When considering an emergent obstacle, board members can review the data, adjust the tasks needed to achieve the goal, or amend the goal.

## Communicating the Plan

Starting with the completed document and progressing through the implementation of its elements, communicating the strategic plan and its progress to residents is critical. First, the plan itself is a reminder of the role of the board and its commitment to the future of the community. Sharing a summary of the plan and its goals for the community provides a focal point for discussion among board members and residents. Second, after engaging them in building the plan, keeping residents informed maintains their engagement and allows them to be appreciative of the plan's progress. Finally, if the plan unfolds over a series of years, producing an engaging annual progress report will maintain the ongoing need to keep residents informed about its progress and ultimate goals.

## Summarizing the Plan

Summarizing the key elements of the community strategic plan and posting the summary in a space accessible to residents is helpful to all stakeholders. A concise one-page summary that includes the rationale for the plan, key elements, and anticipated timelines can be a great tool to keep the focus on the various projects. As progress is made, completed projects can be checked off the list.

Having a concise summary available is a reminder about why the projects were undertaken, their benefits, and the role of the association in improving the lives of its residents.

## Communicating Progress

In addition to reporting strategic plan progress at regular board meetings, information should be communicated regularly via appropriate channels to all residents. Committee reports and board minutes can be shared on community websites or internal social media and can be the basis for creating more reader-friendly updates to post on the community's existing channels. For strategic plans that have many elements, a separate strategic plan page on the community's website can be an excellent and helpful source of information for residents. The key element is communicating progress regularly.

## Developing Annual Progress Report

Reporting progress toward strategic plan goals annually is also critical, especially for multi-year projects. While regular communiques maintain interest and reflect continual progress, annual reports combine those smaller accomplishments into a larger, more significant, more impressive attainment. This helps maintain momentum and should instill pride as homeowners are reminded about and realize anew the plan's impact and ability to improve their community association.

Annual progress reports can be a compilation of data gathered by the board through committee and task force reports throughout the year. They should be reader-friendly, using appropriate graphics such as colorful charts and graphs to convey information in an engaging manner. The report can be posted on the community website and via internal private social media channels.

## Reaping the Benefits

Many tomes are written about the benefits of strategic planning. From a business standpoint, I have witnessed repeatedly its benefits in my company and with our clients. The process of developing, drafting, and executing a strategic plan requires engagement, listening, and problem-solving. In the context of a community association, the strategic planning process provides benefits beyond merely achieving the plan's goals. Developing it requires community input and a dynamic exchange of information between stakeholders in the community, which improves communication.

Through identifying and prioritizing needs and overcoming obstacles, the strategic planning process enhances problem-solving skills in the community. Finally, and most heartening, as the community successfully achieves its objectives, it unlocks the realization of the true power of community. That power is the ability collectively to make positive change.

## Improved Communication

As a community navigates through the strategic planning process, it creates new challenges of communication and strengthens others. Communication is a process that is improved when there is a need to convey information about a topic that unites listeners. Foremost among the communication benefits of the strategic planning process is its expression of the community's long-term aspirations and goals. This allows its members to embrace the common objective of improving the community.

As the execution of the plan progresses, board members and stakeholders are required to commit to thoughtful and appropriate communication and feedback opportunities. This exercise also requires a review of lines of authority within the community, providing both the board and residents with a better sense of community governance. Most importantly, the strategic planning process creates a document that embodies the community association's vision and mission, communicating them and reflecting their related values to current and future residents.

### Enhanced Problem-Solving

Executing the elements of a strategic plan also provides multiple benefits by enhancing problem-solving mechanisms in the community association. The plan development process solicits feedback from inception, enabling the board to identify areas of improvement or that the residents believe would benefit from a new approach.

As plan priorities are set, stakeholders engage in prioritizing and funding identified goals, gaining insight into the community's priorities and the ability to allocate resources.

### Strengthened Sense of Community

Uniting to improve its environment is an empowering experience for a community association. Developing a strategic plan and achieving its goals provide residents with a hands-on demonstration of the benefits of collective action. When the plan is the result of input from the community and reflects the needs of residents, it contributes to a sense of ownership and belonging, the very elements that help define community.

Executing a strategic plan and its elements also enhances engagement of residents by providing opportunities for project delegation and participation. These factors promote communication, problem-solving, and trust in the collaborative process. Moreover, as the progress and improvements from the plan become evident, they underscore the positive role a community association plays in improving the lives of its residents.

## CONCLUSION

Measuring success is part of a larger vision for the community association. It involves engaging in discussions about what the community is, how it works, and what it aspires to become. Even the most successful communities cannot take the future for granted; planning facilitates continued harmony in the community.

Success is ultimately a measure of progress toward goals. For community associations, that journey can be undertaken by creating foundational statements that define the community, engaging residents in discussing the future, and creating a strategic plan. Through this process, the community can begin to unlock its true power to connect residents.

Measuring progress in any community requires a starting point. Many organizations successfully use vision, mission, and purpose statements to define the community and begin planning. The vision statement is a long-term aspirational goal to unite residents in a common cause. Closely aligned and always consistent with it, the mission statement captures related incremental short-term goals. Both are foundations for defining benchmarks essential for measuring growth. Finally, the purpose statement helps explain how the community intends to operate and treat its residents in pursuit of its operations and aspirations.

When a community association has defined its vision and mission and identified related benchmarks to measure, it can begin preparing for the future. Working with residents, the board can initiate the process of assembling a strategic plan that articulates the goals of the community and allows it to implement actions to achieve them.

The planning process provides many opportunities to engage residents about what is important to them and demonstrate the board's role in serving their needs. Once the elements of the plan are drafted, seeking a final round of feedback will further engage stakeholders before the plan's approval by the board. By developing a community plan, the community association will reap ancillary benefits such as improved communication, enhanced problem-solving, and a strengthened sense of community.

As soon as the plan is in place, the board can leverage existing or special committees to assist with its implementation. Following the same thoughtful process used in creating the plan, board members can gather data and track progress toward its goals. Through regular committee reports, periodic plan reviews, and annual update reports, all stakeholders can be kept informed, and momentum can be maintained. As goals come to fruition, they can instill a sense of empowerment and pride throughout the community as residents recognize the purpose of the association and the power of collective action.

## QUESTIONS TO CONSIDER

1. How would you define your community association's vision and mission? If your community has written vision and mission statements, how would you improve them?

2. What future challenges might your community face, and how do they shape the board's vision of what your community needs to, or can, become?

3. How does your community prepare to deal with future challenges?

4. How do your board members engage residents in discussing how the association should operate and treat its residents? How would articulating that in a purpose statement benefit the community?

5. If your community has a strategic plan, how well is it being implemented? If not, would a strategic plan be helpful in meeting the community's future needs?

6. How would engaging residents in shaping the future impact the culture of your community?

7. How does your association committee structure lend itself to identifying functions in the community that could be improved? Could these committees assist in that process?

8. How does your community association measure its performance? Do these measures include goals to address unmet community needs?

9. How does your community association communicate with residents about its operations and ability to achieve its goals?

PART V

# FUTURE PLANS

The future is called "perhaps," which is the only
possible thing to call the future. And the important
thing is not to allow that to scare you.

—TENNESSE WILLIAMS,
American Playwright

## PART V INTRODUCTION

Too often, we retreat to our comfort zones, holding on to the same processes and routines. Although this can provide a sense of familiarity, the reality is that the world around us changes continuously. This change creates possibilities, or, as Tennessee Williams so aptly noted, introduces "perhaps" into our lives.

While fundamental board duties benefit from consistency, that is not the same as allowing processes to ossify. Keeping an eye on the future allows community association boards of directors to identify and respond to emerging needs and changing priorities in their communities. Developing a sense of what is to come helps them evolve appropriately.

A key part of looking toward the future is developing a sense of what it might look like. It may be speculative and malleable, but we can develop a rudimentary picture of it by deducing potential outcomes from today's data and trends. This process can allow a community to plan for future challenges and meet its residents' needs. It is also an important part of reinforcing the ability to adapt over time into the mindset of a community.

If the past is a prologue, boards can expect a growing complexity of regulations that empower or limit their authority. The last twenty years have seen a growing interest in regulating community associations, not always with a positive impact. While some proposals provide a clearer legal framework for community governance, others could impose mandates funded by limited community resources.

Regulatory impositions can emerge at any level of government. Thankfully, just as boards and residents engage in dialogue to shape community rules, they can also speak up and engage to help shape the environment in which associations must operate.

The final question is, within the larger scope of this publication, how can boards of directors put the pieces together to ensure community matters now and in the future? They can start by gleaning from the lessons my company and I have learned over the years. These lessons can be fortified by remembering the keys to success that are within the reach of every community leader. By implementing the board's arsenal of skills, they can collaborate in moving forward to unlock the potential of every community.

Building on the earlier parts of this book that focused on community association concepts, elements of success, challenges, and alternative outcomes, Part V, "Future Plans," focuses on looking ahead, coping with a more regulated future, and putting the pieces together.

## CHAPTER 13

# Looking Ahead

The best way to predict the future is to create it.

—DENNIS GABOR,
Nobel Laureate, Inventor of Holography

## CHAPTER INTRODUCTION

History books and social media memes are filled with flawed predictions about the future. As we do not have a crystal ball, it would be foolish to make claims about it with confidence. Regardless of our inability to predict accurately or confidently, however, what lies ahead for community associations surely is consistent with Dennis Gabor's outlook that "the best way to predict the future is to create it." That is why we work so hard at laying the strongest possible foundation from which to build our communities and measure our success over time in reaching priority goals.

Because community associations offer a unique means to self-govern our neighborhoods, residents are empowered not only to make decisions, but also to change courses when appropriate. As we look toward the future, we can create possible visions of it by looking at the recent history of community associations, reviewing current demographic trends, and extrapolating those trends to create a hypothesis of what is to come. Then, using the power of self-governance, which is the core of community associations, we can make that future a reality.

When we do our best, we can quote Robert Browning confidently: "The best is yet to be."

## FORECASTING THE FUTURE OF COMMUNITY ASSOCIATIONS

Before making any forecasts, it behooves us to look at the present. When extrapolating possible outcomes for the community association model in future scenarios, it is helpful to reiterate and understand its success. The rise of community associations, their popularity with residents, and their benefits have been keys to their rapid adoption as a preferred housing model in growing jurisdictions.

Examining and understanding why they work so well and what is in store for them will likely be more productive if available data are synthesized and evaluated as the basis for forecasting. At the risk of sounding academic, I recommend a process based on the following revision of Bloom's Taxonomy developed at the Vanderbilt University Center for Teaching (see figure 13.1):[1]

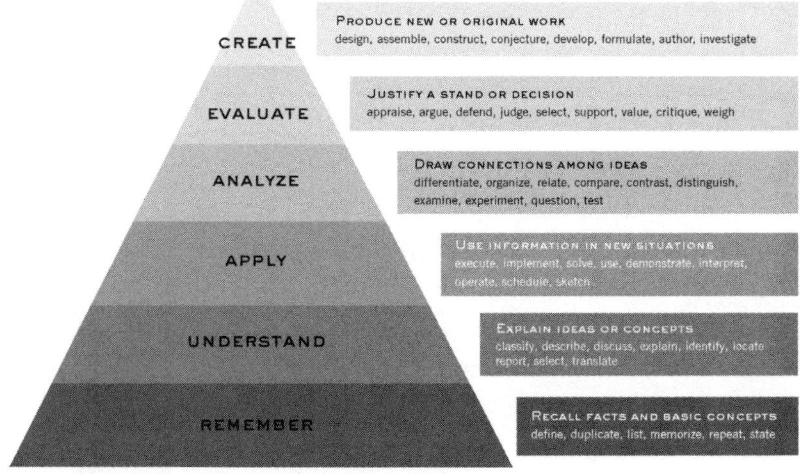


Figure 13.1: Based on the Figure from Vanderbilt University Center for Teaching

By starting at the base of this pyramid and working toward its top, we would *remember* our history and basic data, *understand* happenings and their outcomes, *apply* our information to the task at hand, *analyze* it in drawing conclusions, *evaluate* outcomes, and *create* our forecast for community associations.

Every step in the process of looking ahead involves working with available critical data. To begin with, fortifying a continuing role for community associations in the years ahead benefits from a quick look at current demographic trends that will shape what our communities will look like and how they will house future residents. Factors that include population growth and rate will help predict housing needs, while a review of population trends can lend insight into the types of people who may need them. In short, projections of key data points will allow us to connect the dots regarding possible future outcomes.

Once we understand what has happened, we can work through the process of applying, analyzing, and evaluating our information to create our visualization about how community associations can help address future housing challenges and how they might need to adapt to meet changing demands or preferences. While mapping the future admittedly requires a level of "guestimation," the more important protocol is to be guided by emerging trends to ensure that community associations can not only prepare for the future, but also create it.

It is fascinating to realize that community associations were in their infancy slightly more than fifty years ago but now account for up to 30 percent of housing in the United States. To understand their role in the future, we begin our analysis by looking at their role today, why they continue to grow as a housing model, and the benefits they confer to their residents and the municipalities in which they exist. This snapshot affords us a good basis from which to predict what they might look like tomorrow.

The second part of looking ahead is examining demographic trends. Data points such as population and future housing needs can provide insight into what the future might be. In the last fifty years, the migration of people from America's Northeast and Midwest to the Sunbelt impacted housing development, politics, and even culture. Examining and evaluating current demographic trends enable us to gauge the direction of growth and to infer impacts on community associations. These data points can also help us gauge where people will choose to live, what housing they might prefer, and how community associations could help meet those needs.

Finally, with a foundation of the current state of community associations and insight into future demographic trends, we can apply that information and create visions of what the future might look like for community associations. While today's trends may not continue, they provide us with a basis for looking ahead and understanding the opportunities and challenges community associations might face. Collectively, this can provide guidance about how community associations can build a vibrant future.

## Taking a Snapshot

Before we delve into the future, it is worth examining facts and figures indicating that community associations have played an increasingly important role in housing markets for the last fifty years. Understanding these numbers is a point of departure for exploring future outcomes.

Community associations comprise a sizeable and growing share of the housing market. Interestingly, despite the tired tropes about community associations, residents overwhelmingly report satisfaction with them. What is more, in this time of tight government budgets, their self-funding nature and countless hours of volunteer work financially benefit the areas in which they exist. An understanding gleaned from these figures can help us uncover pathways community associations can use to shape their future. Securing this snapshot involves quantifying community associations, documenting this growing segment of housing, measuring resident support, and estimating the impact.

## Quantifying Community Associations

In 2023, the Foundation for Community Association Research estimated the United States was home to more than 75 million persons in 28 million housing units in approximately 365,000 community associations.[2] It also noted that approximately 58–63 percent of community associations consist of homeowners associations, with 35–40 percent consisting of condominium associations and 3–4 percent in the form of cooperatives. Approximately, 30 percent of housing in the United States is in a community association.

## Documenting the Growing Segment of Housing

That community associations comprise almost 30 percent of housing units in the United States is remarkable, given their emergence only slightly more than fifty years ago. The status quo is a far cry from 1970, when an estimated 10,000 community associations comprised 700,000 housing units—a mere 1 percent of housing units in community associations.[3]

## Measuring Resident Support

There is no doubt about it: Community associations are popular with their residents. Despite frequent stories on local news to the contrary, an overwhelming majority of residents in community associations report satisfaction. The Foundation for Community Association Research's most recent longitudinal survey of community associations confirms anew that 86 percent of residents are satisfied with community association living.

These numbers have remained relatively steady since 2005. Additionally, 82 percent report that their boards work in the best interests of their communities. This, by the way, stands in stark contrast to the approval rating of the U.S. Congress, which, as of 2024, was only 16 percent.[4]

Clearly, community associations are supported by their residents, and this support is a factor in their continued growth.

**Estimating the Impact**

Community associations are governed by elected volunteer leaders who live in communities in which their property values are protected. The impact of these people and circumstances can be measured. In 2023, for example, an estimated 2.5 million residents volunteered to lead their communities by serving as members of boards of directors or on committees.[5] Collectively, they contributed a whopping estimated 100.4 million hours of service.[6] With volunteer time valued at $33.48 per hour, these civic-minded residents provided more than $3.3 billion of service to their communities. That is amazing!

Also impactful are the enforceable rules they create and implement to protect the value of their homes in community associations. Specifically, it is estimated that homes in community associations are worth an average of 5–6 percent more than homes in legacy neighborhoods.[7]

## Summarizing the Data

The snapshot of community associations provided presents some compelling key points. These data points regarding the state of community associations are summarized here:

- Represent a growing segment of the housing market
- Enjoy the support of their residents
- Enhance the value of homes by 5–6 percent
- Are led by volunteers who contribute more than $3 billion in time to their communities

Clearly, community associations enjoy a strong base of support from their residents while providing a wide range of benefits that include volunteer contributions and enhanced property values. The data on which this conclusion is based are essential for our ability to forecast the future of community associations.

## Forecasting the Future

Our analysis of community associations enables us to conclude confidently that they will continue to be a valued part of America's housing stock in years ahead. Their positive role as a housing option for millions of residents is underscored by consistent findings regarding their high levels of satisfaction with the quality of their lives and with the governance overseen by their elected volunteer neighbors.

The challenge is determining what these data can tell us about the ability of community associations to meet housing needs in the future and whether they will remain a popular and viable housing model. This analysis requires us to apply what we know about community associations to what data tell us about what our communities and housing needs will look like over the next quarter of a century. Collectively, these elements will comprise the raw materials needed to make that forecast.

## PLANNING FOR FUTURE CHALLENGES

To connect the dots as we map out the future, we can build from our snapshot of the current role of community associations while considering challenges that might lie ahead. Absent a crystal ball, we can look to projections based on key points that, going forward, will likely impact the housing market and community associations.

Because communities are collections of residents, our future understanding needs to begin with an estimate of how many residents will need housing and what factors will impact them. By looking at some high-level demographic trends, we can build an understanding of what the people who will comprise our future communities will look like and what they will need.

We also need to gauge challenges that could emerge when housing them. As the population continues to expand, issues such as new housing construction, affordability, transportation, and environmental concerns will need to be addressed. Doing so will help us determine whether the flexibility and diversity of housing in community associations can continue to play a role in our future housing needs.

Understanding the projected demographic and housing data will enable us to connect the dots and determine how community associations or other models can help meet the challenges of tomorrow. Generally, the process comprises understanding demographic trends, identifying future housing challenges, and connecting the dots.

## Understanding Demographic Trends in the Next Twenty-Five Years

One way to establish a baseline for the future is to look at demographic trends. These trends can provide an understanding of what the world or at least the country may look like in twenty-five years. What is interesting about demographic change is that many of its aspects accrue over long periods, so jumping to a future date provides compelling points to consider when contemplating the potential role of community associations.

Clearly, an entire treatise could be filled with data and speculation about demographic trends. Leaving that to scholars, our focus will be on clear trends that continue to change and shape who we are, namely, a growing population, an increasingly older population, and one with increasing diversity.

### Growing Population

The world's population is expected to continue to grow over the next quarter-century. In the United States, the total population is expected to increase from 336 million in 2024 to more than 388 million by 2050.[8] Similarly, Canada's population is expected to increase from its current 40 million to more than 45 million in 2050.[9] This continued growth will require finding ways to house a projected 55 million more people before 2050.

## Aging Residents

As the population grows, a greater share of it will become increasingly older. Between 2020 and 2050, the number of persons aged sixty-five and older is expected to increase from 56 million to 85 million in the United States[10] and from 7 million to more than 11 million in Canada.[11]

These older persons will require additional resources to support independent living. What is more, upon retirement, many of them will have to rely on savings or pensions to cover expenses, which can create financial pressures.

## Increased Diversity

Former President Ronald Reagan paid tribute to the richness of diversity when he said, "[W]e draw our people—our strength—from every country and every corner of the world. And by doing so, we continuously renew and enrich our nation."[12] His words still ring true.

Over the next twenty-five years, the United States will diversify increasingly, with increases in representation from nearly all population groups. According to the U.S. Census, our African American population will increase by 30 percent and Hispanics by 60 percent, with the number of persons born elsewhere increasing to 17 percent.

With increasing diversity comes a wealth of opportunities as our communities benefit from a rich variety of points of view, life experiences, and cultural differences. This will empower future communities to address challenges with the help of additional perspectives as everyone learns from each other.

## Identifying Future Challenges

The housing market faces future challenges and opportunities that include not only the demographic changes noted here, but also a growing population, affordability issues, transportation needs, and environmental concerns.

The population of North America is projected to continue to expand, and with it, the need for millions more housing units and accompanying infrastructure to support them. Careful planning is necessary to preclude increased demand for housing resulting in affordability or transportation problems. Closely related are challenges caused by the environmental impact of concentrating housing in windstorm regions and the popularity of the sunny and arid Southwest. Cumulatively, these interconnected factors and many others will impact new home development and underscore the need for strategies to ensure future demands can be met. Before considering solutions to these potential problems, it behooves us to look specifically at housing, affordability, transportation, and environmental concerns.

## Housing

According to the U.S. Census Bureau, the current housing unit consists of approximately 2.5 persons.[13] Given this average, the economy will need to add up to 25 million housing units in the next twenty-five years to accommodate the growing population. Looking back at the previous quarter-century, it seems clear that rapid population growth in the Sunbelt states facilitated the rise of the community association housing model.

Part of the reason for the greater use of community associations is that by providing services to their residents, they lessen the financial burden on local governments.[14] Their ability to do so is a major reason they will remain an option for housing development.

## Affordability

In 2024, the median home price was $495,750 in the United States and $667,317 CAD in Canada.[15] This led to a housing affordability crisis, with residents in each country increasingly priced out of the market.

In addition to mortgage costs, residents in community associations are obligated to pay assessments to support the community and its amenities. Absent a change in income trends, future housing models will need to find solutions to address affordability issues.

## Transportation

As more persons migrate to cities and cities continue to expand, they will require greater investments in transportation and perhaps an examination of the density of development. Take, for example, Dallas, Texas. In 1960, the Dallas-Fort Worth Metroplex had a population of approximately 1.5 million residents.[16] In 2024, that number is estimated at 6.7 million living in approximately 9,286 square miles, which makes it larger than six U.S. states.[17]

Houston is even bigger. Both cities are characterized by sprawling suburbs with single-family homes. To accommodate additional population while keeping commutes somewhat manageable will require more highways, public transit, and other options. This challenge can be seen in growing cities across the continent.

One option is to densify neighborhoods closer to city centers with condominium towers and apartment blocks. The underlying point is that more people take up more area and require greater, more efficient means to get from homes to their work sites.

## Environment

When it comes to the environment, I am not a Malthusian who believes that our food supply cannot keep pace with our growing numbers and that disease, famine, and other calamities are therefore inevitable. I have enough faith in the agility of our economic system and the entrepreneurial spirit of our citizens to know we can adapt and deploy solutions to address many challenges. That said, until such investments and solutions are implemented, environmental impacts could shape the housing markets in the future. Two come to mind, namely, water and natural disasters. As the desert Southwest continues to attract new residents, there is increasing pressure on limited water supplies, which, combined with an ongoing and historic drought, have impacted available supplies and may soon impact development if innovative solutions are not found.

Similarly, oceanfront development remains popular, and as more people flock to seaside abodes, the impact of hurricanes increases. This has been a factor in their rapidly increasing insurance rates. To allow continued development in these areas in the future will require finding solutions to these issues.

## Connecting Dots

As we project demographic and housing trends into the future, several challenges emerge from the data. The picture painted is clear, but we need to connect the dots. A continued growing population will require the construction of millions more housing units. Additionally, an aging and increasingly diverse population will likely demand housing that provides appropriate and diversified amenities and social engagement that will meet their needs—and differences.

Additionally, the need to build housing for an estimated additional 25 million housing units will favor developments that can be built without further financial burden on local governments while providing flexible neighborhood-level rules to promote engagement and address emerging issues. The community association housing model has been well-positioned to meet those needs over the last fifty years and remains a viable option for meeting the challenges ahead. Future planning requires more than identifying trends and projecting them into the future. It requires connecting the dots by recognizing the interconnectedness of trends and planning accordingly.

### MEETING FUTURE NEEDS

The community association model remains ready to meet the challenges of the future. Its strength is twofold. First, it puts the governance of the community directly in the hands of its residents. Second, the structure of a community association is resilient and can be adapted to address the needs of community residents today and in the future.

Community associations provide flexibility. Their self-governance model can be applied to single-family, multi-use, and multifamily developments. This flexibility lends itself to addressing the challenges of meeting the needs for millions more housing units while addressing emerging challenges related to affordability, transportation, and environmental concerns, and accommodating the growing diversity and aging of our population.

Similarly, preparing for this possible future will require focusing on fundamentals. Ensuring adequate funding of association operations and setting aside funds for replacement reserves are critical for associations now and in the future. Because existing associations will need to update and replace infrastructure as their residents age, ensuring funding now will mitigate impacts on aging residents. Such planning for them in the years ahead includes providing for mobility issues and evolving social engagement. Doing so will ensure the community association model continues to meet residents' needs.

Finally, to address the challenges outlined in this chapter, community associations can adapt their governance structures to accommodate changing needs. This can include leveraging community rules to mitigate environmental concerns and addressing issues of limited space for new housing. By recognizing and adapting to the potential needs of tomorrow, the association model will continue to benefit communities well into the future. This means providing flexibility, addressing fundamentals, and expanding and adapting current models.

## Providing Flexibility

Community associations have built-in flexibility to address the current and future needs of residents. Associations can range in size from two or three units to entire communities with thousands of housing units. The common ownership model of community infrastructure also provides a range of benefits to the community and the municipality in which it exists. By providing and paying for their own amenities, community associations expand housing in growing communities while minimizing the impact on local governments. Additionally, the type of community associations that include condominiums, cooperatives, and homeowners associations allow for a mix of housing types at varying price points.

The success of community associations to date sets the stage for their continued growth in meeting future housing challenges. The ability to build communities while minimizing the impact on local government will help meet the demand for millions of additional housing units needed in the years ahead. Likewise, the common ownership elements and ability to impose rules within the community will allow for the emergence of more mixed-use communities that can be built near transportation hubs to mitigate the transportation needs of a growing population.

Finally, as self-governing entities, community associations reflect the values and preferences of their residents. This self-governing model and a commitment to community engagement can allow community associations to adapt to the growing diversity of our communities while incorporating the experiences of their diverse residents.

The flexibility needed by community associations to meet future needs relates to meeting demand, exploring mixed-use developments, supporting aging residents, and accommodating environmental preferences for water conservation and renewable energy.

## Meeting Demand

Community associations are a good option for meeting the projected need for up to 25 million additional housing units in the next twenty-five years. Because they support their own cost of development and infrastructure, they allow growing municipalities to expand. Simultaneously, their diversity of housing types and ability to impose rules within communities will result in varied housing types, price points, and amenities to meet housing needs. These, in turn, potentially will address affordability issues and provide options for aging residents.

## Exploring Mixed-Use Developments

By offering alternatives for those who dislike long commutes and prefer to live closer to the offerings of city centers, mixed-use community associations are an example of how the community association model can meet current and future needs. Mixed-use developments built near or in city centers offer the ability to house more residents closer to employment, entertainment, and commercial hubs while limiting impacts on transportation infrastructure. With amenities such as retail stores, restaurants, and entertainment within the development, such communities promote walking. When such communities are built near transit hubs, they provide additional incentives for residents and visitors to use transit and reduce overall traffic. Additionally, mixed-use developments lend themselves to a mix of housing options at differing price points suitable for the economic diversity of residents.

## Supporting Aging Residents

The community association model has two major advantages for serving an aging population. First, the built-in social component provides a ready-made structure through which residents can combat feelings of isolation that often accompany aging. Similarly, community-based rules can promote community structures that help meet the needs of a growing senior population. New community associations can include accessory dwelling units, or attached "mother-in-law" suites, to allow multigenerational families to care for each other.

Active adult communities across the country demonstrate the benefits for those fifty-five and older by creating engaging communities and amenities that will most likely meet their needs and interests. Scaling this model to create housing options at varying price points can provide additional housing choices for the growing senior population. More specifically, cottage-style communities with common cooking facilities and activity centers are emerging models that can help provide options for aging residents.

## Accommodating Environmental Preferences

Community associations are well-positioned to address and reflect the environmental preferences of their residents. Current and future environmental issues such as water scarcity and sustainable energy are being addressed widely, and solutions can be expanded under the community association model. The ability of community associations to adopt and enforce rules can provide environmental benefits, while common areas can provide space to create wildlife habitats or space for sustainable energy installations.

**Conserving water.** First, many community associations in more arid regions demonstrate their ability to promote more sustainable living. Some communities are being built with gray water systems that allow treated wastewater to be used for landscaping irrigation, thus conserving potable water for its proper use. Additionally, the ability of a community association to regulate property within the community allows residents to adopt natural landscaping rules that require native species for landscaping use, which reduces the use of water for maintaining water-hungry, nonnative plants.

**Renewable energy.** The common ownership element of community associations also lends itself to promoting renewable energy. Common space can be set aside for solar farms, wind power, or other uses that can reduce energy costs. To reflect the changing times, current rules that may inhibit renewable energy installations on individual units can be reconsidered and updated on a community-by-community basis to reflect the evolving needs, interests, and priorities of a community.

**Adapting old rules.** Community associations are sometimes criticized for their perceived anti-environmental rules. Their rules, however, can and should change over time to reflect the changing perspectives of residents. Rules that restrict environmentally friendly practices—such as clotheslines or home solar installations—once considered critical to protect property values, may now seem archaic to some.

Community rules should be periodically reevaluated against current preferences by the community. The community association model's adaptability is an element of its resilience. Being open to adapting rules to meet future challenges demonstrates the value of self-governance.

## Addressing Fundamentals

To remain a relevant housing option, community associations will need to focus on the emerging challenges and opportunities ahead. Having established that community associations remain popular with their residents, associations will need to double down on the fundamentals to ensure they are prepared for tomorrow. In the next quarter-century, communities will face a host of challenges that include aging residents, updating or replacing community infrastructure, and finding novel and timely ways to continue to engage residents. An awareness of what the future holds and how to meet its challenges will ensure community associations can remain resilient in the face of changing demographics and housing needs.

A focus on fundamentals is especially important when considering the future. Building realistic budgets that fund current operations and setting aside funds for reserves are essential. It also is important for boards of directors to understand that aging residents may require the community association to adapt rules, amenities, and activities to meet their needs over time, including by maintaining assessment stability, updating common areas, ensuring accessibility for those with disabilities, and providing appropriate engagement opportunities. Addressing these critical subjects is necessary not only to meet community needs now, but also to prepare to meet them in years to come.

## Ensuring Adequate Funding

Ensuring adequate funding for a community association consists of two critical elements. First is providing sufficient funds to allow for the day-to-day operations of the community. Annual funding includes setting aside funds to maintain common elements, obtain appropriate insurance coverage, and maintain the social fabric of the community. Second is setting aside funds to ensure any future repair or replacement costs of common elements in the community will be covered. These reserve funds ensure that when the time comes to engage in these costly expenses, funding exists to cover the projects.

Failure to fund reserves means the true cost of community association living is not being covered. In such cases, replacement projects that emerge in the future could require higher assessments, a loan, a sizeable special assessment, or a combination of all three. None of these is good.

## Preparing for Aging Residents

Simply stated, current and future community associations should be cognizant of the needs of current and future older residents. For current associations, ensuring sufficient funding for current operating costs and future replacement reserves is critical. Older residents sending their children off to college or transitioning to retirement savings and fixed incomes may be more sensitive (and vulnerable) to unexpected costs such as special assessments or sudden assessment increases.

Committing to appropriate funding today fosters the ability to maintain stable assessments in the future. Likewise, maintaining and adapting engagement programs will help ensure social interaction to combat isolation and foster a sense of community. Both support the mental and emotional health of all residents, but especially of seniors.

Finally, as community common elements undergo repairs or replacement, keeping in mind the needs of aging residents and potential mobility issues will help keep residents active in the community. By addressing these elements or planning for them in future communities, associations can create a supportive environment and remain a relevant housing choice for seniors.

**Maintaining Robust Engagement**

As discussed in chapter 11, community engagement is a critical element that defines the notion of community. Its importance moving into the future cannot be overstated. This is especially true as our communities continue to reflect the nation's growing diversity.

Providing the opportunity to allow residents to connect and build rapport and trust can facilitate understanding in a more diverse future. Moreover, active engagement offers a counterpoint to feelings of isolation that accompany aging and our more digital world. To address these future challenges and ensure community associations remain relevant, providing means for residents to connect is essential.

Engagement is part of the process of building personal relationships and a sense of belonging. It mitigates the tearing of our social fabric in a digital world. Community associations have the ability, through their physical and governance structure, to continue to meet this need.

## Expanding and Adapting Current Models

When anticipating the broad set of challenges to come, community associations are well-positioned to continue to expand housing options, address emergent needs, and successfully serve their residents. To ensure vibrant future community associations, they must remain vigilant in serving their residents while adapting to and addressing changing needs. Preparing for that future will require a thoughtful approach to keeping what works while not needlessly retaining rules or policies that no longer meet the demands of the moment.

Because community associations are empowered to govern themselves, the ability to meet the challenges to come is in the hands of residents and the boards who serve them. Through attentive and responsive governance, communities can continue to secure a bright future. Expanding and adapting current models of community associations is a matter of keeping what works, adapting to change, and securing the future.

## Keeping What Works

Everyone knows (or should know) the maxim, "If it ain't broke, don't fix it." Many aspects of the community association model serve residents well and will continue to provide relevant solutions to meet housing challenges in the future.

Chief among these characteristics is the self-governing nature of community associations. Having the ability to prioritize matters important to the community allows an array of solutions to emerge that reflect the experiences and priorities unique to each community. Whether the issue is affordability, environmental matters, or aging in place, community residents are in the best position to develop solutions to meet their needs. Likewise, the ability of community associations to allow growing municipalities to add new development while minimizing impacts on local budgets is a factor that will help meet the housing challenges to come.

Finally, the ability of community associations as a development model to provide a wide array of housing unit sizes and price points can assist in creating housing solutions for a greater range of buyers entering the ownership market. Preserving and protecting communities' self-governing nature and the flexible, rules-based development that characterizes community associations are keys to their playing a role in meeting future challenges. Generally, keeping what works includes flexible development, changeable rules, and neighborhood governance.

**Flexible development.** The community association model can assist in meeting future housing needs by leveraging its flexible development model. Because of their varying housing options, greater density, and varied resident amenities, community associations can offer future homeowners a rich variety of housing and price points.

Mixed-use developments also offer an approach that allows for more efficient living with shops and entertainment proximate to housing, thus reducing the need for more cars. Leveraging the community association model to build housing that addresses needs at all price points can help meet the challenge of providing the millions of housing units that will be needed in years to come.

**Changeable rules.** The ability of community associations to adopt and enforce rules has many benefits. First and foremost, it helps preserve and enhance property values. Studies indicate that homes in a community association are worth more than those in legacy neighborhoods. Additionally, the ability of the community, working through its board of directors, to adopt or update rules means that emerging issues such as water conservation or alternative energy can be accommodated based on the collective changing preferences of residents. This allows the emergence of multiple solutions to challenges based on the experiences and wishes of a community.

**Neighborhood governance.** Governance works best when it is close to those it serves. The community association model provides for neighborhood-level governance that, when fully realized, allows for effective management of community operations. Data support this finding, with a supermajority of community association residents repeatedly reporting over time their satisfaction with community association living. To continue to thrive, the elements of self-government should be preserved and enhanced. This allows communities to chart their own paths while preserving scarce local and state resources to address other needs.

## Adapting to Change

While the community association model has many aspects that will help ensure its vitality and contributions in the future, changing circumstances will also require community associations to adapt to meet the future needs of residents. As residents age, communities will need to prepare for the issues that accompany that trend. Likewise, as communities age, associations must concurrently plan for addressing repair and replacement costs.

Keeping a close eye on governance fundamentals will help ensure a positive outcome. Similarly, communities should not hesitate to update or overhaul outdated community rules that no longer reflect current preferences. Such adaptability can allow communities to help resolve challenges, including those involving the environment. Finally, demographic changes will require communities to fortify their engagement programs to continue to connect residents in the common cause of building a true community.

**Funding reserves.** All community associations face a time when they have to make major repairs or replace community infrastructure and amenities. Such efforts can be costly and are typically funded by reserve funds that were set aside for that purpose over time. Board members are often tempted to keep assessments artificially low by deferring reserve contributions and putting off major projects. If they do, the expenses will have to be borne by future residents, typically through a costly special assessment. This can hit residents who are aging in place particularly hard, particularly if the assessment comes at or close to their retirement. An element of keeping community associations a viable option is for boards to recommit to community fundamentals that include funding reserves as a means of preparing to pay for these future costs.

**Considering environment.** Not long ago, issues such as renewable energy, water conservation, and other environmental concerns were not priorities for homeowners. The rules from that time reflect this, with restrictions on solar installations, mandates for water-intensive landscaping, and bans on clotheslines. Some communities are seeing a shift in attitudes about these matters as drought and higher energy and water costs impact their pocketbooks.

Community associations have the power to adapt and change rules that no longer suit their residents. For communities in which these issues are a priority, adapting and updating rules positions them to be part of the solution and perhaps reduce utility expenses in the process. Communities can and should use their rulemaking and rule-changing power to address these issues as directed by residents.

## Securing the Future

Community associations can continue to be a dynamic part of securing our housing future. To do so, they must continue to play to their strengths. This includes remaining open to the evolving needs of their residents and remaining flexible in providing diverse housing options at varying price points to accommodate varying market needs. Their flexibility in developing communities with mixed housing options can also help address housing needs and provide greater convenience for their residents.

A key element of securing the future for community associations is a commitment to the fundamentals. Ensuring budgets address current and future costs will help protect aging residents from costly special assessments. Likewise, boards should be open to reviewing rules regularly to adapt to changing economic and social preferences.

This adaptability will allow community rules to remain relevant and address emerging challenges as expressed by resident preferences. The element of community-based, enforceable rules not only protects residential property values, but also provides a mechanism for adapting to current economic and environmental needs. Similarly, facilitating robust community engagement can assist communities in adapting to growing diversity and aging residents. To repeat: Proactive community leadership is key to unlocking the potential that exists in all communities, and it is also how we can ensure positive future outcomes.

## CONCLUSION

When sketching a picture of the future, we can look at board trends and current practices to extrapolate potential outcomes. Such envisioning can help provide us with a preliminary road map to prepare for anticipated challenges. While such an approach does not address all potential variables, it helps position us and our communities to follow the suggestion of Dennis Gabor's assertion that the future is what we create. His wise words imply that community associations must take action to construct a future aligned with their residents' desires. Boards of directors can capitalize on this vision while exercising their ability to unite residents in self-governance, thereby collaborating in shaping their future.

That journey can be guided by a deep dive into the present to understand the elements of the community association model that provide resiliency and allow them to adapt to future challenges. The rapid expansion and popularity of community associations is, in part, rooted in the benefits of self-governance. Fortifying an understanding of community association dynamics positions us to prepare for and shape the future.

Given that understanding, communities can then look to forecasts that lend insight into what future communities will look like and what challenges they may face. Reviewing population trends and housing needs portend their diversity and how they can adapt to meet those changing needs. Indeed, understanding demographic trends and current success allows them to begin to trace the shape of future communities.

Through this process of investigation, reflection, and envisioning, community associations can position themselves to continue to be a leading housing choice with the means to build community well into the future. Predicting that future is difficult, but preparing for it and being open to adaptation and growth can empower community associations to shape their future to benefit their residents.

## QUESTIONS TO CONSIDER

1. How does your board or community consider potential future challenges in its governance or planning for the community?

2. Based on your experience, which elements of community associations support their success?

3. Which elements of community association governance would benefit from change?

4. How does your community association handle reserve funding? Is there any consideration or discussion about how underfunding reserves could impact future costs?

5. What steps does your board take to review rules periodically regarding their relevance or benefit to the community?

6. Has your board ever eliminated a rule that had become archaic or irrelevant? If so, what was the rule, and how was it changed?

7. Does your community consider environmental sustainability in its rule-making process? If so, how?

8. What changes have you seen in your community in the last ten years?

9. What changes do you anticipate seeing in your community in the next ten years?

10. What do you think the biggest challenge to your community will be in the next twenty-five years?

## CHAPTER 14

# Coping with a More Regulated Future

*The government is the strongest of which every man feels himself part of.*

—THOMAS JEFFERSON,
Third President of the United States

## CHAPTER INTRODUCTION

One of the thematic elements woven throughout this book is the importance of participating in one's community association and engaging with others. This is the essence of community. On a larger scale, and perhaps when various factors align just right, the same can be said of government. Jefferson's words are a guide for examining the impact of government on community associations. To paraphrase them, government works best when we engage in guiding it and shaping its results. For residents of community associations and their boards of directors, this statement is especially true. Because community associations have an impact on a family's most valuable possession, its home, they invoke passionate arguments that can swing the pendulum between greater autonomy and greater regulation.

Community associations are primarily entities of state law, but legislative activities and the resulting regulations they impose can come from all levels of government. Understanding how federal, state, and even local units of government can impact them can help their boards of directors comply with any requirements they impose, engage in the process of information, and shape future regulatory proposals.

Like many areas of the economy or society, community associations are subject to a trend of regulations that include state regulatory frameworks. These often provide a clear legal infrastructure that can result in consistency and stability. They can also include a range of regulations that can impact the authority of the community association board or remove an association's ability to act on a specific matter. Whether one agrees with these regulations, the trend is clear: There is an increasingly greater number of proposed legislative acts that can impact community associations.

In the final analysis, it is up to dedicated residents and board members in community associations to, as Jefferson suggests, become part of the legislative process to help inform proposed regulation and ensure its optimal impact. Shaping the debate is a key factor in moving toward a future in which community associations either benefit from effective and efficient regulation or cope with a patchwork of reactionary mandates.

## REGULATING COMMUNITY ASSOCIATIONS

Regulations impacting community associations come from a variety of sources and levels of government. Although most of these regulations are at the state level because they deal with real estate, federal regulatory proposals and municipal ordinances also play a part in creating the regulatory environment.

Understanding how laws and regulations apply to community associations and where they originate can assist boards of directors in their compliance efforts. More importantly, it can also help them engage constructively and positively in the legislative process to shape future regulations that are optimal for community success.

Starting at the federal level, a host of laws and regulations impact community associations. These laws typically encompass broad categories such as fair housing, mortgage qualification criteria, or other broad-based regulations. While not the primary source of community regulation, they are impactful.

The primary source of laws significantly impacting community associations is the state or provincial level. In most jurisdictions, laws impacting real estate are the purview of the state or provincial government.

Finally, municipalities and courts also play a role in regulating community associations. By the very nature of the level of government, their impact is local and limited.

Knowing the range of government impact on a community association can position its board of directors to comply with any requirements and, more importantly, to attempt to amend current laws or pending proposals through legislative engagement. Developing this knowledge begins with an overview of federal, state, and municipal impacts.

## Federal Regulatory Impacts

Federal impacts on community associations tend to originate in broader efforts to address important issues at the national level rather than legislation specifically focused on them. Efforts to ensure fair access to housing for all, regulations about mortgage lending and qualification, and broader corporate governance mandates are perfect examples. Among these are the Corporate Transparency Act (CTA) and regulations established by the Federal Housing Administration (FHA), Fannie Mae, and Freddie Mac.

### Corporate Transparency Act

The Corporate Transparency Act (CTA) is a law enacted by Congress in 2021 to increase awareness about the ownership and operations of businesses. It was part of a congressional effort to combat money laundering, financial fraud, and terrorist financing by ensuring transparency of ownership and limiting the ability to mask ownership through shell companies.

Although community associations were not targets of this law, the definition of a corporate entity in the legislation covers them. The act requires corporate entities to file reports with the federal government that include personal information for beneficial owners, which in the case of community associations, would be the current members of the board. The law has been subject to litigation and attempts to remove community associations from its provisions, but resolution was pending at the time of publication. Failure to comply with the provisions of the CTA can trigger substantial civil and criminal penalties.

**Federal Housing Administration**

The primary mission of the Federal Housing Administration (FHA) is to provide access to affordable mortgages. A common financing vehicle for many first-time homebuyers, it provides affordable mortgages and is usually used to purchase condominiums.

The agency's regulations impose requirements condominium associations must meet for any purchaser to qualify for an FHA-backed mortgage. Although those regulations are not mandatory for condominiums, if they are not met, no FHA-backed mortgages will be issued for purchases in the association. This illustrates the agency's indirect impact on community associations. Such impactful requirements include the following:

- Adequate budget with at least 10 percent of funds set aside for reserves.
- No more than 35 percent of the association area can be commercial.
- At least 50 percent of the units must be owner-occupied.
- No more than 15 percent of the units can be sixty days delinquent in their assessments.

## Fannie Mae/Freddie Mac Criteria

Originally chartered by the federal government, Fannie Mae and Freddie Mac are government-sponsored enterprises (GSEs) that operate as private entities. Their primary role is to maintain liquidity in the mortgage markets by purchasing mortgages and their securitization for investors.

Unlike FHA, Fannie Mae and Freddie Mac provide the vast majority of mortgages issued in the United States. As part of their mortgage qualification criteria, GSEs have standards for loans issued to community associations for homes. If a community association is not in compliance with them, it can be locked out of most mortgage funding for prospective purchasers. Such results exemplify how these two entities impact community associations.

**Fannie Mae Criteria.** Here is a sampling of Fannie Mae's criteria:[1]

- There must be adequate funding for insurance deductibles.
- At least 10 percent of the budget must be for reserves.
- No more than 15 percent of income is from rental or leasing of commercial parking facilities.
- An association cannot need critical repairs.
- An association cannot have unfunded repairs totaling more than $10,000 per unit.

**Freddie Mac Criteria.** Here is a sampling of Freddie Mac's criteria for funding:[2]

- There must be adequate funding for insurance deductibles.
- Less than 10 percent set aside for reserves, provided the association has a reserve study that supports the lesser amount and the association is following its reserve study.
- No more than 15 percent of owners are more than sixty days delinquent in paying their assessments.

- Commercial or nonresidential space may not be more than 35 percent of the total above- and below-grade square footage.
- Extensive reserve study requirements must be funded.

## State Law Impacts

Under their regulatory systems, state and provincial governments potentially have the greatest impact on community associations. The underlying reason for this is that they regulate real estate and a majority of housing issues.

Community associations, as legal entities, are formed under state laws that can impose a host of restrictions on them. As discussed in more detail in the legislative trends section, the current trend in state regulation is to impose greater restrictions on the authority of community association boards of directors.

Generally, state law impacts community associations in very specific ways. First, foundational acts are laws that govern the formation, governance, termination, and operation of community associations. These acts provide a common basis for all community associations formed after their enactment. They provide an enumerated set of powers for the board, establish processes for the formation or termination of a community association, and define other guidelines to ensure their ongoing operation.

State governments also impact community associations through proposals to mandate certain actions or restrict their authority in a given area. These proposals are typically instigated when a board oversteps its authority or takes actions that generate negative publicity. Boards should be aware of these trends to ensure they are not the source of such proposals and to provide input when misguided proposals emerge.

## Municipal Impacts

Local units of government, such as municipalities or counties and the court system, can also impact community associations. The regulatory actions of local units of government can impact only community associations in their respective areas of jurisdiction. Local regulations can include land use requirements, environmental mandates, or other directives. Unique local regulations impacting community associations are exemplified by a county-level building recertification requirement, a county-level community association oversight commission, and bans on short-term rentals.

### Miami-Dade County Building Recertification

Miami, Florida, is a popular vacation and retirement destination. It is also a market that is rich in condominium associations. In 1975, Miami-Dade County officials passed an ordinance requiring condominium buildings to be recertified by building officials after forty years. This requirement was intended to help ensure the safety of aging condominium buildings. One of the first such laws in the country, it seemed prescient in the wake of the Champlain Tower condominium collapse. Soon after that horrific tragedy, the state of Florida adopted similar statewide requirements.

### Montgomery County Oversight Commission

In response to rapid development in the late 1980s, Montgomery County, Maryland, established a Commission on Common Ownership Communities. The commission provides resources for board members, assists in disputes between residents and their associations, and promotes the rights and responsibilities of community association living. Authorized to act with the power of a court for community association disputes within the county, it can also levy fines for violations and settle challenges to rules adopted by a community association board.

### Short-Term Rental Bans

Often-heated debates about short-term rentals and their impact on neighbors and housing affordability have caused many municipalities to ban or regulate them. Exemplified by Airbnb and VRBO, these housing units are typically rented for thirty or fewer days. Their emergence as alternatives to hotels and as ways for investor owners to make money on their units has triggered a wave of regulations.

Because of their growing popularity, by 2024, municipalities had adopted hundreds of local regulations impacting short-term rentals. These can range from outright bans to requiring them to pay taxes similar to those paid by hotels.

## SPOTTING TRENDS IN COMMUNITY ASSOCIATION LEGISLATION

Community associations have long been defined by their ability to self-govern. Residents elect their boards, which are tasked with establishing and enforcing rules for the benefit of their communities and those who live there. This autonomy, however, is the growing focus of regulators at all levels of government. Sometimes, the proposals they consider are the result of a need in the community association space for clearer guidance. Other times, the regulations are the result of perceived overzealous acts by community association boards. As a result, there is a growing trend of more regulation of community associations.

The current trend in the regulation of community associations via state legislation can be classified in three categories, namely, restricting the authority of a community association or its board, mandating or prohibiting specific actions, and updating foundational laws that provide a legal framework for community associations.

These laws ensure consistency among associations in specific jurisdictions and provide baseline requirements for them. Regardless of the intent of such actions, one aspect is certain: Community associations are the focus of a growing array of legislation by state governments.

## Restricting Association Authority

As self-governing entities, community associations are authorized to set and enforce their own rules. This authority allows them to be laboratories for democracy. Each community can adjust its rules to reflect the preferences of its members.

There is a growing trend, however, for state legislatures or agencies to step in and make changes over specific subject matters when those preferences conflict with changing social norms or when boards of directors are perceived as unfair or overzealous. This is evident in legislative proposals that emerge regularly in state legislatures. Sometimes, the focus is on environmental issues such as the impact of electric vehicles. Other times, it is on restrictions such as how much an association can charge to recoup costs imposed on it by the government itself. While not exhaustive, the following examples provide a snapshot of the types of restrictions that have emerged in the last several years.

### Disclosure Fees

Most jurisdictions mandate that prospective homebuyers in a community association be provided a long list of documents referred to as "disclosure documents" or "disclosure packets." The documents provide the prospective purchaser with critical information about the community association. They enable purchasers to determine if a community association is a good fit for their lifestyle and, more importantly, provide them with financial information to assess the fiscal health of the community.

Disclosure documents are an important consumer protection that are required in most states. Because the sale of a home is a private transaction between two individuals, the fee associated with producing the documents is allocated by the market to the buyer or seller. At the urging of other interest groups, such as realtors, many states have proposed capping the fees charged for these documents or requiring community associations to subsidize their production. This increases costs for community associations and limits consumer choices. Accordingly, many management companies have invested in systems to be able to produce these documents in short order to facilitate the sale.

Fee cap proposals can limit choices and force a community association to subsidize the expense of a private home sale.

## Electric Vehicle Charging Stations

Another emerging trend that reflects changing technology and social norms is the emergence of legislation to facilitate installing electric charging stations in community associations, especially in condominiums, where parking may be in a common garage or parking structure. At the time many of these facilities were constructed, electric vehicles were the stuff of science fiction. As a result, most common garages are not wired to allow for individual metering, which creates challenges for both electric vehicle owners and the community association.

An emerging legislative trend is to mandate the provision of charging spaces for electric cars. While the overall goal of such proposals is worthwhile, they definitely have a financial and potential legal impact on communities.

## Artificial Turf

The ability of community associations to enforce rules related to landscaping and yard upkeep positions them well to adapt to changing environmental needs. It seems suboptimal to eliminate their ability to choose approaches that work best for them, including environmentally sustainable solutions such as xeriscaping, hardscaping, or using native plants. Several states, however, are considering limiting the ability of community associations to regulate the installation of artificial turf, which is sometimes made with oil-based ingredients and may have environmental impacts that have yet to emerge.

Legislators' focus on such proposals is important, but it could be harmful. My opinion is that they could reach their purported legislative goals more successfully by providing choices for communities instead of imposing one-size-fits-all solutions that are likely to fail.

## Mandating or Prohibiting Actions

In addition to restricting the authority of a community association, legislation can also mandate that community associations must or cannot perform certain activities. As with other regulatory actions, these laws are intended to address perceived shortcomings in community associations.

Recent trends in community association regulation, for example, were triggered by the tragic collapse of Champlain Towers South in Surfside, Florida; concerns about inadequate funding of community association reserves; and accusations of overzealous enforcement of rules and assessments. Regardless of their intent, the reality is that such proposals impose mandates on the board or its residents for better or for worse, often pertaining to building safety, reserve studies, and rules and assessment enforcement.

### Building Safety

Community association infrastructure ages and will eventually need to be rehabilitated or replaced. This, of course, ensures the integrity and safety of the structures, especially condominium towers. Building safety became a priority issue in many states in 2021 after the Champlain Towers South resulted in the deaths of ninety-eight community association residents.

Although the county in which the association was located had a building recertification requirement, the shock of the tragedy focused attention on building safety and maintenance. Florida imposed new inspection requirements for condominium buildings, and GSEs such as Freddie Mae adopted maintenance requirements for mortgage qualification.

**Reserve Studies**

Reserve studies are critical for community associations because they are linked to building safety. They provide an outlook on future repair and replacement costs for community infrastructure as well as a pathway for setting aside funds for future repairs.

A well-funded reserve plan ensures repairs can be undertaken timely and that financial resources are available to pay for them. These two aspects of planning became an emergent issue as interest in them intensified after the Surfside collapse. In 2024, for example, seven states considered legislation focused on reserve studies and funding.[3] As community associations built over the last thirty years begin to address aging infrastructure, attention to this issue likely will increase.

**Rules and Assessment Enforcement**

Rules and assessments are the bookends that support community associations. Rule enforcement creates and supports a framework ensuring a vibrant and attractive community to protect property values. Rule compliance, when corrective action is not taken, usually results in fines. Assessments, by comparison, pay for community operations, upkeep of community amenities, insurance, social activities, and other expenses. Unpaid assessments impose costs on all residents of the community. As such, assessment delinquencies result in fines, late fees, and, in rare cases, foreclosure.

Without these two fundamental elements, the common ownership model of community associations would begin to unravel. Simultaneously, however, legislators feel pressure to curb association authority in these areas when confronted with rare but compelling examples of overzealous boards and consumer harm. Legislative restrictions on community associations' authority in these areas are not uncommon, as exemplified by the seven states that focused on these issues in 2024.[4] Their actions are a good reminder for boards to act consistently and prudently and consider the impact of overzealous enforcement.

## Updating Foundational Legislation

Typically nonprofit corporations, community associations are supported by a variety of state laws. In their early days, their legal frameworks mostly reflected state nonprofit and corporate laws.

As community associations became more widespread, states began to update their laws to address their unique aspects, including common ownership. A progression of regulatory frameworks emerged that included horizontal property and condominium acts and the Property Owners Association/Homeowners Association Acts. These new laws provided legal frameworks for governing documents, establishing or terminating an association, and consumer protection. Although somewhat technical, they act as the operating system for community associations, a set of instructions that guide and direct community associations in a jurisdiction.

### Property or Homeowners Association Acts

A property owners association or a homeowners association act is a state statute that provides a common framework for homeowners associations. These laws include provisions focused on establishing, operating, and terminating a homeowners association. They also enumerate board powers and can mandate the inclusion of certain provisions in governing documents or restrict the community association's authority in certain areas.

State laws are helpful in providing a standard framework for condominium associations in the jurisdiction. This facilitates consistency regarding topical areas such as board authority, voting requirements, homeowner protections, and assessment collection.

## Condominium Acts

Condominium acts provide a legal framework supporting condominium associations in a jurisdiction. They provide a prospective framework for what elements should be included in condominium governing documents, define board authority, clarify authority in limited cases in which governing documents are silent, and can enhance or restrict the authority of the community association board. As with property owners association acts, condominium acts provide a consistent set of requirements, rights, and obligations for any condominium established after the act's effective date.

## Uniform Common Interest Ownership Act

The Uniform Common Interest Ownership Act (UCIOA) is a model act developed by the Uniform Law Commission.[5] In effect, it is a template designed to help states update their laws governing community associations. UCIOA and its companion Common Interest Owners Bill of Rights provide a process for addressing issues that may arise from outdated or older state laws that govern community associations. If adopted by a state, UCIOA provides a modernized update to supplement existing HOA or condominium acts. Unlike current statutory regimes that typically have different statutes for condominiums and homeowners associations, UCIOA provides one regulatory framework for existing community association models.

The most recent version of UCIOA was updated in 2021 and includes a variety of provisions that deal with the creation, governance, operation, and consumer protections in community associations. Although these uniform acts do not get a lot of attention, they provide a highly structured and informed legal infrastructure to support community associations. As of 2024, seven states have adopted a form of UCIOA.[6]

## SHAPING THE LEGISLATIVE DEBATE

Thousands of legislative measures that could impact community associations are introduced each year in state legislatures across North America. Unfortunately, too often they are written in response to common misperceptions that community associations are unpopular.

The importance of residents of community associations participating in the legislative process to shape the debate cannot be overstated. By expressing their insight and experience and making their feelings known, collectively they can help ensure legislation is grounded in reality and more helpful than harmful.

Having served in the Texas House of Representatives and in the Texas Senate, including as chair of the Senate Committee on Business and Commerce, I know firsthand the impact informed stakeholders can have on pending legislation. If those impacted by legislative proposals do not speak out, legislators will assume, perhaps wrongfully, that certain legislation is acceptable. When they do speak, stakeholders can change the course of a potential law, preferably for the better. Making one's voice heard makes a difference.

Understanding the basics of the legislative process, the situational context in which particular legislation was developed, and the accompanying politics are essential for advocates. Too many of them, for example, lobby for or against a bill too late, sometimes after it was passed and sent to the governor for consideration. Their success can be enhanced by a simple overview of the process and its related deadlines, followed by tracking the progress of the legislation in question.

Many proposals related to community associations emerge from the rare but real situational context in which a board of directors or community has acted inappropriately. Often, they were crafted in response to constituents who complained about the status quo and, consequently, reflect one side of the story. This dichotomy sometimes allows these outlier situations to set the parameters of debate for an issue. By engaging in the process, residents and advocates for community associations can ensure all sides of the issues are presented and considered.

Making community associations' voices heard in the legislative process is crucial to ensuring a fair regulatory regime. Engaging with legislators can seem like an insurmountable challenge, but working with the community's professional partners can help board members and residents learn to identify, interpret, and track legislative proposals before suggesting how to improve them.

Suggestions can be made while visiting legislators and/or with their staffs at their respective state capitol or district offices. Inviting them to community association events is also an opportunity to influence their perspectives on the benefits of community associations. Finally, writing, emailing, or calling state or provincial elected officials to express opinions about community association matters can yield positive results. The bottom line is sharing experiences and insights to better inform the process.

The legislative process is designed to reflect the views of the majority rather than of a few disgruntled, opportunistic, or ill-advised persons. Accordingly, it is imperative that community associations collaborate in presenting a united front while seeking to impact pending legislation. This can be done by organizing informal groups of local community associations or joining one of many membership or trade organizations that represent community association interests. Collectively, these approaches will help ensure all voices are heard and any new legislation regulating community associations is balanced and appropriate.

## Being a Squeaky Wheel

We all know the saying that the squeaky wheel gets the grease. While there is debate about the attribution of this quote, it is worth considering. Rephrased, it means, "you don't get what you don't ask for."

The legislative process is not a spectator sport. It is captivating because it has the potential to impact our lives for the better or for the worse. Legislative proposals can emerge from a variety of sources, including responses to a negative individual experience. Generally, however, legislation is typically a response to a request to address a perceived need.

Because legislators are tasked with considering a broad array of topics, they cannot be experts about everything. In this environment, it pays to be the squeaky wheel—or risk not getting attention for our issues. Less metaphorically, it pays to engage in the process to ensure all sides of the issue are considered, that unfortunate examples of bad actors do not set the parameters of the debate, and that as citizens we share our experiences to ensure a balanced debate and optimal outcome.

## Outliers Driving Legislation

When it comes to community associations, it is not uncommon for a specific act by an uninformed or overzealous board to trigger a legislative response. The Great Recession of the mid-2000s provides examples of this phenomenon. The economic downturn was triggered, in part, by too many unqualified mortgages. The resulting downturn impacted the housing market with plummeting home values, and residents were left without jobs and with mortgages worth more than their homes. Community associations struggled as residents lacked the means to pay assessments.

To fulfill their duties to their communities, some boards were forced to take ultimate steps in assessment collections, including foreclosing on homes to collect monies owed. There were publicized cases of homeowners having their homes foreclosed for seemingly nominal amounts owed. These cases resulted in legislation that would limit or even possibly remove the ability of associations to use foreclosure as a tool for collection assessments.

These rare but clearly impactful examples rightfully raise eyebrows and demand action. Similar examples can be found regarding issues that include landscaping, clotheslines, and political campaign signs.

While overzealous board actions require a response, they feed the misperception that community associations are not supported by residents and are unpopular. Moreover, when a proposal is the result of one of these bad actor examples, it can result in an equally harsh response. These matters are best resolved by a well-informed debate and are examples of why the process should matter to all community associations.

**Two Sides to Every Story**

We know that a supermajority of residents is satisfied with community association living. By engaging in the legislative process, they can provide legislators with a more holistic view of the roles and benefits of community associations. The best voices to shape a legislative debate about community associations are those who live in them or who serve on their boards. Their failure to do so could result in only one side—the negative side—of the story being heard.

Examples of overzealous boards should not be ignored. When searching for legislative solutions to perceived problems, success is more likely when all aspects of the issues are considered and discussed. Those with experience in community association governance are the most credible source of that information. Only then will both sides of the story be heard.

**Input Matters**

As a former legislator, I can attest that hearing from constituents and stakeholders about legislative issues is a valuable resource. This is especially true when the information conveyed is based on experience. That is why the insights and perspectives of board members and residents are crucial resources needed to shape the debate and guide outcomes about community association legislative matters. When there is an issue that would impact the community, speaking out makes a difference and can guide the process to more favorable outcomes. Truly, input matters.

## Understanding the Process

Community association residents may be interested in the actions and, therefore, in the processes of city, county, state, and federal officials. Because this is not a treatise in advocacy at all levels, however, my focus herein will be on the one I know best, namely, state government. Rest assured that most of the content can be applied to the others.

One of the first questions raised by beginners in the legislative process is, "Where do I begin?" At first, the process can appear overwhelming. Because the makeup and practices of legislatures differ throughout the country, step one is to understand when, how often, and for how long they meet; their process for holding committee hearings and for passing legislation and sending it to the governor for consideration; how funding is decided; and, finally, whether seeking a gubernatorial veto would have a positive or negative impact on the bills in question.

While some may consider such information elementary or technical, it actually is essential. It is surprising—if not amazing—to realize how many advocates fail because they simply are too late or ill-informed. Too often, for example, they ask legislators to take a stand on a bill that has already been passed (or has failed)—sometimes after the legislature has adjourned. Other times, they may ask state officials to vote for or against a bill that is being considered in Congress (or vice versa).

Adopting a means for identifying and tracking legislation of interest is essential. A good place to start is the official website of the particular legislature. There, you will likely find rich resources for accessing schedules, directories, deadlines, and legislation. Identifying a bill of interest will be helpful only if one determines how to track its progress through the legislative maze, which includes committee hearings, voting in one or two chambers (depending on the legislature's makeup), and the often overlooked but equally important step of the governor's consideration and possible veto.

A plan of action is the heart of advocacy. It is wise to organize a team of like-minded persons who can collaborate in reaching out to legislators; attending and perhaps testifying at hearings; developing one-pagers of persuasive, memorable, significant information; and following up to express appreciation for support or for listening.

Whether the object is to support, oppose, or amend legislation, advocates must be well-informed not only about the issue at hand, but also about related records of legislators. Studying their records of voting on related matters will be useful in determining how to approach them. This could range from thanking them for past support and asking them to support similar legislation to trying to persuade them to take a different stand.

Engaging in the legislative process also benefits from building relationships with elected officials and their staffs. Interacting with them is an opportunity to bolster one's credibility by demonstrating community engagement and expertise or experience in a particular policy area. Especially when advocacy is a long-term commitment, relationships should be developed during the interims between legislative sessions. That is when legislators and their staff members have more time for briefings, visiting sites, and attending social or informative events.

Finally, and equally important, is to ensure compliance with state laws that govern legislative engagement. This includes registering as lobbyists under certain circumstances and observing limitations on spending and gifts.

These basics should be helpful as we turn to more specific aspects of the process, namely, tracking legislation, focusing on what's important, and responding to critical caveats.

**Tracking Legislation**

All states have state legislative websites where one can look up, read, and, in some cases, track, legislative proposals, often referred to as bills. Unfortunately, however, many are not updated in real time, so depending on them completely to track the process can lead to negative results when, for instance, the starting time or location is changed unexpectedly. Other times, they do not reflect reality regarding when events will occur. By way of example: A bill might be scheduled for consideration at a 10 a.m. committee hearing, but it is one of thirty on the agenda, and the agenda order might not be followed. Worse, the hearing might be recessed if it overlaps with the scheduled legislative session, meaning it will not resume until afterward. This could be one hour or even twelve hours later! The moral of the story is: Develop relationships with legislators and staff members, especially committee staff members, who can advise you about a more realistic schedule.

Tracking legislation usually is not restricted to one bill, but, rather, to those in the issue area. Advocates primarily interested in legislation that would limit the authority of community association boards of directors, for example, would also be smart to track other related bills.

A bill is more than a number. It is identified by the chamber in which it is introduced, and, sometimes, a bill can be introduced in both chambers, which results in two numbers. "Senate Bill 40," for example, could be a "companion" (identical) to "House Bill 6." To complicate matters further, each could be amended dramatically differently in its respective chamber, but, in the end, only one could be passed—usually, the one that is passed first.

That means the second chamber would receive and consider a bill that differs from its own version. Members then would have to adopt the newly received bill or amend it. If the originating chamber does not concur with the amendments, its sponsor can move to appoint a conference committee of members from both chambers who would work out the differences before asking their respective colleagues to accept them. This is complicated, but nobody said it was easy!

Beginners often make the mistake of tracking a bill through one chamber without realizing that it must pass both, unless the jurisdiction has a unicameral legislative body. If legislation requires funding, then the appropriations bill must also be monitored. Successful advocacy in those cases would require not only getting the bill passed and approved by the governor, but also getting it funded.

## Focusing on the Important

Each session, legislators review hundreds, if not thousands, of bills about a vast array of topics, but only a few are relevant to the interests of community associations. Focusing on the important means association advocates should address only issues that impact them directly and for which their perspective would be helpful. A proposal that would limit the authority of community association boards of directors, for example, would merit their attention, while one about business regulation in general is not something the association would have a vested interest in commenting on as an entity.

As a rule, the greater the impact of the proposal on an organization, the more likely their participation is needed and their perspectives impactful on a debate. For community association advocates this means focusing on issues that impact them generally and specific proposals that impact their expenses and revenue or their land use and environmental policies.

**Issues impacting associations.** When issues impact community associations, board members and residents should feel compelled to share their insights, perspectives, and experiences. Their failure to do so not only deprives legislators of the benefit of their expertise, but it can also result in undesirable results for residents. Subjects on which their participation is critical include legislative proposals that would restrict recouping costs for mandatory disclosure documents, criminal or civil penalties for board members, and restrictions on foreclosure authority.

Community association board members are in a strong position from which to articulate how such proposals would impact their ability to govern and support the community.

**Proposals impacting association expenses and revenue.** Community associations have fixed and variable expenses that must be covered. Because they adopt assessments to pay for services needed for a community's operation, their ability to enforce assessment obligations is essential for their well-being.

It is appropriate for a community association to provide input about the impacts of legislative proposals that would restrict or remove the associations' ability to collect required funds. Given their responsibilities, they are in the best position to explain how limiting associations' ability to recoup the expenses associated with collecting past-due debts can increase costs for all homeowners.

When examples of association bad acts related to assessments emerge, they should not be ignored. Instead, they should be explained in context by good actors who know those negative actions are exceptions and that not all community associations should be punished because of isolated cases.

**Land use and environmental issues.** When legislation relating to land use and the environment impacts community associations, advocacy from board members and residents is important. Water use restrictions that affect communities disproportionately, for example, certainly merit their attention. Similarly, land use proposals that may negatively impact the area surrounding a community may also warrant their engagement, especially if their property values could be affected.

The threshold for engaging is whether there is a clear relationship between the proposal and the impact on a community. When there is, engagement is in line with board members' responsibility to preserve and protect the association.

## Considering Critical Caveats

Participatory government is a fundamental right of citizens in a democracy. Community association board members who engage in public advocacy, however, must consider important caveats, especially if it is, or can be perceived as political. Regulations can vary depending on whether the activity is at the local, state, or federal levels of government. Before engaging, they would be smart to check with their legal counsel to determine if they are within their authority to act. Generally, they should act within their roles, avoid endorsements, and be sensitive to hot-button issues.

**Acting within roles.** Board members should act only within their roles as elected representatives of a community. The opinion of an individual board member is his or hers alone. The board speaks only on behalf of the community and only when a majority is aligned. This is an important consideration when addressing a legislative issue. Offering one's opinion as a board member is acceptable only if it is qualified in the context of that person's experience without speaking for the community.

If board members want to provide input on behalf of a board of directors or a community, they should first schedule a public discussion, vote on a position, and consider the extent of participating in the legislative process.

**Avoiding endorsements.** Participating effectively in legislative processes and building positive relationships inevitably result in invitations to also participate politically. This can include invitations to host political gatherings or endorse candidates, especially incumbents who have been helpful or who are like-minded. This can be a slippery slope, because declining such requests could harm those relationships but accepting them can cause problems for board members in their official capacities. There is a fine but important line that should not be crossed between acting individually and officially.

Because community associations reflect a diversity of political alignments, they should be reticent in aligning with any candidate or advocating for candidates in an election. Similarly, the nonprofit status of a community association may prohibit the use of community funds to support candidates or political action committees. This is an area in which communities should seek guidance from counsel. Remembering that the board represents all residents of a community, regardless of political alignment, reinforces the need to exercise caution and act with an even hand.

**Dealing with hot-button issues.** Hot-button issues are those that arouse strong, if not passionate, support and opposition. Learning to identify them is wise, but knowing how to deal with them appropriately is even wiser. These can include myriad topics ranging from the public display of the Ten Commandments or Confederacy statues to placing partisan yard signs. The problem for community associations is that a single resident or small group who is irate about board actions regarding controversial issues can turn to legislators for a favorable resolution. In such cases, a local problem can evolve into an issue with statewide impact, sometimes with negative implications for community associations.

Political signs have long been a hot-button topic in community associations. Boards should approach this issue with caution, especially in the current political environment. As a private entity, a community association may have the authority to regulate or ban political signs, depending on its jurisdiction. States such as Pennsylvania allow them to prohibit signs, while others allow associations to regulate the time, place, manner, and size in which they can be displayed.[7]

Underscoring these limitations is the reality that boards can regulate signage only if they are authorized to do so in their governing documents. Reviewing and understanding what the community governing documents specify about this or any other hot-button topic is a must for any community association.

## Engaging Elected Officials

The legislative process thrives when concerned citizens engage in public debate about issues. With more than 75 million people living in community associations, their governance and operations is a popular subject for regulatory proposals. For residents or elected board members in community associations, providing feedback regarding those pending legislative proposals is critical to ensure optimal outcomes.

While engaging in the legislative process, sometimes it is easy to get caught up unwittingly in the politics that define the day-to-day workings of elected bodies. Understanding the difference between political and legislative participation can preclude partisan challenges within communities and running afoul of nonprofit statutes and of restrictions imposed by governing documents. It is also essential to participate in the legislative process effectively and build relationships that facilitate opportunities for being heard.

## Defining Engagement

Living in politically divisive times seems to impact our ability to listen to each other. Divisiveness, however, should not be an excuse for not exercising our rights to petition our government and provide feedback about important legislative proposals.

Community association board members should be aware not only of the types of engagement, but also of their impact on communities. Differentiating legislative engagement from political engagement can help them set the boundaries for their participation and help them avoid any pitfalls by staying within legal boundaries.

**Legislative engagement.** Legislative engagement is the process of engaging with elected officials to express views or provide feedback about legislative proposals. Citizens are empowered to express their views, and most elected officials welcome their doing so. This engagement can include making a telephone call, writing a letter, or sending an email with the goal of supporting, opposing, or amending pending legislation.

Individuals can engage in the legislative process with few obstacles. Board members acting collectively to express their opinions and contact legislators should remember the caveats identified earlier.

**Political engagement.** Political engagement means participating in the electoral process by supporting a candidate, donating to a campaign, or participating in an election-related event. Because it can create issues for the community and the association's corporate status, board members cannot be too cautious in following the letter of the law and their governing documents.

Partly because community residents reflect a diversity of political opinions, political engagement should be left to individuals in a community rather than undertaken as an association. When a board engages politically, it risks creating needless division in the community and noncompliance with laws and governing documents.

A community association, speaking through its board, should resist endorsing candidates or using community association funds for any type of political activity associated with an election. Board members should always bear in mind that as nonprofit corporations, community associations are bound by restrictions that may impact the community if it engages in these activities.

**Compliance.** If there is any doubt about whether the board's engagement is political or legislative, board members should ask for clarity from legal counsel. They must act only with the utmost confidence that their actions are appropriate and comply with statutes and rules. These legal restrictions will vary, depending on whether the legislative or political engagement is at the municipal, state, or federal level. When in doubt, it is always best to get advice from a professional.

## Participating Effectively

When a legislative issue emerges that may impact a community association, responsible board members should feel obligated not only to speak out, but also to reflect a united voice of reason. The process is complicated, especially because there is no golden rule or one-size-fits-all approach to participating effectively. What works in one situation or for one person may not work for another, so strategies must be tailored and targeted.

Any general advice should be taken with a grain of salt, with the assumption that exceptions will always be the rule. There are many effective means of outreach, but a few formalities and best practices can ensure maximum effectiveness. Generally, participating effectively is a process that includes identifying and targeting elected officials and their staffs; writing, calling, or meeting with them; and always being respectful.

**Identifying elected officials.** The process begins with identifying the appropriate officials to contact, whether directly or through staff members. The importance of the latter should not be overlooked, for they often are the unsung heroes who analyze legislation and advise their bosses what to say and how to vote.

Most of the legislation impacting community associations is introduced by a state or provincial government official. Every state/provincial jurisdiction has a website where advocates can search for their elected representatives. The sites typically allow users to enter their addresses to see a display of the names of elected officials who represent that location.

**Targeting elected officials and staff.** The best next step is to call the official's office to determine his or her preferred means of receiving feedback from constituents. Some prefer in-person visits, while others prefer telephone calls, emails, or letters. Similarly, some prefer feedback from individuals, while others prefer hearing from groups, whether at meetings or via petitions. Taking time to gather this information can pay large dividends and save much time. More importantly, it empowers advocates to target the elected officials and their staff members by attempting to reach them via their preferred channels of communication.

Many legislators appreciate receiving one-page briefings about issues and in-person briefings scheduled either for their own staffs or for groups representing various legislative offices. This approach also saves time for advocates and legislators.

Being effective means doing what is best to inform and/or persuade a targeted official, not doing what is easiest for an advocate. It may be easier, for example, to send a quick email than to write a formal letter or pay a visit, but in this day and age, the truth of the matter is that those quick emails can get lost among the thousands received by elected officials from their districts and beyond.

**Writing to elected officials.** Writing to elected officials is one of the most impactful means of expressing a point of view. It provides them with a written or emailed statement of a constituent's view about a pending matter. Although some persons believe a handwritten note is more personal, handwriting may be difficult to read—and the longer the letters or emails, the more likely they will not be read completely. Count me among those who favor typed letters because they are easier to read and do not cause me to spend time deciphering handwriting.

Bear in mind, however, that there are exceptions to every rule. A Texas legislator regularly and strongly advised advocates to type, not write, letters, and to craft them individually rather than send copies of form letters. She was favorably impressed to the contrary, however, by a package from the American Association of Retired Persons (AARP) that violated her two rules. It contained 200 copies of a beautifully handwritten letter—each with a different signature, a printed name, contact information, voter registration number, and precinct number. The handwriting was her mother's! (Guess how she voted!)

Nevertheless, an impactful letter reflects the following best practices:

- Concise
- Easy to read
- Easy to understand
- As informative as it is persuasive
- Clearly expresses the writer's intent or request
- Excludes extraneous information
- Connects the issue to the elected representative's district
- Includes the sender's complete contact information

A typical letter or email to an elected official follows this format:

- Formal greeting: Dear Representative:/Dear Senator:
- Introduction: Name of person or organization writing
- Connection: Connection to the elected representative's district
- The issue: Name or number of the bill in question
- The ask: What the official is being asked to do
- The why: Why the official should support the ask
- Conclusion: A brief thank-you

I highly recommend one-page letters with attachments, if necessary. Many recipients read or glance at only the first page of a letter, but also take the time to look at attachments. Advocates who feel compelled to share extensive written information should present it in the best possible reader-friendly formats and packages.

Emails should follow the same best practices, especially those regarding attachments, but they should be as short as possible. To repeat: Sending emails risks their getting lost among the thousands of unsolicited messages from nonconstituents, spam, etc. This is especially true if they are sent to a governmental email address that likely reaches staff, not the official. Writing letters may be more time-consuming, but they are more likely to be effective.

**Calling elected officials.** Calling can be effective, especially as a follow-up to a written communication. The question is, will the caller reach the elected official or a staff member? Regardless of the person reached, the outcome can be productive. Most elected representatives I know strive to be informed about feedback from constituents and get at least a general tally of the calls for or against specific legislation.

Callers should prepare the same way they would develop a written communication because the points to be expressed are the same and should be just as concise and organized. They should request to speak to the appropriate staff member responsible for the issue that is the subject of the call. Once connected to that employee, callers should make the following points:

- Identify self by name and appropriate title.
- Define the issue in question.
- State the purpose of the call.
- Describe the action requested of the elected official.
- Secure the staff member's contact information.
- Arrange for follow-up.

As for a written communication, a polite, professional, and respectful approach facilitates the message being received well.

**Meeting with elected officials.** Meeting with an elected official is the most dynamic means of engagement because it is interactive in real time and impacted by nonverbal messages ranging from body language to seating arrangements and decor. Attentive advocates can learn much simply by observing an elected official's reaction as information and requests are articulated.

Especially because their time is so limited, legislators are more likely to meet with their own constituents and refer nonconstituents to their respective elected representatives. During legislative sessions, their schedules are regularly disrupted by unforeseen conflicts, including hearings and meetings. When they are, advocates typically meet with staff representatives. Those interactions can be equally productive, especially when they are with those who will write issue briefs and make recommendations related to legislation.

Scheduling meetings with legislators is far easier to accomplish when they are in their districts between regular or special legislative sessions. In many cases, those meetings can be scheduled for longer periods and generally are more relaxed. Regardless of the time, place, or circumstances, the following suggestions should be helpful for anyone hoping to meet with a legislator:

- Determine how to make a good first impression.
- Prepare thoroughly.
- Know the related background and record of the legislator.
- Be ready to answer questions.
- Arrive at least ten minutes early to sign in.
- Have enough copies of business cards and written information.
- Be respectful, pleasant, likable, and accommodating.
- Explain the purpose of the meeting and the importance of the issue.
- Provide appropriate facts, figures, examples, and anecdotes (orally and in writing).
- Request specific action or support.
- Specify how officials can facilitate a positive outcome.
- Offer assistance regarding issues.
- Do not overstay your welcome.
- Make a good last impression.

Making a positive, memorable last impression can be even more important than making a good first impression. Talk and act positively to preclude the obvious negative alternatives: What if they do not even remember who you are or what you said? What if they remember you but do not like you? What if your presentation results in a determination to oppose you?

If faced with disagreement, remain professional, but consider providing additional follow-up information, perhaps from another advocate or group. Under no circumstances should a legislator or staff member be warned or threatened for disagreeing. Do not emulate the passionate advocate who told a woman senator, "If you don't agree with us, we're going to take the marbles out of your bag!" Oh, my!

Above all, remember that "tomorrow is another day": You might disagree today but be on the same side in the future. In other words, do not burn your bridges over a single disagreement.

After the meeting, it is smart to send a thank-you note or email that reiterates the points made and offers additional assistance or information. That is also a good time to regroup for a debriefing that will include sharing perspectives about how the meeting progressed and the best ways to follow up and plan future interactions.

**Respecting officials and staff.** When communicating with elected officials or their staff members, it is important to be professional and respectful and treat the elected official's staff with the same courtesy as the official. Many legislators are former staff members, and similarly, today's staff members may be tomorrow's legislators. Being polite to everyone is not only basic, but also can be productive in the short- and long-term.

Advocates who express hostility can be counterproductive. A professional approach is most likely to impact the process positively. When legislators have been approached by disgruntled or unhappy residents, board members addressing their issues should go out of their way to make positive impressions by being polite and respectful—even when talking about their detractors.

## Building Relationships

When we must make an important decision, we typically get advice from friends, family, and colleagues whose opinions we trust and with whom we have shared experiences. The same can be said about the legislative process. Ongoing engagement and providing informed, accurate, and honest input over time builds credibility. There is a benefit in maintaining civic engagement, becoming a trustworthy source of information for elected officials, building relationships with other community associations, and shaping the regulatory environment for community associations. This is a long-term, multi-faceted strategy that includes playing the long game, leveraging industry groups, and—yes!—running for office.

**Playing the long game.** Successful legislative advocacy can have a cumulative effect. Advocates who individually or in groups provide accurate, relevant, and trustworthy information over time gain credibility and influence. Playing the long game in this manner may be time-consuming, but it is productive. Elected officials want to do what is best for the people they serve and welcome diverse points of view that help them make the best decisions about the many different topics they consider.

Those who establish themselves as credible sources of information and expertise can enhance their ability to shape the legislative process while building relationships with elected officials. To be successful in this regard means providing information that is accurate, not exaggerated, and reliable. Because this is representative government, lawmakers are expected to vote to meet the best needs and interests of their districts, not of their own. Any information that will reinforce such positions is likely to be appreciated.

Playing the long game also involves inviting elected officials to visit the community, especially during legislative interims, to see association governance and operations first-hand. Building successful communities benefits from such a long-term commitment to civic engagement.

**Leveraging industry groups.** A soloist can be beautifully moving, but that voice joined with a choir can be even more so—and drown out background noise. Similarly, community associations can be more "moving" when they join forces by leveraging industry groups.

Problems, issues, and challenges seldom occur in isolation. If a community association is impacted, others are likely impacted too. Whether an issue in question is being addressed at the local, state, or federal level, its impacting only one community is as unlikely as it is rare. Even if it is the result of an unhappy resident reaching out to an elected official, the resulting action could impact many associations.

Joining with other community associations—through informal groups or by joining one of the many industry trade groups advocating for them—can increase individual impact. Such organizations unite communities and help coordinate responses to legislative proposals that impact them. What is more, these groups provide coaching for effective legislative engagement and tracking, networking opportunities, and board member education. Membership in these groups is not expensive, and it can help board members leverage their communities' interests and enhance their success.

**Running for office.** Public service is the lifeblood of our democracy. Locally, volunteer community association board members, city council members, county commissioner courts, boards of education, and other elected bodies thrive from having a pipeline of passionate candidates. Those who succeed at those levels sometimes aspire to higher office, perhaps in state legislatures or the U.S. Congress.

Involvement in the legislative process may inspire advocates for community associations to run for office. It has happened before: The 53rd speaker of the U.S. House of Representatives, the Honorable John Boehner, got his start in public service when he ran for president of his community association board in the 1980s. Closer to home, my experience in community association management and legislative engagement caused me to realize I could serve even more families in significantly more ways by serving in the Texas Legislature, first as a state representative and later as a state senator. I remained in such capacity for twenty-four years.

Current community association board members gain valuable experience in governing that can benefit others if that passion leads them to run for local, state, or even federal office. With millions of Americans living in community associations, leveraging that experience to serve in a higher office would benefit many.

## CONCLUSION

Coping with a more regulated future is a challenge that we can meet by dealing effectively with the federal, state, and municipal regulations imposed on community associations; spotting trends in community association legislation; and shaping the legislative debate.

Community associations are impacted by legislation and regulations adopted by federal, state/provincial, and local governments. Each level of government has a particular focus that can reach into our communities and shape our associations. Emerging trends point to a greater focus on areas of building safety, assessment collections, and reserve funding. It is important to work as a community to pay attention to governing fundamentals so as not to become an example of the need for further regulation.

The emergence of legislative proposals that impact our community associations is inevitable. We who have experience and insight into community association living should embrace our civic responsibility to engage elected officials in shaping the process and ensuring optimal outcomes. The trend of increasing community regulations will continue regardless, but it is better to have a seat at the table than to be on the menu.

### QUESTIONS TO CONSIDER

1. What federal, state, or local regulations does your community deal with most frequently?

2. How would you describe the regulatory environment for community associations in your state or province?

3. What are the most useful regulations impacting community associations in your jurisdiction?

4. How do legislation and regulations support your community's success?

5.  What are the most burdensome regulations for your community? How would you change them?

6.  If you could pass one law that would fix or improve something in your community association, what would it be?

7.  How does your community association stay abreast of changing laws?

8.  What issues, if any, have compelled you or your association to reach out to an elected official?

9.  How would you describe your interactions with elected officials?

10. Has your community ever engaged in supporting or opposing legislation in your jurisdiction? If so, what was the issue, and were the efforts successful?

## CHAPTER 15

# Putting the Pieces Together

Every day is sort of a jigsaw puzzle. You have to make sure
that you're putting the most important things first.

—JULIA HARTZ,
Cofounder, Eventbrite

## CHAPTER INTRODUCTION

Governing a community can seem very much like the proverbial puzzle Julia Hartz references. When addressing challenges and priorities, it certainly helps community association board members to, as she suggests, "put the most important things first."

It begins with mapping the journey from a point of departure that ensures the community moves forward in the proper direction. Unity along the way is imperative and made possible only by collaborating effectively with residents at every step of the process.

Always bearing in mind the important role community associations play for a growing number of homeowners is the foundation for motivating everyone to participate and affirming the significance of our work. Despite the many memes and jokes that come at our expense, we can build upon the reality that a vast majority of persons living in community associations are satisfied with their boards and with their neighbors. Underscoring the importance of our service, we can set the starting point for the journey and a course that focuses on needed improvements, listening to residents, and engaging everyone in social and community-related activities.

The next action to fall into place is remembering the keys to success. This includes communicating effectively to inform residents about the community's work and many benefits. It also entails keeping the focus on the community. By recognizing the contributions of residents, focusing on community processes, and finding ways to connect and have fun, we provide residents with actions that magnify the value and benefits of community.

Finally, as the board moves the community forward, it can experience the empowerment of taking that extra step to work toward a brighter future. Investing in board education, conducting resident pulse surveys, and focusing on the big picture will help set the course for future success and prosperity.

The remarkable aspect of community associations is that as self-governing entities, what they wish to accomplish is within their grasp. It simply requires putting the pieces of the puzzle together and, as Hartz suggests, focusing on the most important things first. Some of the subjects in this chapter were discussed earlier, but they are referenced anew herein to relate them to the most important task of all, that is, putting the pieces together to map the journey toward a better and brighter future for a community association.

## MAPPING THE JOURNEY

Humans are social creatures, and we thrive when we make connections and feel part of something larger than ourselves. In its modern incarnation, community is where we live, work, and socialize. Having emerged over the last fifty years as the preferred means to provide housing and build community in North America, community associations house more than 75 million persons—and their number is growing. To strengthen our communities and ensure they remain relevant to their residents, we can begin putting the pieces together to map the journey for our communities.

That journey begins by remembering that community associations matter. Housing close to one of every four homeowners, community associations provide a host of benefits for their residents and their surrounding areas. Irrespective of negative publicity, they remain popular by continuing to prove how they serve residents. Mapping the journey is facilitated when there are frequent reminders of those benefits and the important roles of community association boards.

The next step in mapping the journey is to find a starting point for communities interested in improving their associations. As self-governing entities, community associations have the power to chart their own courses, change, and respond to the needs of their residents. The starting point will be different for each community, but the underlying commonality is the epiphany that the community has the ability to shape its future.

Finally, with a refreshed understanding of the importance of community associations and a set starting point, board members and residents can move together toward their destination. Although there may be many paths depending on the state of a community association, the destination is a shared point for a vibrant and engaging community.

## Remembering Why Community Matters

As the preferred housing choice for millions of residents, community associations are poised to retain that status—and perhaps improve it—in the future. Sometimes challenged by negatively inclined reporters, board members should be ready to describe their explosion in growth over the last fifty years. It is not a coincidence that more than a quarter of housing in the United States is in community associations. Longitudinal surveys consistently remind us that residents enjoy the benefits of community associations, that the volunteer time of elected boards provides value, and that the flexible, self-governed approach allows communities to change with time. For these reasons and a multitude of others, the outlook is bright. What is more, it is relatively easy to remember why community associations matter and why we should welcome every opportunity to tell our story.

## Residents Favor Community Associations

While social media may be populated with negative stereotypes of community associations, survey data tell a different story. Their popularity with their residents is based on the very purposes for which they were created and reflects the good work of countless board members over the years. Residents favor their community associations largely because of the good work of board members. Extolling their virtues is as easy as it is important.

We who work or volunteer in our communities should readily share our story with the media and residents. The easiest way to do this is to cite the results of the Foundation for Community Association Research's Homeowner Satisfaction Survey, which has been conducted for close to twenty years. Highlights are listed here:

- 86 percent of residents of community associations rate their experience positively.
- 87 percent of purchasers noted buying a home in a community association would not impact their decision or make it more likely they would purchase the home.
- Community associations are home to almost one in four households in the United States.
- 82 percent of community association residents report positive interactions with their professional community managers.
- Community association residents cite neighborhood appearance and safety as the top benefits of association living.

## Board Members Add Value

Surveys indicate not only that residents enjoy living in community associations and have positive views of their boards of directors, but also that board members add value through their impressive volunteer time to their communities. From a civic engagement standpoint, the numbers on volunteer board service are staggering. Millions of residents volunteer their time each year to serve on their community association boards, dedicating their time to help advance community interests. Noteworthy survey facts include the following:

- 82 percent of residents believe their boards serve in the best interests of their communities.
- 82 percent of residents have a positive relationship with their community boards.
- Approximately 2.5 million volunteers serve on community association boards of directors.
- Board members contribute 100 million hours of service annually at a value of $3.3 billion.

## Community Associations Are Adaptable

Community association boards of directors can adapt and update rules periodically to reflect the evolving needs, preferences, and values of their communities. Their look, feel, and safety are linked to rules that govern myriad matters ranging from visitor parking to yard upkeep.

Neighborhood appearance and safety are two of the most cited benefits of community association living. These points underscore the importance of the board establishing and enforcing rules that help preserve and enhance property values. This is one of the factors that support the finding that homes in community associations are worth more on average than those in legacy communities.

## Finding the Starting Point

Determining how to prioritize challenges or opportunities can perplex new or continuing board members. Fortified with the knowledge that community associations matter, however, they should be ready to take the next step, namely, finding the starting point for preparing for a brighter future.

The goal of any board, volunteer, or resident of a community association should be to find ways to make the community a better place. This can be as simple as adopting an attitude of assuming the good intent of others or as complex as committing to take action on a long-standing opportunity to make an improvement. Regardless of the scope or scale, I subscribe to the Chinese proverb that "a journey of a thousand miles begins with a single step." Moving forward by applying ideas gleaned from this book or other sources can be facilitated by bearing in mind the following best practices:

- Do not pursue change for the sake of change. If the processes, governance, and operations of the community are going well, do not fix what is not broken.
- If inspired to undertake a project or embrace a goal for the community, determine if there is support for it. The best way for boards to serve their residents is by ascertaining how they think and responding to their needs, interests, and preferences.
- Build consensus and trust by engaging residents in the governance process.

These actions empower board members as they benefit from collaborating with residents to make better decisions. The result should be significantly more pleasant, positive, and productive than responding to their social media posts.

## Not Fixing What Is Not Broken

Simply stated, change for the sake of change is not good. Quoting Bert Lance, a former presidential advisor, Texans often say, "If it ain't broke, don't fix it." Amen.

New community association board members sometimes easily fall into the trap of changing the governance or operations only because they can, to demonstrate their newly acquired power, or based on their mistaken beliefs that a change in administration automatically means a change in policies and procedures. Sustainable change in a community, however, comes from consensus. If the operations, programs, and governance of a community are working well, then changing policies or projects significantly only adds complexity and resources where they are not needed. Just as it is important to reflect on how the board and community serve its residents, it is equally essential to know when things are working well and to maintain and monitor them—not necessarily change them.

## Tracking the Pulse of the Community

Think about how we lived a mere twenty years ago. There were no smartphones, social media, or electric cars. Most of us still used paper maps or early navigation devices because Google Maps on cell phones was not an option. The point is that how we live and what we value change over time. A community association that recognizes this positions itself well to adapt to those changes.

For all boards, the best way to ensure the community's journey is on the right path is to track the pulse of the residents. One of the many positive changes brought about by technology is that most community associations have private social media applications that can be used to survey residents periodically. The resulting data can be used to evaluate the direction of the community and the relevance of existing rules. An informed board can work to keep the association responsive and relevant to its residents.

### Focusing on Engagement

When the connections between a board and its community are tenuous, they erode the potential of the community association and can cause residents to question its value.

Community associations provide value by enforcing rules and maintaining the physical infrastructure of the neighborhood. Board members have so much more potential, however, to connect with their residents and build a sense of community. As highlighted in chapter 11, they should share a perspective on ways to engage residents and the benefits that flow from focusing on community engagement. Connecting neighbors and providing for a social or other engaging structure should always be part of their focus.

## Determining the Destination

One of the truly amazing aspects of community associations is that they are self-governing entities. That means each community can chart its own path pursuant to powers granted to it in the governing documents and by statutes. The fact that those governing the community are neighbors facilitates their timely responsiveness to the needs and interests of residents. This gives board members wide latitude to set priorities that reflect the desires and preferences of their residents.

Determining a destination provides an open opportunity to improve life in a community. Based on my experience in community association management, I recommend three priorities that help board members determine and achieve their goals: staying current, acting on resident preferences, and building a bench of future leaders for the community.

### Staying Current

It is easier for a board to stay on track when it is current about its powers and any developments in regulations that may impact its authority. A helpful best practice is for board members to review their governing documents annually to ensure they are familiar with their responsibilities and authority in the community. Any questions that arise during this review can be sent to qualified counsel for clarification. This ensures the board acts within its scope of power, understands its boundaries, and has answers vetted by a licensed legal professional.

Boards should also keep abreast of developments such as court cases, legislation, and other regulations that may impact their governance. Good sources for information about this topic are industry membership groups and local counsel. Especially because ignorance of the law is no excuse, monitoring these changes continually facilitates the board's staying on the right path to achieve its goals for the community.

## Acting on Resident Preferences

The problem boards face when they fall into a comfort zone of maintaining the status quo is being out of sync with changing resident preferences and priorities. Issues that were once important to residents may have evolved with culture changes, technology, or other forces that impact how we live.

To remain current while providing timely, relevant governance, the board should engage in periodic pulse surveys. These can provide data about where the board should focus its attention or direct resources to address what is important to those it serves. More importantly, having survey data about resident priorities empowers board members to justify their actions.

## Building a Deep Bench

Our earlier discussion about engagement and the benefits it accrues to associations should be helpful to board members interested in building a deep bench of future community leaders. As they engage residents in the governing, operational, and social activities of their communities, they will likely experience opportunities to whet their interest in assuming leadership responsibilities. Assuming their service is productive and satisfying, they can develop into experienced, qualified board members who are prepared to implement community goals.

Anyone who has served on a community association board knows it can be a significant investment of time and energy. Sometimes, some members stay on because they cannot recruit suitable successors. Building a deep bench of future leaders provides the community with fresh leadership, energy, and greater trust in the line of succession.

## REMEMBERING KEYS TO SUCCESS

Governing a community association requires juggling multiple demands ranging from rules enforcement, budgeting, operations, dealing with upset residents, and other day-to-day challenges. As a result, getting sidetracked by greater goals is easy.

Remembering the keys to success, namely, communicating, focusing on the community, and leveraging professionals, can provide some respite from those pressures and time to home in on planning the best future possible. Especially when daily demands pull board members too far from long-term goals, taking the time to focus on fundamental processes can help restore balance in the board's workload.

Communicating effectively is a key element to board success. It is as important to communicate accomplishments as it is to work toward them. Aristotle was right (and has been quoted for centuries!) when he argued that nature abhors a vacuum. He could have added, however, that gossip, by comparison, loves one. In communities in which communication is lacking, some residents may "fill in the space" by conjecture, while others can wonder what is the point of having an association. Sharing the work of the board, its accomplishments, efforts of volunteers in the community, and social functions reminds residents of the benefits of their community association and underscores its relevance.

Relatedly, the familiarity of community association living can push discussions about community policies into the realm of personal differences. Focusing on the community and its processes mitigates the emergence of personality conflicts and keeps the focus on debating the merits of current proposals. The board is a collective entity that serves the collective interests of the community. Focusing on the community not only facilitates constructive engagement, but also models language and behavior for participants. If it is true that conflict breeds conflict, then it also must be true that professionalism inspires professionalism.

Finally, board members need not work in isolation. They have access to a vast array of professional services that support them in their efforts. The nature of community governance touches on myriad subjects including legal matters, insurance, community operations, financial management, and customer service. Effective boards leverage professional business partners to assist them in areas that may be of technical or require a level of professional expertise or license to undertake. These professionals, including community managers, are resources to help the board continue its success.

Communicating, focusing on community, and leveraging professionals are the three keys to success, which are discussed here.

## Communicating

Communities are about connections and relationships. The best way to make connections and strengthen relationships is to communicate regularly, consistently, and effectively. This kind of communication is a key to success. Although chapter 10 focused on various ways community associations could tell their stories to internal and external audiences, the tips here expand on the importance of ensuring residents have access to reliable information about their communities. This requires using multiple channels, being consistent, and maximizing technology.

## Using Multiple Channels

The diversity of a community association extends into the realm of technical savvy. Residents of various ages may be more attuned to different channels of communication. Accordingly, informing a community about the board's work, community accomplishments, or other news entails transmitting messages via channels of communication favored by the targeted resident. This includes cross-posting information to community social media and websites, email, and at central locations such as community clubhouses. Using multiple channels increases the likelihood of connecting with residents regardless of their preferred channels.

Communication is also a key element of engagement. The more residents know what the community has to offer and what board members are doing, the greater the likelihood of their engaging in activities and meetings.

## Being Consistent

When it comes to communication, consistency is key. Any communication plan should focus on building a consistent and sustainable flow of information. Many of us still like to pore over the newspaper with our morning cup of coffee, a good, quiet time to connect with what is happening in the world. It is part of our daily routine.

Few community associations may need to communicate daily, but they should do so regularly and consistently, preferably by setting a regular schedule. If that effort includes an emailed eNewsletter, for example, residents can expect and even look forward to receiving it at the scheduled time. Scheduled communiques set expectations and, most importantly, keep residents informed about progress and events in the community.

## Maximizing Technology

Most of us are now comfortable with the growing role technology plays in our daily lives. It is amazing how much we rely on our smartphones for banking, booking travel, food deliveries, global communication, and even to check on community association accounts. I still marvel at the extent of what we can do on this little device we carry with us.

Maximizing technology for communication is increasingly necessary. Boards should use community websites, email, and private social networks to engage residents and enhance the availability and accessibility of information. This includes not only reporting community news, but also providing secure access to resident account information and the ability to book amenities or even make maintenance requests.

## Focusing on Community

Focusing continually on the best interest of the community is the essential key to success in keeping peace and maintaining momentum at meetings or regarding operations and governance in general. Indeed, it keeps everyone centered on what matters and steers discussion away from the personal or political, the self-serving or egocentric.

A few of the means of maintaining this focus can be simple. The more they become part of the fabric of the community, the easier they will be to continue. Consider recognition, for example. Too often, the board focuses on rule enforcement, and residents focus on when, how often, why, and how fairly and consistently those rules are enforced. Although this is a valuable and necessary part of community governance, it certainly is not the only priority, nor does it need to crowd out recognition of residents or others who make positive contributions to a community.

Similarly, focusing on a community's processes and implementing them professionally means that rules are enforced fairly. Finally, board members should govern consistently. They should work collectively, using their authority in the best interest of residents and with a common understanding of their communities' goals. This supports a community-wide understanding of the work and value of the board and the benefits of community association living.

## Recognizing Contributors

Community is built on a feeling of belonging. One of the best ways to foster it is to recognize and celebrate residents' contributions to a community. Finding ways to create positive incentives can not only build connections, but also be a proactive means to highlight community association living.

Many associations, for example, have rules related to yard upkeep. Instead of focusing on the negativity of rule violations, boards can focus on the positive. This can be accomplished by announcing monthly awards for the most attractive yard, most beautiful flowers, or best holiday decorations. Such competitions create a fun, competitive atmosphere while engaging families in beautifying properties. They build connections between a community and its residents and also highlight examples for others to emulate.

Recognitions can be extended to other areas as well, such as honoring residents who help neighbors or volunteer for community activities.

From the points of consideration and announcement of awards to actual presentations to honorees and related publicity, the entire process highlights the benefits of community associations and provides valuable community news to share within and beyond the community.

## Focusing on Process

The governance role of the board of directors is essential for the success of a community association. In executing the host of governance and operational duties, board members can rely on another key to successful governance: focusing on community processes. Their being familiar with both their role in the community and any processes that are part of its governance process can help build upon their shared understanding. In dealing with duties such as an appeal of a rule violation, for example, their efficient and fair execution is part of focusing on the process and working for respected outcomes. Their doing so empowers them to resolve disputes more fairly while building trust with residents.

**Remembering to Have Fun**

Regardless of how diligently a board strives to create fair and effective leadership for a community, from time to time there will be moments that require dealing with difficult people or situations. It is important for board members to take their roles seriously while also taking the time to find balance and even enjoyment in their work. Assessment collection, rule enforcement, and operational tasks are essential and must be not only done, but also done well. Concurrent with those duties, however, is an opportunity to go beyond the basics and create a truly embracing community environment. Building a social structure, connecting residents, and finding ways to enhance day-to-day living helps sustain energy and positivity for hours of volunteer work. Sustainable and successful leadership requires an element of finding pleasure and reward in one's work.

## Leveraging Professional Support

Leveraging resources for a successful community is facilitated by the board and residents having an arsenal of support on which to draw. A key element of community success is engaging and working with the many professionals who are on call to help communities navigate legal, operational, technical, and financial matters. In my earlier overview of the many professionals who are or should be on hand to assist, I noted that they are an integral part of building a successful community. Accordingly, I would be remiss not to revisit this issue when contemplating ways to boost a community's success.

To ensure good governance and operations, board members can and should call upon these professionals. Having a qualified attorney on hand to counsel the board about legal matters is critical. We can roll our eyes at this and fret about the cost of legal services, but, in the end, an ounce of prevention is worth more than a pound of cure. Likewise, the larger the community association, the harder it is for a board to handle all aspects of operations without professional advice and assistance.

Community managers are the most likely source of support for board members. Their specialized education prepares them to implement board directives and apply their knowledge, insight, and experience to keep a community running smoothly.

Finally, we increasingly see issues emerge in older associations that did not budget adequately for future expenses. Planning for the future of a community requires the support of financial advisors who can help the board plan funding to replace valued amenities and infrastructure when the time comes. To repeat: Community is about connections, and connections with key professionals are part of the process of ensuring a successful future.

**Engaging Attorneys**

Community association board members are charged with the duty to govern a corporation. In the case of large community associations, this can encompass adopting multimillion-dollar budgets, managing numerous employees, and juggling the rights of residents. When confronted with a challenge that touches on legal matters, board members should not hesitate to engage legal counsel. A qualified attorney can help them navigate the many challenges and the ramifications of each available option for action. Costs of legal advice typically are far, far less than the costs of possible litigation or the impact of negative publicity for a high-profile dispute with a resident.

A side benefit to building a relationship with legal counsel is that it can lead to other benefits, such as information about new laws and access to education and training resources.

## Hiring a Community Manager

Having devoted most of my professional career to establishing and strengthening the community management profession, I can, without hesitation, extol its virtues in supporting a community. The volunteer leaders who serve as community association board members sometimes are overwhelmed while dealing with a variety of governance, administrative, operational, and financial issues. By hiring a professional community association manager, they can shift that burden to a dedicated professional who has expertise and training in critical areas of community management.

What is more, many management companies offer an array of technological solutions to support their community clients. These can include accounting software, private social networks, and other tools to add convenience and security to the community. Many community managers also have extensive contacts with the many other professional colleagues who serve communities, and they can help the board find the right partner for any given project.

## Investing in the Future

Few working people, regardless of profession or occupation, ignore their futures and simply hope their retirements somehow will work out. Most of us budget and set aside what we can to ensure funds will be there when we need them. The same is true for community associations. The community infrastructure and amenities that make our neighborhoods so appealing have a finite life. It is important, and yet another key to success, to prepare for that day by funding community reserve accounts.

This responsibility can be both a technical and a political undertaking. Many boards face pressures to keep assessments as low as possible, sometimes foregoing adequate funding reserves. Ignoring or unjustifiably delaying the task of funding future repairs is a roll of the dice. Because it may cost significantly more to pay for items later, wise and responsible board members set aside modest amounts over long periods. This precludes their having to rely on special assessments when the time comes for repairs or replacements. To help boards navigate this path, reserve specialists and other financial advisors are ready to set up a community for success.

## MOVING FORWARD

Starting a new journey can take a bit of courage, but it always begins with the first step. To maximize the success of a community association, board members should reflect on their optimal destination, that is, on what they would like to achieve for the families they represent and what they want their legacy to be. Collectively, they must move beyond the day-to-day governance that is critical to the functioning of the community and includes assessment collections, rules enforcement, and regular board meetings. Moving from good to great requires their taking that one extra step. It can be big or small, but at its core is a commitment to make the community a better place to live and one in which residents feel well represented.

The first step in moving forward is setting a goal to go the extra mile, to move the association forward one step at a time. Board members do not have to change everything about their communities, especially if they are working well, but it may help if they ask themselves, "When our service is completed, what would we like to have contributed and accomplished?" By starting from that point and collaborating to coalesce around a goal or project, they can apply agreements reached by consensus and lessons learned along the way to become more adept, efficient, and productive.

The second step is to focus on working for a better future. Board members have a challenging job to do together, and the scope of issues that emerge in their associations can seem endless. It is never too late, however, for them to add to their arsenal of skills.

The wealth of continuing education opportunities available online and in person for board members can be undertaken at little or no cost. Continuing to sharpen their governance acumen will facilitate their dealing with future challenges and free their time to invest in moving the community forward.

Finally, in charting a new course for moving the community forward, they should take time to reflect on jobs done well. Such mindfulness can help refresh the group's motivation and fortify them to continue to pursue progress. Too often, they simply move from one project to the next without taking time to reflect on the journey and what takeaways they can glean from it. Investing time and effort to assess and celebrate progress is essential to continued success.

Generally, then, moving forward entails taking that extra step, working for a better future, and charting a new course.

## Taking that Extra Step

Volunteer board members are the unsung heroes of community associations. They devote themselves to maintaining and enhancing the community experience for all residents. There are times when their regular governance duties fill the time allocated for fulfilling their responsibilities, but to take the community from good to great requires taking that extra step.

The fundamental duties required to keep the community functioning certainly are a priority. Achieving a sustainable, connected, and vibrant community, however, sometimes requires accomplishing just one extra goal, perhaps by trying something new. Board members can begin this process by engaging in an annual review of governing documents, rules, and goals before exploring ways to move beyond the daily tasks to address issues that matter most to residents. This process will move forward as they strengthen their foundation of knowledge and insight, try something new, and build on success.

## Strengthening the Foundation

Staying current about the board's authority, function, and challenges is a prerequisite to taking an extra step and moving the community forward. Over time, one's recollection of board authority or responsibilities can atrophy. Making time annually to review and discuss the board's authority, study governing documents, and discuss any concerns is a healthy way for boards to strengthen unity and focus. This exercise can include discussing any challenges or events that have transpired since the last review and applying lessons learned to future challenges.

## Trying Something New

Taking the next step to improve a community often requires trying something new. Board members and residents take a variety of pathways toward tackling something outside the box. Trying something new is a great way to break out of old habits. To improve the tenor of ponderous and formal board meetings, board members could consider adding a social period before or after to promote fellowship and share snacks and drinks.

Similarly, if the focus of the community has been solely on rule enforcement and other foundational tasks, they can look for ways to create great connection and cohesion in the community through social or community service events. Such strategies can create a sense of shared purpose and connection that are critical to vibrant communities. It is not about reinventing the wheel, but rather, about looking for small steps that can help the board and community build the confidence to try new approaches to community challenges.

## Building on Success

When striving to strengthen the community, not every approach will take root. That is why it is important to take a variety of extra steps to find ways to respond to the needs of the residents. As the process plays out and the board listens and builds the community the residents desire, success becomes a catalyst for continual improvement. The underlying principle is that to unlock the potential of a community association, board members and residents need to reflect on the elements that will define their community, work toward building them, and enjoy the small victories along the way.

## Working for a Better Future

In the final analysis, the goal of a community association is to preserve and enhance the value of the homes within it while connecting its residents. This mission can be summarized as neighbors working together for a better future. For boards and residents alike, the community association model presents an opportunity to build sustainable connections and processes for a happy present and a vibrant future. This thesis is sometimes overlooked, but it is the promise that exists in each community association. Boards can work toward that future by investing in self-improvement, focusing on the big picture, and adapting as preferences and values change over time. Keeping these principles in mind can help communities stay on the right path as they grow and evolve.

### Investing in Self-Improvement

It is never too late to continue to add to one's arsenal of skills. Board members have a challenging job, particularly because scope of issues that emerge can seem endless. The wealth of online and in-person continuing education opportunities can be undertaken at little or no cost.

Continually sharpening their governance acumen will make dealing with future challenges less difficult and free up time to invest in moving the community forward. It enables board members to become more efficient in the governing process and to hone expertise over time. As they engage in continuing education and reflect on the success of past actions, they learn to work smarter, not harder.

**Focusing on the Big Picture**

Throughout the process of working for a better future, it is important to remember there are sometimes multiple routes to the same goal. The key to working through the dynamic process of community association governance is keeping the bigger picture at the forefront. Despite the many opinions that exist in all community associations, most residents will likely agree on the importance of sustaining the vitality of the community and exploring ways to improve it.

When conflicting views arise, it is helpful to remember this factor that unites the community. Ultimately, projects and priorities that enjoy majority support from the board and are sustainable from a resource standpoint should win the day. Keeping in mind the big picture can facilitate putting the pieces together and working toward a brighter tomorrow.

**Adapting to Change**

A critical element in working for a better future is recognizing that change is inevitable. Over time technology, cultural trends, and personal preferences evolve. With that evolution comes a need to ensure that the rules of the community and its objectives continue to align with the desires and preferences of residents.

The remarkable aspect of community associations is that they are self-governing. The board has the power and the responsibility to adapt community rules to meet the preferences of residents today and into the future.

## Charting a New Course

One of the elements of a community association that inspires me is its ability to chart its own course. The key to putting the pieces together to unlock a community's potential is making use of this authority to work toward the common interest. The destination can be as simple as committing to improve upon current operations or as aspirational as building a connected and empowered neighborhood. The choice is there for each and every community association board.

The only obstacle is the time constraints imposed on boards as volunteer leaders. That is why it is important to apply lessons learned and work to be efficient and fair in governance. As communities chart new courses, they can leverage their autonomy to choose their next adventures while moving past challenges and distractions and serving the community.

## Choosing the Adventure

Invested in the ability to self-govern, community associations have the power to choose their own adventure when planning their neighborhood's future. This ability creates space for boards creatively to approach neighborhood improvements and community engagement activities. The driver should be the needs of the community as determined by the board while listening to residents and observing community trends.

Actions can range from enhancing common areas to implementing sustainability initiatives. Similarly, the board can choose to foster connections among residents through social events or communication platforms as a means of strengthening community ties. Doing so allows the board to adapt, innovate, and serve residents in ways that reflect the community's vision.

## Moving Past Distractions

Perhaps the biggest drain on community efforts to move forward is the board members or residents who relish being the contrarians. Moving past such distractions requires more than ignoring them. Only by listening to everyone openly and attentively and responding respectfully and appropriately will board members deal with them effectively. To continue to represent and move the community forward, they must listen and address concerns reasonably without allowing empty criticisms to sap community momentum. When needed, professional assistance can help resolve issues that may arise from difficult residents.

## Serving the Community

It is true that challenging residents can demand much of board members' time, but, as elected representatives, they must serve the entire community. Sometimes, one complaint can seem to carry the weight of ten compliments, but the reality, supported by years of survey data, is that a supermajority of residents are happy with their community association. Focusing on the big picture and, of course, remembering that we cannot please everyone all of the time will allow leaders to focus on serving everyone. At the end of the day, the role of the community leader is to respond to the majority interests in a community.

## CONCLUSION

Putting the pieces together, it is evident that community association governance benefits from deliberation, mindful thinking, and strategic actions. Coupled with a passion for creating the best environment possible for community residents, these are the hallmarks of a committed board of directors. Like the metaphorical puzzle noted by Julia Hartz, governance requires leaders to prioritize what matters most. That process begins by laying a strong foundation and then adding finer details.

Moving toward a new destination requires identifying the starting point and mapping the journey while understanding the hopes, values, and priorities of the residents served. Engaging in sustainable and thoughtful communication, recognizing resident contributions, and fostering a sense of belonging are part of that journey.

Success is measured not only by the day-to-day oversight of community operations, but also by focusing on investing in building a healthy, connected community. Ultimately, self-governing community associations have the power to shape their future—a future in which the pieces fall into place through committed leadership, thoughtful planning, collaboration, and a shared vision of a thriving community.

---

## QUESTIONS TO CONSIDER

1. Does using a puzzle as a metaphor for handling community governance and challenges help a board prioritize its actions?

2. What is the importance of mapping the community association's future? Can mapping impact a board's approach to governance?

3. How would focusing on improved communication and resident recognition impact your community association?

4. How has your board used its self-governing authority to chart a path for your community?

5. Why should a board track the pulse of residents' preferences? How can technology facilitate this?

6. What would be the impact of investing in training and development for your board members?

7. How does your community balance its responsibilities regarding rule enforcement with the need to foster positive connections and social engagement in your community?

8. How does your board decide when change is necessary?

9. In what ways has engaging professional support benefited your community?

10. Do attorneys and community managers help boards better serve their residents?

11. How does your board build a foundation for future leadership?

# CONCLUSION



This is not the end. It is not even the beginning of the end.
But it is, perhaps, the end of the beginning.

—WINSTON CHURCHILL,
Former British Prime Minister

Community associations have been and will continue to be a popular choice for homebuyers for many years to come. From an economic standpoint, they allow a developer to build a condominium building or a complete community and empower it with self-governance and the ability to fund many of its own functions. Beyond economics, community associations provide a built-in framework for social interaction, which is the heart of the concept of community.

In a world increasingly disrupted by technology, social change, and politics, community still matters. Having discussed unlocking the benefits of community, we can be inspired by the words of the great Winston Churchill in that this is not the end, but it is perhaps the end of the beginning. May this book inspire community leaders to unlock the potential that exists in their respective communities.

The knowledge that community associations remain popular with their residents should be at the forefront as a community begins its journey to unlock its potential. More than 70 million homeowners in the United States live in a community association, and that number is growing. Data gathered over time continue to demonstrate that the preference and satisfaction for the lifestyle are stable, with a supermajority of residents expressing satisfaction. Despite the memes and even jokes at their expense, community associations are enjoyed and supported.

As board members and residents collaborate to unlock the potential of their communities, they would be wise to review the conceptual discussion of community and the four key areas we explored herein, namely, elements for successful communities, dealing with community challenges, exploring alternative outcomes, and planning for the future.

The first, as discussed here, is to remember that the work of community association leaders matters. The years-long data about community surveys tell a story of success. Although community volunteers too often forget this fact as they engage in their day-to-day work, they should be heartened by knowing their efforts are supported and appreciated by a strong majority of residents.

When examining the elements of successful communities, it is important to remember the functions of community governance. The element that allows board members to focus on moving the community forward is their understanding of their roles and their commitment to focus on the powers allocated to them in their community's governing documents. Memory and habit can cause a board to drift away from its mission. To refresh their focus, boards can and should periodically review their roles and defined powers.

Similarly, the board's focus should be on governance. Depending on the size of a community, its amenities, and the time available to board members, operations can be a burden. Hiring professional community association managers can allow a board to concentrate on its role while benefiting from experienced and capable support. Boards should also leverage professional advisors, including lawyers, accountants, community managers, reserve professionals, and others, to support and inform their success.

The reality that it is impossible to please all residents at all times should be a reminder of the key element of overcoming challenges. That one special resident who often opposes every board initiative can sap a board's energy and burn its time. Even more challenging, problematic boards or board members also must be dealt with effectively and carefully. Successful boards deploy strategies of listening, dialogue, and professional support to address such matters.

Similarly, the need for a board to remain focused on the big picture and not engage in petty community politics keeps progress on track. Finally, as nature reminds us, every community should think about and prepare for responding to a natural or human-made disaster.

I am a strong believer in the power of story. Sharing experiences and lived truth helps others understand a person's perspective and can help foster understanding and promote alternative outcomes. The same is true for our community associations. We can either define our communities and share our stories or allow someone else to do it for us. When it is the latter, the result is the same tired stereotypes of community associations. In every community, however, board members and residents are collaborating to improve their neighborhoods every day. Sharing their stories, communicating the work of the board, and recognizing resident accomplishments can frame the community to its residents and its critics in a more positive light. What is more, responding to media inquiries respectfully, accurately, and as thoroughly as possible can help ensure the community's point of view is part of the report.

Of great importance when addressing community matters is the priority of engaging and connecting with residents. This true asset of community associations too often takes a back seat to day-to-day operations and governance challenges. Engaged residents report a higher level of satisfaction, and a happy resident is more likely to focus on continuing positive progress than on finding board actions to criticize.

Engaging residents in planning for the future of their communities is our fourth key element, and it is critical. Such feedback can facilitate stakeholder support for future projects. As their engagement shapes the future, measuring progress and sharing news about accomplishments help create a virtuous cycle. The resulting process illustrates the role of community associations in protecting and enhancing property values in a community.

Successful communities need to prepare for a better future. It is easy to work within the confines of our comfort zones, doing the same thing repeatedly, ad nauseam—but change is constant. Making community matter for residents requires a continual exchange of information and processing of feedback. People choose community association living to protect their property values and amenities and because of their ability to self-govern. When leaders do not keep a finger on the pulse of residents' preferences, state legislatures stand ready to substitute their ideas at the expense of community autonomy. To address matters of community, it is important to listen, adapt, and communicate. The best advocates for community are their leaders, whether the audience is internal or external.

We close where we began by agreeing with Churchill's perspective that this is not the end, but rather, a beginning. Community matters, and community leaders and residents alike have a stake in its ongoing success. Accordingly, community leaders, residents, managers, and allies should set their sights on finding ways, large or small, to make their communities better places for all. Amen.

# ACKNOWLEDGMENTS

The process of writing a book can be a long journey, and it requires support from many people. As in earlier books, I begin by thanking my wife, Helen, who is my best friend and most trusted colleague. Her encouragement led me to write my first book and to continue my journey to share my passion about community with you.

We are grateful for the support of my five children, Joey, Jeff, Will, Kirsten, and Kellen. They support my pursuit of service and share my commitment to embrace the importance of community. I agree with Lee Iacocca, former Chrysler CEO, who said, "The only rock I know that stays steady, the only institution I know that works, is the family."

I am also blessed with the industry's most talented leadership team, namely, my extended family at Associa. I especially appreciate the contributions of Andrew Fortin, who helped me craft and conceptualize the framework for this book. Without him, this book would not have been written. A respected leader in the community association industry who joined our Associa team many years ago, Andrew displays a unique mix of deep industry knowledge, passion for community, kindness, and humor. Above all, I appreciate his leadership and friendship.

Thanks, too, to our executive team leaders, including Jon Hunter, Andrew Brock, Brian Kruppa, José Maldonado, Chelle O'Keefe, Helen Eden Carona, Angela Frieling, Shannon Streenz, and many others, who tirelessly collaborate with me in executing a vision for our company and shaping the future of community.

Literally, millions of volunteers govern their community associations daily. I am in awe of their commitment to civic engagement and grateful to have dedicated my career to supporting their success. My gratitude extends to the developers and members of our industry's professional associations who continue to raise the bar for those who serve communities.

Finally, I thank Associa employees, past and present, for their important roles in growing Associa into a global leader in community association management. Their hard work benefits not only our team and our colleagues, but also the millions of homeowners they serve every day by strengthening community and connecting residents.

It is also imperative to acknowledge the countless volunteers who work tirelessly each day to encourage, support, and grow the community. I look forward to our ongoing efforts to build on our successes and to continue to learn how to serve others better as we help create a brighter future for them.

# Sample Homeowners Association, Inc.

## RESOLUTION NO. ____

## CIVIL CONDUCT OF PROPERTY OWNERS, RESIDENTS, AND BOARD MEMBERS

### Recitals

WHEREAS, Article __, Section __ of the Bylaws of the SAMPLE Homeowners Association, Inc. ("Association") assigns to the Board of Directors ("Board") the power to exercise for the Association all powers, duties, and authority vested in or delegated to the Association and not reserved to the membership by other provisions of these Bylaws, the Articles of Incorporation, or the Declaration; and,

WHEREAS, Article ___, Section __(_) of the Bylaws empowers the Board to adopt and publish rules and regulations governing the use of the Common Area and facilities, and the personal conduct of the members and their guests thereon, and to establish penalties for the infractions thereof; and,

WHEREAS, the Board has established the goal of conducting the business of the Association with high levels of dignity, civility, and respect for the Association as an entity and for the individual members of the Association, Board, and any Committees (for the purposes of this Resolution, the term "Board member" shall also encompass any committee members that have been duly appointed by the Board of Directors); and

WHEREAS, the Board of Directors has decided to establish a code of conduct for its Board, committee members, property owners, and residents with regard to conduct at meetings in order to further its efforts to accomplish its goal.

NOW, THEREFORE, BE IT RESOLVED that the Board adopts the following Code of Conduct as its formal policy:

1. DIRECTION AND CONTROL OF MANAGEMENT AND LEGAL COUNSEL

    a. The Association's employees, directors, officers, and agents are expected to treat Property Owners and Residents in a courteous and businesslike manner. Likewise, Property Owners and Residents must at all times deal with the Association's employees, directors, officers, and agents in a courteous and businesslike manner. Property Owners and Residents shall not communicate with the Association's employees, directors, officers, or agents in a rude, abusive, harassing, intimidating, or threatening manner. This includes both written and verbal communications, emails, etc.

    b. The Association's Property Manager ("Manager") works under the direction of the Board of Directors, pursuant to a written contract. The Board of Directors shall appoint one or two members to be the Manager liaison and to communicate with the Manager on matters outside of the Board meetings. If no one has been appointed, the Manager liaison shall be the Board President. The Manager and Directors do not work for the individual Property Owners or Residents, and Property Owners and Residents are prohibited from attempting to direct or interfere with the work of the Manager, or the Directors, which is done on behalf of the Association. Property Owners should submit any comments or questions they have regarding the Association's operations to the Manager in writing so that the association has a record of the outreach.

c.   The Association's legal counsel works at the direction of the Board of Directors. The Board of Directors shall select one or two members to be the legal liaison and to communicate with legal counsel. If no one has been appointed, the Manager liaison shall be the Board President. No Property Owners or residents should attempt to direct or interfere with legal counsel.

d.   The Association's contractors work under the supervision of the Manager, who is serving at the direction of the Board of Directors. Property Owners and Residents may not direct or interfere with the work of any Association contractor.

e.   Concerns about contractors must be submitted to the Manager in writing. Concerns about the Manager's performance or about the Association's policies must be submitted to the Board of Directors in writing.

f.   The Board will appoint a Board member to receive complaints about the Manager. If no one has been appointed, any concerns or complaints should be directed to the Board President.

2.  PROHIBITED CONDUCT

a.   No Board member, Property Owner, or Resident shall interfere with the system of management established by the Association's governing documents, the Board by resolution, and the Management Agent through contract.

b.  No Board member, Property Owner, or Resident shall interfere with the duties of any employee of the Association or harass, threaten or attempt through any means individually to control or intimidate an employee of the Association. Each Board member, Property Owner and Resident shall maintain a professional relationship with the staff and Management Agent of the Association. No Board member shall use the Manager for personal or personal business projects.

c.  No Board member shall be in violation of the Association's governing documents, including its rules and regulations, for any reason.

d.  Board members shall not use positions as Board members for their own private gain (or for the individual advantage of their friends or supporters) as distinct from the common interest of all property owners.

e.  No Board member shall receive any compensation from the Association for serving as a Board member, except for reimbursement of appropriate and authorized out-of-pocket expenses.

3.  CONDUCT AND DECORUM AT MEETINGS

a.  Board members shall exercise their best efforts to attend and be on time at all meetings or functions of the Association and shall plan to be in attendance at all times during the proceedings. Whenever a Board member knows in advance that he/she cannot attend a meeting, will be late for a meeting, or will have to leave a meeting early, he/she shall exercise their best efforts to inform the President and the Manager in advance of the meeting.

b.  If a Board member is absent from three (3) consecutive regular meetings of the Board, he/she agrees that he/she cannot properly serve the Association and will voluntarily resign from the Board unless good cause for the absences is provided to and approved by the Board.

c.  Board members, Property Owners, and Residents shall not use inappropriate language or verbal tone during their debate of the issues. Any actions (including physical gestures or body language) or comments designed to insult, demean, or attack the personal character of any member of the Board, the Board of Directors, or the Manager as an entity or any person in attendance shall be strictly prohibited. Board members owe a special duty of civility to the Association's membership and shall be particularly courteous to the individual members at all times during official functions of the Association. If a Board Member is approached by a Property Owner or Resident regarding a community issue(s), the Board Member shall listen to the comments/concerns raised and then direct the Property Owner or Resident to submit the comment or question in writing to the Association's Manager.

d.  The President shall have the unilateral authority to enforce the Code of Conduct or may do so in response to the unseconded request of any other member of the Board if the President agrees with the request. The first step of enforcement shall consist of the President issuing a call to order to the particular member of the Board, who then must obey the directive immediately; however, the member called to order shall have the right to appeal the President's ruling, which appeal shall be open to debate and vote of the entire Board of Directors.

e.  In any instance of a flagrant or repeated violation of this Code of Conduct, the President may unilaterally issue a ruling to that effect against the offending member and may require the offending member of the Board or the Property Owner or Resident to leave the premises of the meeting. Any such ruling shall not be appealable by the offending person and must be immediately obeyed, unless another member of the Board wishes to appeal the President's ruling, in which case the appeal shall be open to debate and vote of the entire Board of Directors.

f.  The Board of Directors further reserves additional enforcement powers, as set forth in the Association's Governing Documents.

4.  DUTY OF RESPECT

a.  All members of the Board of Directors owe a duty of respect to the individual Board members, whether present or absent from a meeting, the Board of Directors as an entity, particularly with respect to its formal votes and formally approved policies, and the Association. Once the Board formally votes on a matter, no member of the Board shall engage in any unauthorized activity which undermines the ability of the Board to successfully effectuate the results of the vote. The duty of respect owed to the Board and the Association requires dissenting members to work within the formal procedures of the Board to voice their disagreements and/or modify or rescind the previously adopted votes or approved policies with which they disagree.

b.  All Board members shall recognize that their individual behavior is a reflection upon the Board of Directors and the Association; therefore, they shall at all times refrain from any public conduct within the community, which would bring the Board of Directors or the Association into disrepute.

5. CONFIDENTIALITY REQUIREMENT

    a.  All Board members shall recognize that matters pertaining to the Association's business conducted in executive session should be kept confidential and not disclosed to the community membership or to members of the public at large. The same applies to any written communications from legal counsel denoted as a confidential document. Board members shall not disclose Confidential Information (as that term is defined below) under any circumstances to any person not on the Board without the express consent of a majority of the Board voting at a duly convened meeting of the Board of Directors.

    b.  In any instance when a Board member might be confused about the confidentiality requirements and in order to minimize the possibility of inadvertent disclosure, Board members shall consult with the President before making any disclosure to any third party, which might arguably release any Confidential Information covered by this Resolution, as that term is defined below.

    c.  All Confidential Information is the property of the Association. Board members shall keep in strict confidence any and all information, documentation, records and devices which contain Confidential Information, and, upon the expiration of the Board member's term, shall return all Confidential Information in his/her possession to the Association and shall keep confidential all nontangible Confidential Information.

d.  For the purpose of this Resolution, the term "Confidential Information" shall mean any information related to:

    a.  communications with the Association's legal counsel or professional consultants;

    b.  pending litigation;

    c.  pending matters involving formal proceedings for enforcement of the governing documents or rules or regulations of the Association; and

    d.  pending negotiations for transactions involving the Association and agreements containing confidentiality requirements.

6.  ENFORCEMENT

a.  The Board is responsible for self-governance including the investigation of any claims of misconduct made about any member and disciplinary action for any claims of misconduct found to be valid. Any alleged violations of this Resolution shall be handled in accordance with the Governing Documents and the applicable governing state legislation (*insert specific citation*).

## RESOLUTION ACTION SHEET

Policy Resolution Number ______

    Code of Conduct:

    Date of Adoption:

The above-referenced Resolution was adopted by the Board of Directors as of the date set forth above.

    Signatures:                    Vote: (Y/N)

    Director

    Director

    Director

    Director

    Director

    ATTEST:

    Secretary                    Date:

# Sample News Release

Friendly Acres Homeowners Association: News Release
Contact: Scoops McNewson
Email: friendlyacres@example.com
Phone: 231-555-5555

**Friendly Acres Homeowners
Association Raises $100,000 for Toys for Tots**

**[Friendly Acres, TX] – [11/24/25]** – The Friendly Acres Home-owners Association (FAHOA) is proud to announce that its Third Annual Toys for Tots Fundraising Campaign was an overwhelming success, raising more than $100,000 to benefit children in need this holiday season.

The month-long campaign featured a series of engaging community events, including a high-energy Fun Run, a lively Silent Auction, and a festive Community Vendor Fair. With the participation and generosity of Friendly Acres residents, local businesses, and volunteers, this year's campaign exceeded its ambitious fundraising goal, ensuring that countless children will receive toys and gifts to brighten their holidays.

"This event showcases the power of community spirit," said Priscilla Jones, social chair of the Friendly Acres Homeowners Association. "We couldn't have done this without the dedication of our neighbors, the creativity of our vendors, and the generosity of our donors. Raising more than $100,000 is proof that when we come together for a worthy cause, we can accomplish extraordinary things."

The Fun Run, held at Friendly Acres Park, kicked off the month of giving, drawing participants of all ages for a morning of fitness and fun. The Silent Auction featured contributions from local artisans, businesses, and residents, while the Vendor Fair offered holiday shopping and entertainment, drawing visitors from across the region.

The funds raised will directly support the Toys for Tots program operated by the U.S. Marine Corps Reserve, which distributes toys to children whose families are facing financial hardships during the holiday season.

The Friendly Acres Homeowners Association extends its heartfelt gratitude to all who contributed their time, talent, and treasure to make this event a success. For more information about the FAHOA or how to get involved in future events, please visit (INSERT WEBSITE OR CONTACT INFORMATION).

•  •  •

Friendly Acres Homeowners Association is a master-planned community located in Anytown, TX. Developed by Community Construction, Inc. in 2004, it contains more than 3,000 homes and noteworthy amenities. Residents of Friendly Acres appreciate its numerous community centers, pool center, and walking trails. With more than 6,500 residents as of November 2024, Friendly Acres is the premier community attracting buyers and families across the region.

•  •  •

###
Follow us on social media:
X: (INSERT)
Facebook: (INSERT)
Instagram: (INSERT)
Threads: (INSERT)

# NOTES

## Chapter 1


1. Francis Newton Thorpe and The Avalon Project, *Mayflower Compact: 1620. Agreement Between the Settlers at New Plymouth* (United States Government Printing Office, 1909).

2. Richardson B. Gill et al., "Drought and the Maya Collapse," *Ancient Mesoamerica* 18, no. 2 (2007): 283–302, https://doi.org/10.1017/S0956536107000193.


## Chapter 2


1. "History of Homeowners Associations," FindLaw, November 16, 2023, https://www.findlaw.com/realestate/owning-a-home/history-of-homeowners-associations.html.

2. *Community Associations Remain Preferred Places to Call Home: 2022 Homeowner Satisfaction Survey* (Foundation for Community Association Research, 2022), https://foundation.caionline.org/wp-content/uploads/2022/08/FCARHomeownerSatisfactionSurveyResults2022Final.pdf.

3. *2023 U.S. National and State Statistical Review* (Foundation for Community Association Research, 2023), https://foundation.caionline.org/wp-content/uploads/2024/01/2023StatsReviewDigital-002.pdf.

4. During construction of an association and for set periods, a board may be appointed by the developer until certain thresholds are met, at which time the association transitions to resident control.

5. *Community Associations Remain Preferred Places to Call Home.*

## Chapter 3

1. Nevada Revised Statutes 116.31034(19): "Each member of the executive board shall, within 90 days after his or her appointment or election, certify in writing to the association, on a form prescribed by the Administrator, that the member has read and understands the governing documents of the association and the provisions of this chapter to the best of his or her ability . . ."

2. *Rights and Responsibilities of Association Board Members* (Illinois Department of Financial and Professional Regulation: Division of Real Estate, August 2022), https://idfpr.illinois.gov/content/dam/soi/en/web/idfpr/ccico/pdfs/rights-and-responsibilities-of-association-board-members.pdf.

3. "Homeowner Education, CAI Board Leader Certificate," Community Associations Institute, accessed March 14, 2025, https://www.caionline.org/HomeownerLeaders/Pages/RightsandResponsibilities.aspx.

## Chapter 4

1. California Civil Code 4753. Clotheslines: "(a) For the purposes of this section, "clothesline" includes a cord, rope, or wire from which laundered items may be hung to dry or air. A balcony, railing, awning, or other part of a structure or building shall not qualify as a clothesline. (b) For the purposes of this section, 'drying rack' means an apparatus from which laundered items may be hung to dry or air. A balcony, railing, awning, or other part of a structure or building shall not qualify as a drying rack. (c) Any provision of a governing document, as defined in Section 4150, shall be void and unenforceable if it effectively prohibits or unreasonably restricts an owner's ability to use a clothesline or drying rack in the owner's backyard."

2. Arizona Revised Statutes 33-1816. Solar energy devices; reasonable restrictions; fees and costs: "A. Notwithstanding any provision in the community documents, an association shall not prohibit the installation or use of a solar energy device . . ."

3. 42 U.S. Code Chapter 45.

4. Added in 1974.

5. 4 U.S. Code Chapter 5.

6. For more information about CAI, visit: www.caionline.org.

7. For more information about Associa board resources, visit: https://hub.associaonline.com.

8. Find out more about Florida approved board training organizations here: https://www2.myfloridalicense.com/lsc/documents/ ListofApprovedProviders.pdf.

9. Andrei Tcacenco and Dre Anderson, *Welcome to the Board* (Nevada Real Estate Division), https://red.nv.gov/uploadedFiles/rednvgov/Content/ CIC/Program_Training/Presentations/welcometotheboard.pdf.

10. For more on the Albert Mehrabian Communication Model, visit: https://www.google.com/search?client=safari&rls=en&q=albert+ mehrabian+communication+model&ie=UTF-8&oe=UTF-8.

## Chapter 5

1. Patricia Armstrong, *Bloom's Taxonomy* (Vanderbilt University Center for Teaching, 2010), https://cdn.vanderbilt.edu/vu-sub/wp-content/uploads/ sites/59/2010/06/19134035/Blooms-Taxonomy.docx.

2. According to the Community Associations Institute, state-level certifications exist in California, Arizona, Illinois, Florida, and Nevada.

3. States with licensing or registration requirements for community managers include Alaska, Connecticut, Florida, Georgia, Illinois, Nevada, and Virginia.

## Chapter 6

1. My intent in sharing my experiences and observations of client associations engaging professionals is to give you insights or a framework to clarify the process. Please note: I am not an attorney, and nothing printed herein should be considered legal advice.

2. CAI's directory of credentialed professionals is available on the CAI website: www.caionline.com.

## Chapter 7

1. "What Is Mediation?," Office of Civil Rights, accessed March 14, 2025, https://www.commerce.gov/cr/reports-and-resources/eeo-mediation-guide/what-mediation.

2. Barbara Kate Repa, "Arbitration Basics," NOLO, updated January 15, 2025, *https://www.nolo.com/legal-encyclopedia/arbitration-basics-29947.html.*

## Chapter 8

1. *Community Associations Remain Preferred Places to Call Home: 2022 Homeowner Satisfaction Survey* (Foundation for Community Association Research, 2022), https://foundation.caionline.org/wp-content/uploads/2022/08/FCARHomeownerSatisfactionSurveyResults2022Final.pdf.

2. "Congress and the Public," *Gallup News*, May 1, 2023, https://news.gallup.com/poll/1600/congress-public.aspx.

3. Linda Robertson, "Defrauded HOA Trying to Unravel the Mess," Florida Realtors, August 22, 2023, https://www.floridarealtors.org/news-media/news-articles/2023/08/defrauded-hoa-trying-unravel-mess.

4. California Civil Code, (4825), (5000) and (4930(a)).

5. Nevada Revised Statutes, 116.31083(6).

6. Code of Virginia, 55.1-1949(d), 55.1-1816(d).

7. Nevada Revised Statutes, 116.31036(2): "A removal election may be called by units' owners constituting at least 10 percent, or any lower percentage specified in the bylaws, of the total number of voting members of the association. To call a removal election, the units' owners must submit a written petition that is signed by the required percentage of the total number of voting members of the association pursuant to this subsection and that is mailed, return receipt requested, or served by a process server to the executive board or the community manager for the association. If a removal election is called pursuant to this subsection . . ."

8. Arizona Revised Statutes, 33-1813.

9. California Corporate Code, 7222(a).

10. Florida Statutes, 720.303(10).

11. North Carolina General Statutes, 47F-3-102 (applies to HOAs), North Carolina General Statutes, 47C-3-103 (applies to condominiums)

12. Code of Virginia, 13.1-860.

13. Jandra Sutton, "How to Do Battle with Our Homeowners Association," *Washington Post*, November 16, 2023, https://www.washingtonpost.com/home/2023/11/16/homeowners-association-hoa-violations-fights/.

14. For more information about the Condominium Authority of Ontario, visit: https://www.condoauthorityontario.ca.

## Chapter 9

1. "The Changing Threat of COVID-19," CDC National Center for Immunization and Respiratory Diseases, February 23, 2024, https://www.cdc.gov/ncird/whats-new/changing-threat-covid-19.html.

2. For more information about the Federal Emergency Management Agency, visit: https://www.fema.gov.

## Chapter 10

1. Megha Shah, "Traditional Media vs. New Media: Which Is Beneficial," TechFunnel, updated September 6, 2024, https://www.techfunnel.com/martech/traditional-media-vs-new-media-beneficial/.

2. "Number of Internet and Social Media Users Worldwide as of October 2024," Statista, https://www.statista.com/statistics/617136/digital-population-worldwide/.

## Chapter 11

1. For more information about the National Night Out, a project of the National Association of Town Watches, visit: www.natw.org.

## Chapter 12

2. Jen Croneberger, "Mission, Vision, and Purpose: The Difference," *Forbes*, May 4, 2020, https://www.forbes.com/councils/forbescoachescouncil/2020/03/04/vision-mission-and-purpose-the-difference/.

3. Croneberger, "Mission, Vision, and Purpose: The Difference."

4. Catherine Bailey, Catherine Tilley, and Anna Lelia Sandoghdar, "What Makes a Great Corporate Purpose Statement," *Harvard Business Review*, September 11, 2023, https://hbr.org/2023/09/what-makes-a-great-corporate-purpose-statement.

5. Sushma Raman, "How to Write a Strategic Plan" (Harvard University), https://projects.iq.harvard.edu/files/hks-communications-program/files/pp_how_to_write_a_strategic_plan.pdf.

6. G.T. Doran, "There's a S.M.A.R.T. Way to Write Management's Goals and Objectives," *Management Review* 70, no. 11 (1981): 35–36.

## Chapter 13

1. Patricia Armstrong, *Bloom's Taxonomy* (Vanderbilt University Center for Teaching, 2010), https://cdn.vanderbilt.edu/vu-sub/wp-content/uploads/sites/59/2010/06/19134035/Blooms-Taxonomy.docx.

2. *2023 U.S. National and State Statistical Review* (Foundation for Community Association Research, 2023), https://foundation.caionline.org/wp-content/uploads/2024/01/2023StatsReviewDigital-002.pdf.

3. *2023 U.S. National and State Statistical Review.*

4. "Congress and the Public," *Gallup News*, April 2024, https://news.gallup.com/poll/1600/congress-public.aspx.

5. *2023 U.S. National and State Statistical Review.*

6. *2023 U.S. National and State Statistical Review.*

7. "Study: Homeowners Associations Are Booming," National Association of Realtors, March 14, 2024, https://clips.cato.org/sites/default/files/Cato_NAR_Homeowners.pdf.

8. "U.S. and World Population Clock." United States Census Bureau, https://www.census.gov/popclock/.

9. "Population of Canada," *The World Counts*, https://www.theworldcounts.com/populations/countries/canada.

10. Jonathan Vespa, Lauren Medina, and David M. Armstrong, "Demographic Turning Point for the United States: Population Projections for 2020 to 2060," United States Census Bureau, March 2018.

11. Jennifer Ferreira, "This Is What Canada Will Look Like in 20 Years—Are We Ready for an Aging Population?," *CTVNews*, December 12, 2023, https://www.ctvnews.ca/canada/this-is-what-canada-will-look-like-in-20-years-are-we-ready-for-an-aging-population-1.6652355.

12. Ronald Reagan, Medal of Freedom Remarks, January 19, 1989.

13. "America's Families and Living Arrangements: 2023," United States Census Bureau, November 2023, https://www.census.gov/data/tables/2023/demo/families/cps-2023.html.

14. Ron Cheung and Rachel Meltzer, "Homeowners Associations and the Demand for Local Land Use Regulation." *Journal of Regional Science* 53, no. 3 (2013): 511–534.

15. "Nearly Half of U.S. Households Can't Afford a $250,000 Home," National Association of Home Builders, May 17, 2024, https://www.nahb.org/blog/2024/05/housing-affordability-pyramid.

16. The Dallas Fort Worth Metroplex refers to the great metropolitan area that includes the cities of Dallas, Fort Worth, and their surrounding suburbs.

17. Those states include Massachusetts, Hawaii, New Jersey, Connecticut, Delaware, and Rhode Island.

## Chapter 14

1. *Project Standards Requirements* (Fannie Mae, 2023).

2. "Freddie Mac Seller/Servicer Guide, Series 5000, Topic 5700: Property," Freddie Mac, accessed March 6, 2025, https://guide.freddiemac.com/app/guide/topic/5700.

3. Phoebe E. Neseth, "Update: First Quarter Community Association State Legislative Trends," Community Associations Institute, March 27, 2024, https://advocacy.caionline.org/update-first-quarter-community-association-state-legislative-trends.

4. Neseth, "Update: First Quarter Community Association State Legislative Trends."

5. The Uniform Law Commission: The Uniform Law Commission (ULC, also known as the National Conference of Commissioners on Uniform State Laws), established in 1892, provides states with nonpartisan, well-conceived and well-drafted legislation that brings clarity and stability to critical areas of state statutory law. ULC members must be lawyers, qualified to practice law. They are practicing lawyers, judges, legislators and legislative staff, and law professors, who have been appointed by state governments as well as the District of Columbia, Puerto Rico and the U.S. Virgin Islands to research, draft, and promote enactment of uniform state laws in areas of state law in which uniformity is desirable and practical.

6. States with existing UCIOA–based statutes: Alaska, Colorado, Connecticut, Delaware, Minnesota, Nevada, Vermont, and Washington.

7. Midlake on Big Boulder Lake v. Cappuccio, 449 Pa. Superior Ct. 124 (1996), 673 A.2d 340.

# INDEX

Figures and tables are indicated by an italicized *f* or *t* following a page number.

# ABOUT THE AUTHOR

**JOHN J. CARONA SR.** A native Texan and the grandson of Italian immigrants, John Carona grew up in East Dallas and was an entrepreneur from the age of twelve. He worked three jobs to pay his way through college and is a proud alumnus of the University of Texas at Austin.

In 1979, John Carona founded the firm known today as Associa, then a small property management boutique in Dallas providing limited property management services to apartments and condominiums. Today, the company is the largest community management company in North America, operating 300+ offices with more than 15,000 employees in the United States, Canada, Mexico, and Brazil.

As one of the founders of his industry, Carona is widely respected as an authority, innovator, and exemplar of excellence. In recognition of his innovation and success, he was honored with the prestigious EY Entrepreneur of the Year Award for the Southwest Region in 2014. Under his leadership, Associa has been named a Great Place to Work® in the United States for eight consecutive years beginning in 2017. It is a Gold Star winner of the "U.S. Best Managed Companies" designation awarded by Deloitte and the *Wall Street Journal*, having earned the honor for the fifth consecutive year in 2024.

Enthusiastic about giving back to the industry in which he made his career, Carona added "author" to his resume in 2013 with the publication of his first book, *In the Common Interest: Embracing the New American Community*. It provides a history of the industry and a compelling narrative of why community associations are on the rise in the United States and abroad and what the future holds for the industry. He released his second book, *In the Common Interest 2: Embracing Five Star Customer Service,* in 2019, providing insight into the service delivery model that underlies his firm's success.

In addition to his real estate businesses, Carona has been in the banking industry for decades, first serving as an advisory board member to East Park National Bank and then as a shareholder and board member of First Associations Bank. He helped lead the successful sale of that bank to Pacific Premier Bank of Irvine, California, where he served as a member of the board for seven years.

In 2015, Carona furthered his ventures in banking by acquiring First National Bank of Kemp, followed in 2023 with the acquisitions of Texas Brand Bank and Rice Bancshares, which he then combined to create Harmony Bank.

Beyond business and entrepreneurship, Carona has long been passionate about service to others. In 2007, he created Associa Cares, a 501(c)(3) charitable organization that provides support for victims of natural and human-caused disasters. He also founded Associa Supports Kids, a program that educates and advocates for child safety and wellness.

He has held numerous advisory and board positions with a variety of civic organizations in Texas, including the Children's Health System Foundation and The Episcopal School of Dallas, and has lent significant financial support to a host of organizations, including Baylor University, the University of Texas at Austin, and Fair Park First.

Also an accomplished legislator, Carona served five terms in the Texas Senate and three in the Texas House of Representatives. His statewide legislative leadership roles included serving as chair of the

Senate Transportation and Homeland Security Committee and chair of the Senate Business and Commerce Committee. He also was elected president pro tempore of the Texas Senate, authored or sponsored more than 900 bills that became law, and received more than 200 public service awards. *Texas Monthly* twice named him one of the "Ten Best Legislators."

While running his international business and serving his community and state, Carona has remained focused on his family. He lives in Dallas with his wife, Helen, and is the father of five children and the grandfather to eight grandchildren. An avid art collector, he enjoys traveling with his family, ranching, and hunting.